The **AA** Best Drives
Ireland

Written by Susan Poole and Lyn Gallagher

Published by AA Publishing, a trading name of Automobile Association Developments Limited, whose registered office is Fanum House, Basing View, Basingstoke, Hampshire RG21 4EA. Registered number 1878835.

ISBN-10: 0-7495-4430-9
ISBN-13: 978-0-7495-4430-0

The contents of this publication are believed correct at the time of printing. Nevertheless, AA Publishing accept no responsibility for errors, omissions or changes in details given in this guide, or for the consequences of readers' reliance on this information. This does not affect your statutory rights. Assessments of the attractions and so forth are based upon the author's own experience and contain subjective opinions that may not reflect the publishers' opinion or a reader's own experience. We have tried to ensure accuracy, but things do change, so please let us know if you have any comments or corrections.

A CIP catalogue record for this book is available from the British Library.

Colour separation: Daylight Colour Art, Singapore
Printed and bound by G. Canale & C. S.P.A., Torino, Italy

Find out more about AA Publishing and the wide range of travel publications and services the AA provides by visiting our website at www.theAA.com

First published 1992
Revised second edition published in this format 1998
Revised third edition 2000
Reprinted June 2001
Reprinted 2004. Information verified and updated
Reprinted February 2005
Reprinted 2006. Information verified and updated

Opposite: *South Cross detail, Kells*

A02490

CONTENTS

ABOUT THIS BOOK

This book is not only a practical guide for the independent traveller, but is also invaluable for those who would like to know more about the country.

It is divided into four regions, each containing between four and ten tours. The tours start and finish in the towns and cities which we consider to be the best centres for exploration. Each tour has details of the most interesting places to visit en route. Highlighted panels dotted throughout each tour cater for special interests and requirements and cover a range of categories – for those whose interest is in history, wildlife or walking, and those who have children. There are also panels which highlight scenic stretches of road along the route and which give details of special events, crafts and customs.

The route directions are accompanied by an easy-to-use map at the beginning of each tour along with a simple chart showing how far it is from one town to the next in miles and kilometres. These can help you to decide where to take a break and stop overnight, for example. (All distances quoted are approximate.)

Before setting off it is advisable to check with the tourist information centre (addresses are given after the symbol [i] at the end of town entries) at the start of the tour, for recommendations on where to break your journey and for additional information on what to see and do, and when best to visit.

Tour Information
See pages 185–92 for addresses, telephone numbers and opening times of the attractions mentioned in the tours, including telephone numbers of tourist offices.

Hotels and Restaurants
See pages 160–79 for a list of recommended hotels and restaurants en route for each tour.

Business Hours

Banks: there are many bureaux de change in Ireland, but banks are the best place to change money. Opening hours vary, but most are open 10am–4pm, with some extended hours, including limited Sat morning opening, in Northern Ireland. Foreign exchange counters in the main airports give good rates: Belfast International, 5–8pm, may vary; Dublin, open Mon–Fri 5.30am–9pm, Sat 5.30am–midnight, Sun 5.30am–10pm; Shannon, open daily 6am–9.30pm; Cork, open Mon–Fri 6.45am–8pm, Sat 9am–5pm, Sun 9am–8pm. There is also a wide network of automatic cash points where you can use credit and bank cards. Post offices: in the Republic, standard post office opening times are generally Mon–Fri 9am–5.30pm; Sat 9am–1pm. The General Post Office in O'Connell Street, Dublin, is open Mon–Sat, 8am–8pm and 10am–6.30pm on Sun and bank holidays. Post boxes are green; Republic of Ireland stamps must be used.

In Northern Ireland, standard opening times are Mon–Fri 9am–5.30pm, and Sat 9am–12.30pm. Throughout Northern Ireland sub post offices also close one other afternoon each week. Post boxes are red; British stamps must be used.

Credit Cards

Throughout Ireland American Express, Visa and MasterCard, are widely accepted, though not by some smaller restaurants and independent traders. Personal cheques can be cashed using a Eurocheque card. A few bed and breakfast establishments may expect to be paid in cash.

Currency

The currency of the Republic of Ireland is the euro, divided into 100 cents, with notes in denominations of 5, 10, 20, 50, 100, 200 and 500 and coins in denominations of 1, 2, 5, 10, 20 and 50 cents, plus 1 and 2 euros. Northern Ireland uses the pound sterling, divided into 100 pence, with notes in denomina-

tions of 5, 10, 20, 50 and 100 and coins in denominations of 1, 2, 5, 10, 20 and 50 pence, plus £1 and £2. Large companies and businesses around the border will often accept either.

Customs Regulations

Standard EU customs regulations apply when travelling between the Republic or Northern Ireland and another EU country, and if crossing the border between the two. Travellers may import or export goods for their personal use, up to certain limits depending on whether the goods were bought in ordinary shops (tax paid) or duty-free shops.

Electricity

220 volts AC (50 cycles) is standard. Sockets for small appliances are the three-pin flat or two-pin round wall types.

Embassies and Consulates

Embassies in the Republic: Australia: Fitzwilton House, Wilton Terrace, Dublin 2 (tel: (01) 664 5300); Canada: 65 St Stephen's Green, Dublin 2 (tel: (01) 417 4101); UK: 29 Merrion Road, Dublin 4 (tel: (01) 205 3700); US: 42 Elgin Road, Dublin 4 (tel: (01) 668 8777).

Consular offices for Northern Ireland: Australia High Commission, Australia House, The Strand, London

WC2B 4LA (tel: 020 7379 4334); Canada: Honorary Consul, Unit 3, Ormeau Business Park, 8 Cromac Avenue, Belfast BT7 2JA (tel: 028 9127 2060); New Zealand: Honorary Consul, Ballance 118A, Lisburn Road, Glenavy, Crumlin, BT29 4NY (tel: 028 9264 8098); US: US Consul General, Danesfort House, 223 Stranmillis Road, Belfast BT9 5GR (tel: 028 9038 6100).

Emergency Telephone Numbers
In both the Republic and Northern Ireland, dial 999 for police, fire or ambulance.

Entry Regulations
When planning your trip to Ireland, remember that the Republic of Ireland and Northern Ireland (which is part of the UK) may have different passport and visa requirements. For this reason, you should check before you leave your home country.

Health
There are no special health requirements or regulations for visitors to the Republic or Northern Ireland. It is best to take out medical insurance, though EU visitors are covered by a reciprocal agreement. British visitors should contact the post office for an EHIC (European Health Insurance Card) form, which replaces form E111.

Motoring
For information on all aspects of motoring in Ireland, including accidents, breakdowns and speed limits, see pages 158–59.

Public Holiday
(R) Republic only
(NI) Northern Ireland only
1 January – New Year's Day
17 March – St Patrick's Day
Good Friday & Easter Monday
1st Monday in May – May Day
Last Monday in May (NI)
1st Monday in June (R)
12–13 July – Orangemen's Day (NI)

Traditional pub music session

1st Monday in August (R)
Last Monday in August (NI)
Last Monday in October (R)
25 December – Christmas Day
26 December – St Stephen's Day (Boxing Day)

Route Directions
Throughout the book the following abbreviations are used for roads:
M – motorways
Northern Ireland only:
A – main roads
B – local roads
Republic of Ireland only:
N – national primary/secondary roads
R – regional roads.

Telephones
To call a number in Ireland, first dial the International access code: Australia 0011; Canada 011; New Zealand 00; UK (for the Republic only) 00. Then dial 353 for the Republic or 44 for Northern Ireland, and then the full number (omitting the first zero of the area code).

For international calls out of Ireland dial 00, then the country code: Australia 61; Canada 1; New Zealand 64; UK 44; US 1. Then dial the full number omitting the first zero.

Glass and metal call boxes have largely replaced the old blue and cream ones in the Republic, and red boxes in Northern Ireland. Phones using cards (bought at newsagents) are widely available.

Time
Both the Republic of Ireland and Northern Ireland follow GMT, or GMT plus 1 hour from late March to late October.

Tourist Offices
Republic of Ireland Tourist Board (Bord Failte): Suffolk Street, Dublin 2 (tel: (01) 605 7700).
Northern Ireland Tourist Board: St Anne's Court, 59 North Street, Belfast, BT1 1NB (tel: 028 9023 1221).
Tourism Ireland now has joint tourist offices abroad, which include:
Australia: 5th Level, 36 Carrington Street, Sydney, NSW 2000 (tel: (02) 9299 6177).
Canada: 2 Bloor Street West, Suite 1501, Toronto, Ontario M4W 3E2 (tel: (416) 925 6368)
UK: 103 Wigmore Street, London W1U 1QS (tel: 08000 397000).
US: 345 Park Avenue, New York, NY 10154 (tel: 800 223 6470).

MUNSTER

The province of Munster is made up of the counties of Waterford, Cork, Kerry, Limerick, Clare and Tipperary. Its fertile ever-changing landscapes form a microcosm of Ireland.

Soaring, surf-fringed cliffs rise above tiny coves and sandy beaches. Mountains, awash with colours of rhododendrons and the delicate hues of heather, are slashed by deep gaps and scenic passes. The Knockmealdown and Comeragh ranges guard east Munster, while to the west the peaks of Macgillycuddy's Reeks include Ireland's highest, 3,400-foot (1,036m) Carrauntoohill. The Slieve Mish range marches out to the tip of the Dingle Peninsula, and the Galtees, Slieve Felims, and Silvermines straggle across the interior.

A variety of fish fill Munster's rivers: the mighty Shannon that draws a watery line along the boundaries of counties Kerry, Clare, Limerick and Tipperary; the Lee that rises in the hills of Gougane Barra and flows eastward to split into two forks that make an island of Cork city's centre; the tidal Blackwater whose scenic beauty has earned it the title of the 'Rhine of Ireland'; and the Suir, Slaney and Nire whose waters trace their way across eastern Munster.

The beautiful Italian Gardens on Garinish Island benefit from the warming effects of the Gulf Stream (Tour 6)

Fertile fields are ringed by stone walls and verdant woodlands. Small fishing villages along the coast and prosperous inland market towns dot the landscape. Three of Ireland's largest industrial cities and most important ports – Waterford, Cork and Limerick – ring the coastline, while inland lies the great Golden Plain of Tipperary.

Ancient ringforts, dolmens, and cairns predate recorded history, while massive castles, monasteries and round towers speak of Christians, Vikings and Normans. The stone promontory fort of Dunbeg stands guard on the Dingle Peninsula, while adjacent fields contain the still-intact beehive huts of early Christians. The lofty Rock of Cashel is a reminder both of the days of Celtic kings of Munster and of the coming of Christianity.

The breathtaking scenery and the juxtaposition of history with progress leave the visitor with an almost overwhelming sense of the enduring nature of the region. There is a feeling that time has not stood still in this ancient land, but is marching on into eternity, its past a solid foundation for the future.

Tour 1

The strange barren landscape of the Burren is the most evocative sight of this region, though the towering grandeur of the Cliffs of Moher forms another unforgettable vista. For history lovers, Clare is a county of castles. Ennis, which readily claims the affection of the visitor, is the base for the tour.

Tour 2

From the Viking city of Limerick, this tour takes you west along the banks of the Shannon estuary, tracing the footsteps of the mighty Desmond clan who left massive castles in their wake. The route turns south, where history merges with culture in northern County Kerry and continues east and north for medieval ruins in Newcastle West and the picturesque beauty of Adare.

Tour 3

Turning east from Limerick city, it is not such a long way to Tipperary town, in the heart of that county's Golden Vale. Further east is the great Rock of Cashel, with its impressive ruins and folk village, then on to Thurles, Roscrea and Nenagh.

Dunguaire Castle looks out over Kinvarra Bay (Tour 1)

Tour 4

Tralee is the gateway to a tour of the antiquities of the Dingle Peninsula, through tiny seaside villages and over the breathtaking Connor Pass to Dingle town. Prehistoric forts, beehive huts and a drystone oratory that has stood watertight for over 1,000 years are only a few relics of this magical place.

Tour 5

The 107-mile (172km) Ring of Kerry takes top billing on this tour as you travel from one scenic wonder to the next. Mountains, lakes, sandy beaches and offshore islands form an unforgettable panorama, and Killarney town has its own fair share of splendid lakes, antiquities and legends.

Tour 6

From Kenmare, this tour takes you south to Glengarriff and the semitropical Italianate gardens on Garinish Island. It continues along the wild seascapes and mountain passes of the Beara Peninsula.

Tour 7

This tour takes you to Blarney to kiss the famous stone and northwest through historic towns before turning east then south for Cahir's Norman castle, the

spectacular drive across The Vee, Lismore's fairy–tale castle perched above the Blackwater river, and Youghal's harbour, haunted by Sir Walter Raleigh.

Tour 8

Turning south then west from Cork, the splendours of West Cork unfold along this tour. Delightful little coves and sandy beaches are backed by wooded hills. A turn inland takes you through a mountain to remote Gougane Barra.

Tour 9

After exploring historic Bantry, with its great house and attractive harbour, the route takes you to picturesque Skibbereen, with a side trip to tiny Baltimore, a village which has seen more than its fair share of violence, and circles the unspoiled peninsula that stretches as far as Mizen Head, the southernmost mainland point of Ireland.

Tour 10

Waterford is the starting point for a journey along dramatic coastal cliffs and coves, past picturesque castles, panoramic mountain views, and lush farmland. The Vee opens up unforgettable views of heather-covered mountains and bogs and Tipperary's fertile landscape.

Clare

The pleasant town of Ennis, the capital of County Clare, winds around low hills astride the River Fergus. It was at the forefront of the struggle for emancipation, and has strong associations with Daniel O'Connell and Eamon de Valera. The Riches of Clare Exhibit in the Clare Museum has enthralling displays on all aspects of Clare life.

2/3 DAYS • 159 MILES • 256KM

SPECIAL TO...

The Irish music and dance tradition is particularly strong in Co Clare, and the Glór Irish Music Centre in Ennis is a state-of-the-art concert venue where you can hear the top Irish performers. For Irish set dancing, go along to the town's friendly ceili at Cois na hAbhna (tel: 065-682 2347), any Wednesday night from May to October.

▶ Take the **N85** for Lehinch. After 9 miles (14km) turn left at Inagh on to the **R460** for Milltown Malbay. After another 9 miles (14km) turn right on to the **R474** for Milltown Malbay.

❶ Milltown Malbay, Co Clare
The coastline of County Clare is better endowed with cliffs and rocky foreshore than with beaches, but there is good bathing at White (or Silver) Strand. Close by is Spanish Point, which owes its name to the unhappy fate of shipwrecked sailors from the Spanish Armada, executed by Sir Turlough O'Brien in 1588.

Milltown Malbay feels like a seaside resort, even though it is a little inland. It is an important centre for traditional music.

▶ Take the **N67** to Lehinch.

❷ Lehinch, Co Clare
The busiest resort in Clare, Lehinch earns its reputation from its splendid beach, good for bathing and popular for surfing. The name Lehinch comes from the Irish name for peninsula, as it has water on three sides. Its name today is perhaps most often associated with the championship golf course.

Across the bay lies Liscannor, birthplace of John Phillip Holland, the man who developed the submarine into a

working naval vessel in 1900. In appreciation of his achievement, the US Navy erected a commemorative stone at the small fishing harbour. From here the *Moher Princess* departs to view the Cliffs of Moher from the water, sometimes watched by the local dolphins.

▶ Take the **R478** for 6 miles (10km) to the Cliffs of Moher.

❸ Cliffs of Moher, Co Clare
These awe-inspiring bastions of rock rise sheer from the sea to a height of nearly 670 feet (200m) and run relentlessly for

The precipitous Cliffs of Moher, home to flocks of sea birds

5 miles (8km). The great Irish naturalist Robert Lloyd Praeger, writing in the 1940s, suggested: 'If you want to feel very small, go out in one of the canvas curraghs on a day when a ground swell is coming in from the ocean, and get your boatman to row you along the base of those gigantic rock-walls. The rollers and their reflections from the cliffs produce a troubled sea on which your boat dances like a live thing, like a tiny cork, and the vast dark precipice above, vertical and in places overhanging, seems to soar up to the troubled sky. It is a wonderful experience.'

Generations of visitors have not failed to be impressed by

the monumental quality of these cliffs. In 1835 Sir Cornelius O'Brien MP built O'Brien's Tower as an observation point for 'strangers visiting the Magnificent Scenery of this neighbourhood' on the highest point of the cliffs and overlooking a rockstack called Breanan Mor. Today's visitor has the advantage of a visitor centre, which has leaflets explaining the history and geology of the area, as well as giving information about walks and bird life.

i *Visitor Centre (seasonal)*

RECOMMENDED WALKS

The best way to appreciate the full grandeur of the Cliffs of Moher is on foot. A walking guide for the path starting at O'Brien's Tower is available from the visitor centre. The Burren Way stretches for 20 miles (32km) along the 'green roads' of this magical limestone landscape, passing many ruined churches and stone forts and monuments along the way. The Mid Clare Way is a 60-mile (100km) route from Quin that encircles Ennis and traverses some beautiful and varied landscape.

SPECIAL TO...

There are varying accounts of just how many dolphins inhabit the Shannon Estuary and waters off Co Clare – some say 50, some say 100 – but whatever their number, they have become a major attraction. Enquire locally about dolphin-watching cruises.

▶ *Continue on the R478, turning left to bypass Lisdoonvarna, and follow the coastal route, R477, by Black Head to Ballyvaghan, 25 miles (40km).*

4 Ballyvaghan, Co Clare
Ballyvaghan is an attractive village, focused on a large harbour used for a small fishing fleet, for sailing and for boat trips to the islands. Close to the village is a cluster of holiday homes in traditional style, known as 'Rent an Irish Cottage', which is a popular feature of this area. As a centre for contemporary and traditional craftspeople, this is a good place to look for quality souvenirs.

▶ *Take the N67 up Corkscrew Hill for 10 miles (16km) to Lisdoonvarna.*

5 Lisdoonvarna, Co Clare
Lisdoonvarna has long been synonymous with the art of

FOR CHILDREN

The Burren is widely known for its potholes and caves but only experienced potholers can attempt to explore most of them. Aillwee Cave, south of Ballyvaghan, is perfect for a memorable family visit. Guided tours are informative and often amusing, and passages are safe and lit throughout. The reception building has been built to blend in with the remote and beautiful environment.

SCENIC ROUTES

The descent to Ballyvaghan, down Corkscrew Hill, provides a wonderful combination of the extraordinary Burren rock formations with the little village of Ballyvaghan, its white-washed cottages and harbour and the wide expanse of Galway Bay beyond. Kinvarra and Finavarra Head are to the right, Gleninagh Mountain and Black Head to the left.

fragrant bounty is the Burren Perfumery at Caron. In a lovely remote location, it also features visual presentations in its floral centre and herb garden.

FOR HISTORY BUFFS

In 2002, to mark the 1,000th anniversary of the inauguration of Brian Boru as High King of Ireland, a special heritage trail, The Footsteps of Brian Boru, was launched. It highlights 31 important sites associated with the monarch who routed the Vikings and led a prosperous and cultured society, as well as his descendants, the O'Brien clan. Many of those sites are within the area of this tour, but the Brian Boru Visitor Centre, is a little to the east at Killaloe. An excellent colour brochure, available from tourist information centres, gives full details, plus lots of fascinating historical information.

▶ *Take the Corofin road, R476, for 4 miles (6km), then turn left on to the R480 for Ballyvaghan. Turn right and follow the N67 to Kinvarra.*

7 Kinvarra, Co Galway
Kinvarra is a fishing village in Galway Bay, and the hill above gives splendid views of these much-loved Irish waters. Dunguaire Castle – the 7th-century seat of the King of Connacht, Guaire Aidhneach, a man of celebrated hospitality – stands on a promontory in Kinvarra Bay. The 17th-century tower house and bawn that now stands here was built by his descendants, the O'Heynes.

Southeast of Kinvarra, near Gort, is Thoor Ballylee, where Yeats lived, a place of great symbolic importance to the poet. You can climb the 'narrow winding stair', and see an audiovisual presentation on Yeats's life and times. Yeats often visited Coole Park, home of Lady Gregory, co-founder of

'matchmaking', and festivals are held to persuade traditionally reluctant bachelor farmers to the altar. The town has a great reputation for fun and good company, which is at its height in September when the harvest is gathered in. It also has Ireland's only active spa. The Spa Wells Health Centre has a Pump House and a variety of health and recreational facilities.

▶ *Take the R476 for 5 miles (8km) to Kilfenora.*

6 Kilfenora and the Burren, Co Clare
You will already have passed through part of the Burren, but here at Kilfenora, the Burren Centre puts this unique landscape and its plants into context. May is the best time to see the wild rock garden of flowers that covers the Burren, crowding together in crevices or covering the limestone out-

The wild and treeless Burren landscape is eerily beautiful

crops in profusion. It is not only the abundance of the plants that makes the Burren so special, as bright blue gentians blossom in the shallow turf and mountain avens, clear white with golden centres, tumble across the limestone terraces. The Burren also harbours a profusion of rare varieties. Species normally found only in the Arctic or at high altitude, such as the alpine saxifrage, appear in the Burren, but so does the dense-flowered orchid, which is a Mediterranean plant. Twenty-two varieties of orchid grow here, favouring a unique ecosystem created by a combination of factors, including fast drainage into the limestone, mild, moist weather conditions, the absence of grasses and the control of hazel scrub by goats. Drawing on this natural,

The house-painter's art – an appropriate mural for this shop in Kinvarra

the Abbey Theatre in Dublin. The house, where many of the figures involved in the literary renaissance met, was demolished in 1941, but the beautiful woods that appear in much of Yeats' work are in state care and the former stables contain an interpretative centre and tearoom.

▶ Turn right for Gort. After 4 miles (6km) bear left, and go through Tirneevin to Gort. Take the **N18** for Ennis and after 6 miles (10km) follow the **R462** for Tulla. Half a mile (1km) further on, turn right on to the **R532** for Ennis, then after 2 miles (3km) turn left for Quin.

8 Quin, Co Clare
A Franciscan friary, of which altars and tombs, a graceful tower and cloister remain, was built by the MacNamaras in the 15th century, on the site of a 13th-century castle. It also incorporates the buildings of a large Anglo-Norman castle. Close by, Knappogue Castle is

typical of hundreds of medieval castles that are scattered throughout Clare, many of them the preserve of the MacNamara family. The present castle has Georgian and Regency extensions. Set in pretty gardens within its well-planted demesne, it combines the atmosphere of sturdy stronghold and comfortable home.

Craggaunowen is close to Quin, too. An enterprising historical project has been built up around Craggaunowen Castle, a restored 16th-century tower house with replicas of furniture and tools of the period. The project lifts the lid off many of the skills of the past, including the construction of wattle-and-daub buildings, and weaving and cooking techniques. There is a reconstruction of a *crannóg*, or defensive lake dwelling, used by the Celts in the 6th and 7th century. Another replica is that of the boat St Brendan the Navigator is said to have used for his legendary transatlantic voyage in the 6th century. In 1977 Tim Severin sailed the Atlantic in this replica, proving that St Brendan could have

discovered America centuries before Columbus's landfall.

▶ Take the Limerick, road **R469**, turning right after 4 miles (6km) on to the **R462**. After 6 miles (10km) turn right on to the **N18** for Bunratty and Ennis.

SPECIAL TO...

Medieval banquets have become a very popular ingredient of many holidays in the Shannonside region. In the atmospheric surroundings of Bunratty, Knappogue or Dunguaire, medieval feasts or banquets are served with pageantry, costume, music and rhyme, with the emphasis on plenty of fun. The history of the castle dictates the mood and content of each of the entertainments.

9 Bunratty, Co Clare
One of Ireland's most popular tourist destinations, Bunratty's completely restored Norman-Irish keep sits four-square by the main road, its stout defences, including three

'murder holes' over the main door, defying entry. In fact, this is the most inviting of castles and, furnished with Lord Gort's magnificent medieval collection, it gives a colourful insight into the life of a 15th-century keep. In the grounds is Bunratty Folk Park, which re-creates 19th-century life, both in the small cottages and houses of the region, and in a village street. The scenes are enlivened with traditional crafts in action – bread-making, candle-making, thatching, milling and basketweaving. Ballycasey Craft Workshops

for contemporary craftsmen and women are close by.

Towards Limerick is Cratloe, where a mighty oak forest once supplied the timbers for Westminster Hall in London and the Grianan in Ulster. Cratloe Woods House, a good example of the Irish longhouse dating from the 17th century, is the family home of descendants of the O'Briens.

▶ *Take the **N18** for 14 miles (23km) back to Ennis.*

Bunratty Castle combines history with entertainment

River Shannon
Rambles

2 DAYS • 112 MILES • 179KM   The Celts were the first to recognise Limerick's strategic position when they built a fort at the lowest ford of the River Shannon. In the 18th century the city developed its present form, but then suffered a period of decline in the 20th century. Renovation has now restored much of its earlier style, notably at The Georgian House on Pery Square. King John's Castle and its excellent visitor centre tops the attractions. St Mary's Cathedral, founded in the late 12th century by the King of Munster, is filled with antiquities.

(See also Tour 3.)

In military use from 1200 to 1922, King John's Castle gives a magnificent insight into Limerick's eventful history

i *Arthur's Quay, Limerick*

▶ *Take the **N69** west for 17 miles (27km) to Askeaton.*

FOR HISTORY BUFFS

Limerick's history comes to life in King John's Castle, aided by costumed characters. Built in the 13th century as an instrument of royal authority and a military stronghold, it has been converted into an international visitors' centre. The centre has an audiovisual overview of Limerick's long history, and historical exhibits and archaeological remains covering some 800 years.
The excavation of archaeological treasures beneath the castle floor has provided added fascination since the dig began in 1990.

BACK TO NATURE

About 11 miles (18km) west of Limerick on the N69, turn south for 2 miles (3km) on a signposted, unclassified road to reach Currahchase Forest Park. This was the estate of poet Aubrey de Vere (1814-1922). The grounds contain fine landscaped gardens and an arboretum with exotic plants, as well as the tombstone that marks his pet cemetery. A nature trail leads through the estate, one of the finest in Ireland, past native Irish trees and plants, and the picnic area is an ideal spot for lunching in the open.

❶ Askeaton, Co Limerick
A Middle Ages stronghold of the Desmond clan, Askeaton sits on the River Deel. Alive with echoes of the past, ruined Desmond Castle inhabits a rocky islet in the river, right in the village centre. Its last defending Earl of Desmond fled to the Kerry Hills when the castle and the town fell to British troops in 1580. The impressive Great Banqueting

Hall measures 90 feet by 30 feet (28m by 9m) and at the south end there is a small chapel.
On the east bank of the river, cloisters enclosed by black marble pointed arches and supported by cylindrical columns are all that is left of a 15th-century Franciscan friary.
At Kilcoran, to the east, the Celtic Theme Park and Gardens features re-created historic buildings.

3 Glin, Co Limerick

The Fitzgeralds, powerful
Earls of Desmond, dominated
this village, and ruins of their
Castle of Glin still overlook
the Shannon estuary. It was
fiercely defended in 1600 but
fell to the English forces after
two days of intense fighting.

*Glin Castle is a mixture of 18th-
century and Victorian Gothic
architecture*

The Desmond holdings here
have passed without interrup-
tion for more than seven centuries to the present Knight of
Glin, whose home, Glin Castle
(not to be confused with the
Castle of Glin), contains a fine
collection of Irish paintings,
furniture and decorative arts.
The Castle (now a hotel),
pleasure grounds and walled
garden are open to the public.

About 1 mile (1.5km) west
of the village, look for the
Gothic-style Glin Castle Gate
Lodge, a pleasant tea-room and
craft shop, where cast-offs from
the castle are often scattered
among craft items.

The castellated building
overlooking Glin pier is
Hamilton's Tower, a 19th-
century folly built by one Dr
Hamilton to give employment
to Irish famine victims.

▶ *Continue west on the N69
for about 4 miles (6km)
to Tarbert.*

4 Tarbert, Co Kerry

A car ferry across the Shannon
to Killimer in County Clare
departs from the wooded
headland that juts into the
river's estuary at this quiet
little village, a real timesaver
for travellers who want to
avoid Limerick traffic.

▶ *Take the unclassified coastal
road to Ballylongford, then
the R551 to Ballybunnion.*

▶ *Follow the N69 to Foynes.*

2 Foynes, Co Limerick

The most scenic portion of the
coastal drive along the Shannon
begins in this small seaport,
though these days, its waters
play host to luxury yachts as
well as commercial ships. The
first steamship to depart its
docks was a blockade runner
providing uniforms made in
Limerick for Confederate
forces during the American
Civil War. During the late 1930s
and 1940s, Foynes was the
home port for a transatlantic sea
plane service, and the
renowned Flying Boat Museum
presents an audio-visual show
along with mementoes of those
pioneering days in the world of
air travel.

▶ *Continue west on the N69
for another 8 miles (13km)
to Glin.*

5 Ballybunnion, Co Kerry
The ruins of Ballybunnion
Castle stand on Castle Green in
this popular Atlantic coast resort
town. It is the fine beach, however, that draws visitors, as well
as the network of souterrains
(subterranean passages) near
Castle Green, and invigorating
clifftop walks.

Just north of the town are

the remains of a promontory fort
overlooking Doon Cove. The
18-hole golf course is an
attraction for amateurs and
professionals alike.

▶ *Continue southeast via the*
R553 to Listowel.

Castle ruins point skyward above
Ballybunnion's beach

RECOMMENDED
WALKS

Magnificent seascapes add to
the exhilaration of cliff-top
walks from Ballybunnion to
Doon Point north of the
strand. To the south is the
lovely Doon Cove.

6 Listowel, Co Kerry
The castle in this bustling market town was the last to hold out against Elizabethan forces in the Desmond rebellion. When it finally fell in 1600, the entire garrison was put to the sword. Two fine Gothic-style churches dominate the town square, and the old Protestant church has been converted into an information centre. Take a look at a wonderful bit of plaster fantasy, the 'Maid of Erin' figure on the Central Bar that sits on one corner of the square. Local craftsman Pat McAuliffe and his son created this monument and other works around the town and in Abbeyfeale.

It was from a window of the Listowel Arms Hotel on the square that Charles Stewart Parnell, campaigner for Home Rule, made one of his last public appearances just three weeks before his death in 1891. Fans of the noted playwright John B Keane should head for his pub in William Street, where he is often to be found mingling with the locals, or engaged in the storytelling for which he is famous. Lord Kitchener, of Khartoum fame, was born 4

The ancient fortress, from which Newcastle West takes its name, stands on the wide main square

miles (6km) northwest of town at Gunsborough in 1850.

[i] *St John's Church (seasonal)*

> SPECIAL TO...
>
> Listowel has spawned such noted authors as John B Keane, Bryan MacMahon, George Fitzmaurice and Maurice Walsh, and this literary heritage is imaginatively portrayed in Seanchaí – Kerry Literary and Cultural Centre, next to the castle. The town is host to hordes of aspiring writers, poets and playwrights during its Writers' Week, held in late May or early June, with a week of workshops, lectures and theatre productions.

▶ *Take the R555 southeast to Abbeyfeale.*

7 Abbeyfeale, Co Limerick
In the foothills of the Mullaghareirk Mountains, this little market town grew from

the Cistercian abbey founded here in 1188. The only traces of the abbey have since been incorporated into the Catholic church building. The town square has a statue of Father William Casey, parish priest and leader of the tenant farmers' fight against landlordism in the mid- and late 1800s.

▶ *Take the N21 northeast to Newcastle West.*

8 Newcastle West, Co Limerick
Adjacent to the town square of this bustling market town are the ruins of a Knights Templar castle dating from 1184. Burned in 1642, its two 15th-century halls, peel tower, keep, bastion and curtain wall have survived. While the Great Hall is largely in ruins, the Desmond Banqueting Hall is almost perfectly preserved, complete right down to a vaulted basement, and now serves as a cultural centre for recitals, concerts, lectures and exhibitions.

You can see Irish Dresden porcelain being made at the factory and showroom in Dromcolliher, some 9 miles

(15km) southeast of town via the R522.

▶ *Follow the N21 northeast for 8 miles (13km) to Rathkeale.*

9 Rathkeale, Co Limerick
The poet Edmund Spenser and Sir Walter Raleigh first met in Rathkeale at Castle Matrix, built in 1440 and named after an ancient Celtic sanctuary that once occupied this site. The castle has furnishings authentic to its era and an outstanding library with many rare books. There is also a unique collection of documents about the 'Wild Geese', Irish chieftains and soldiers who fought with European armies in the 17th and 18th centuries.

▶ *Continue northeast via the N21 to Adare.*

10 Adare, Co Limerick
With its neat thatched cottages and broad main street, Adare is

One of the delightful cottages that have made Adare one of Ireland's prettiest villages

likely to come closer to the romantic image of the 'quaint little Irish village' than any other in the country, although its appearance is decidedly English. Credit for its beauty must go to the third Earl of Dunraven, who had a passion for early Irish architecture and local improvements.

The ancestral home of the Dunravens, Adare Manor, stands at the northern edge of town and is now a luxury hotel. In the heart of the hotel's golf course are the ruins of a castle on the banks of the River Maigue, a Franciscan friary dating back to 1464 and the 15th-century Desmond family

chapel (check with the golf club before visiting).

In the village, remains of a 14th-century Augustinian friary sit near the fine 14-arch bridge across the River Maigue. The Adare Heritage Centre in Main Street has interesting displays on the area's unique history, including realistic models and an audiovisual show (in several languages). Guided tours leave from here in summer.

i Heritage Centre (seasonal)

▶ *Take the N21, then turn left on to the N20 back to Limerick.*

SPECIAL TO...

Frank McCourt's Pulitzer Prize-winning novel, *Angela's Ashes*, was set in Limerick, and an evocative exhibition, in the old coach house of The Georgian House, includes a full-size reconstruction of the McCourt's home.

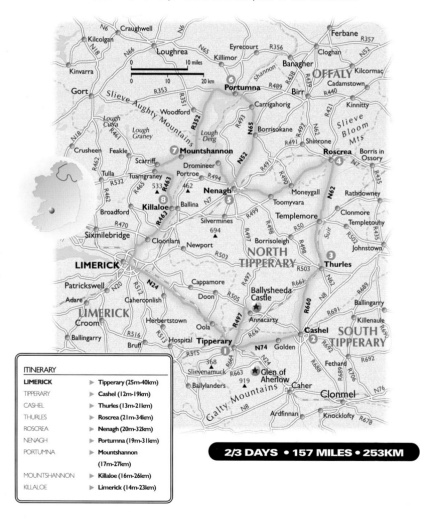

TOUR

3

Ancient Castles
& Lake Odyssey

Limerick is a large and lively city with a long history of momen-tous events. (See also Tour 2). The Limerick Museum in St John's Square tells the story from the Stone Age onwards, and the famous Hunt Museum, in Rutland Street, holds more than 1,000 Irish antiquities and examples of medieval art.

2/3 DAYS • 157 MILES • 253KM

[i] Arthur's Quay, Limerick

FOR HISTORY BUFFS

Eleven miles (17.5km) northwest of Limerick via the N18 west, then north on the R462 to Sixmilebridge, is the Craggaunowen Project, a fascinating historical complex. There is a superb example of a 16th-century fortified house, and the adjacent lake holds a reconstructed crannog, a prehistoric dwelling built on an artificial island. Housed in a glass structure near by, the tiny leather boat *St Brendan* is an exact replica of the vessel in which the saint crossed the Atlantic in AD700 and was used by Tim Severin and his modern-day crew to retrace the legendary voyage.

▶ *Take the N24 southeast for 25 miles (40km) to Tipperary.*

❶ Tipperary, Co Tipperary
In the heart of Ireland's fertile Golden Vale, Tipperary town is an important dairy farming centre. It figured prominently in the 19th-century Land League campaigns to legalise land ownership for Irish tenants, and today it is a thriving market town, and an excellent base for hill walking in the nearby Slievenamuck and Galty mountains. The major point of interest in town is St Michael's Church, Gothic in design and noteworthy for its fine lancet windows and west door.

About 8 miles (13km) north of town via the R497 and R505, the well-preserved circular keep of Ballysheeda Castle stands on a hillside 1 mile (1.5km) north of Annacarty village. South of Tipperary, via the R664, is the Glen of Aherlow, one of Ireland's most scenic places.

[i] EXCEL Centre

▶ *Follow the N74 to Cashel.*

SPECIAL TO...

The GPA Bolton Library, in the grounds of St John's Cathedral in Cashel, has a fine collection of more than 12,000 rare books, including two leaves from Caxton's press of 1486, and examples of early Irish printing.

❷ Cashel, Co Tipperary
Ecclesiastical ruins on the Rock of Cashel dominate the town of Cashel (see Tour 10), but also of interest are the Cashel Folk Village, and the ruins of the Dominican friary, which was rebuilt in 1480 after destruction by fire, both in Chapel Lane. Be sure to see the lovely 13th-century east window. The Bishop's Palace, set in enclosed grounds in Main Street, was built for Protestant archbishops

Bru Boru Heritage Centre is an imaginative presentation of Irish crafts and culture

and is a splendid example of 18th-century architecture. It is now a hotel. Bru Boru, at the foot of the Rock, is a heritage and cultural centre which showcases Irish music and dance.

ℹ *Heritage Centre*

▶ *Take the **R660** north for 13 miles (21km) to Thurles.*

3   **Thurles,** Co Tipperary
It was in the Hayes Hotel in this old Anglo-Norman town that the Gaelic Athletic Association was founded in 1884. Bridge Castle, at the

western end of the Suir river bridge, and Black Castle, near the town square, are remnants of Butler clan castles. In the 19th-century Catholic cathedral the lavish use of marble, especially in the altars, gives a special beauty to the interior.

St Mary's Famine Church is now home to a museum with rare items relating to the famine and a military collection.

Holycross Abbey, a 12th-century Cistercian centre, set on the east bank of the Suir, 4 miles (6km) southwest of Thurles, has been restored as the parish church.

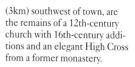
▶ *Take the **N62** north for 21 miles (34km) to Roscrea.*

4 **Roscrea,** Co Tipperary
One of Ireland's Heritage Towns and a good base for climbing and hill walking in the nearby Devil's Bit and Slieve Bloom mountains. Its most outstanding attraction is the Roscrea Heritage Centre in an annexe to Damer House, a town house dating from the early 18th century, set within the walls of an 11th-century Norman castle and narrowly saved from demolition in the mid-1970s. There are panoramic views from the top of the gate tower, and, inside, the magnificently carved staircase is stunning. The house is lavishly decorated and furnished and holds mementoes of life in the town through the ages. Available from the Heritage Centre is a booklet detailing a walking tour that incorporates the ruins of St Cronan's Church and Round Tower, and a High Cross, all of which date back to the 12th century.

At Monaincha, 2 miles (3km) southwest of town, are the remains of a 12th-century church with 16th-century additions and an elegant High Cross from a former monastery.

▶ *Take the **N7** southwest for 20 miles (32km) to Nenagh.*

5 **Nenagh,** Co Tipperary
Originally a Norman settlement, Nenagh served as a mid-19th-century garrison town, and finally evolved into a prosperous market town with many traditional shopfronts. One of the town's major features is the circular keep of Nenagh Castle, a mostly 1860 structure incorporating portions of a larger castle built in the early 1200s. The 100-foot-high (30m), 53-foot-wide (16m) keep, with walls up to 20 feet (6m) thick, formed part of the curtain wall of the earlier castle. Winding stairs set into the thickness of the wall lead to the roof. Nenagh's Heritage Centre is located near the castle in the old Governor's House and county gaol. There is a marvellous 'Lifestyles in Northwest Tipperary' exhibition, as well as visiting art and photographic exhibits. Nenagh Friary, in Abbey Street, was founded in around 1250 and features a 13th-century church.

Six miles (10km) northwest of Nenagh, via the R494, then the R495, Dromineer, on Lough Derg, is a lively centre for fishing, sailing and watersports.

ℹ *Connolly Street*

The River Suir lends an air of tranquillity to historic Thurles

---

SCENIC ROUTES

Six miles (10km) south of Nenagh, via the R500, look for the signposted turnoff for Step viewing point, near Silvermines village, at the foot of the Silvermines Mountains. The drive up to the viewing point is very scenic, and it culminates in panoramic views – the perfect place for a picnic.

towers at each corner and the lovely formal gardens.

About 7 miles (11km) south of Portumna via the N65 and the R493, the village of Terryglass, on the shores of Lough Derg, has a lovely old stone church and the ruins of a 13th-century castle. There are boats for hire and facilities for lakeside picnics.

BACK TO NATURE

Portumna Forest Park is a marvellous 1,000-acre (405-hectare) wildlife sanctuary that counts red and fallow deer among its many inhabitants. There is an observation tower beside the lake, and several other viewing stands, a nature trail and a picnic area.

▶ Turn south on the **R352** to follow the shores of Lough Derg to Mountshannon.

FOR CHILDREN

At the little town of Mountshannon children can embark on an island adventure – hire a boat at the pier to visit the mysterious holy island of Iniscealtra.

▶ Head northwards on the **N52**, then turn left on to the **N65** and continue for 19 miles (31km) to reach Portumna.

FOR CHILDREN

Lough Derg is a natural paradise for children. Its many islands and tiny inlets invite exploration, fishing is excellent, and watersports are a favourite pastime for locals and visitors alike.
The best places for access and facilities on the lough are Dromineer, Portumna, Mountshannon and Killaloe.

The massive keep of Nenagh Castle is mostly Victorian

⬤6 Portumna, Co Galway

This small lakeside town at the northern end of Lough Derg is a popular centre for fishing the lake and the River Shannon, as well as a major base for cruisers. The impressive ruins of Portumna Castle stand in its demesne, laid out as an attractive forest park, on the edge of town. Built in 1609 by the Earl of Clanricarde, it was destroyed by fire in 1826, but has been restored and is open to the public. Of special interest are the Renaissance doorway with gunholes on one side, the Jacobean gables, the square

⬤7 Mountshannon, Co Clare

The River Shannon, in the course of its 230-mile (370km) rambles, forms several lakes, of which Lough Derg is the largest, stretching some 25 miles (40km) in length and sprinkled with numerous islands and islets. The drive down its western shore is delightful, with the lake in view much of the way and never more than a short detour to the east.

At the little town of Mountshannon, hire a boat at the pier to visit the Holy Island of Iniscealtra and the remains of an early Christian settlement, including a round tower and no less than five churches.

▶ Continue southwest on the **R352** to Tuamgraney, then turn southeast on to the **R463** to reach Killaloe.

8 Killaloe, Co Clare
This charming little village stands at a fording point of the River Shannon at the lower end of Lough Derg. The churchyard of St Anne's is said to be the ancient site of Kincora, the palace of Irish King Brian Boru and his O'Brien descendants. In the church grounds, St Molua's Oratory, estimated to be 1,000 to 1,200 years old, reposes in safety after being rescued when its Friar's Island home was threatened by submersion in a hydroelectric development. The 12th-century Church of Ireland St Flannan's Cathedral is noteworthy for its ornately carved Irish Romanesque doorway. It has an Ogham (ancient Celtic writing) stone that also has runic writings and a crude

crucifix possibly formed by a Viking convert. There are traces of a ringfort on the southeastern side of Crag or Cragliath hill.
  Killaloe has been declared a heritage town, and its Brian Boru Heritage Centre tells a fascinating story.
  The Shannon remains an important feature of the town, with fishing, boating and water sports.

ℹ️ *Killaloe Heritage Centre*

▶ *Follow the **R463** southwest to return to Limerick.*

Killaloe village has an important ecclesiastical heritage

Beehive Huts &
Coastal Splendours

Known for its Rose of Tralee Festival in late August, Tralee is an important business centre and the principal gateway for the Dingle. Its many attractions include historic streets, fine churches, the 'Kerry the Kingdom' Museum (including a 'time travel experience'), and the National Folk Theatre, Siamsa Tíre.

2/3 DAYS • 97 MILES • 156KM

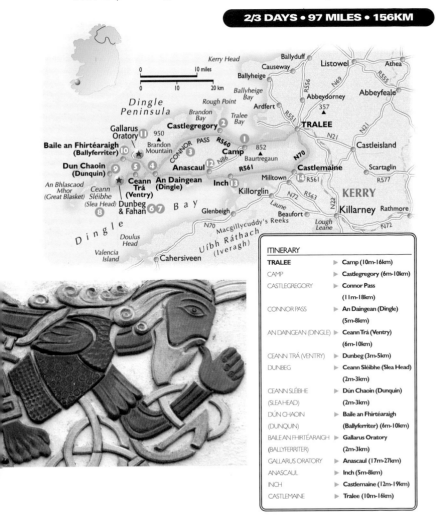

ITINERARY		
TRALEE	▶	Camp (10m-16km)
CAMP	▶	Castlegregory (6m-10km)
CASTLEGREGORY	▶	Connor Pass (11m-18km)
CONNOR PASS	▶	An Daingean (Dingle) (5m-8km)
AN DAINGEAN (DINGLE)	▶	Ceann Trá (Ventry) (6m-10km)
CEANN TRÁ (VENTRY)	▶	Dunbeg (3m-5km)
DUNBEG	▶	Ceann Sléibhe (Slea Head) (2m-3km)
CEANN SLÉIBHE (SLEA HEAD)	▶	Dún Chaoin (Dunquin) (2m-3km)
DÚN CHAOIN (DUNQUIN)	▶	Baile an Fhirtéaraigh (Ballyferriter) (6m-10km)
BAILE AN FHIRTÉARAIGH (BALLYFERRITER)	▶	Gallarus Oratory (2m-3km)
GALLARUS ORATORY	▶	Anascaul (17m-27km)
ANASCAUL	▶	Inch (5m-8km)
INCH	▶	Castlemaine (12m-19km)
CASTLEMAINE	▶	Tralee (10m-16km)

i *Ashe Memorial Hall, Denny Street, Tralee*

FOR CHILDREN

A great attraction for children is the narrow-gauge Tralee/Blennerville railway that runs along part of the long-abandoned Tralee/Dingle line on a 5-mile (8km) round-trip.

At Blennerville is a restored windmill, while at the Tralee end, adjacent to the platform, is the Aqua Dome, a palace of water-based fun.

▶ *Take the N86 west, with the Slieve Mish mountains on your left, to Camp.*

FOR HISTORY BUFFS

Five-and-a-half miles (9km) northwest of Tralee via the Ballyheige road (R551) is imposing Ardfert Cathedral, which dates from the 13th century. A niche in the building holds the 13th- or 14th-century effigy of a bishop unearthed here in 1830, and there is an ogham stone in the graveyard. The tiny village of Fenit, 8 miles (13km) west of Tralee via the R558, is thought to be the birthplace of St Brendan the Navigator (AD484–577), who, according to some, may have reached the shores of America long before Christopher Columbus.

❶ Camp, Co Kerry
In the village, turn off the main road west towards the mountains to reach Ashe's pub, the epitome of everyone's image of what an old-time Irish pub should be – smoke-darkened wood, low ceilings, a peat fire glowing on the hearth, and the Ashe family carrying on a tradition of generations.

▶ *Go back for a ½ mile (1km) before turning left on to the R560 west to Castlegregory.*

❷ Castlegregory, Co Kerry
There are fine beaches at Castlegregory, which sits at the neck of a spit of land dividing

The dramatically beautiful Slieve Mish Mountains

BACK TO NATURE

Tucked away in the mountains near Castlegregory, Gleann Ti An Easaigh/Glenteenassig Forest Park is a feast for the naturalist. It lies a little over 13 miles (22km) west of Tralee on the R560 to Castlegregory. Watch for signposting at Aughacasla and turn left into the mountains for 3 miles (5km). Alive with rushing streams and tiny lakes, the park is the habitat of many species of wildlife, as well as a refuge for a wide variety of birds. Mountain walks yield panoramic views of Tralee Bay and the western tip of the peninsula, with a perfectly positioned picnic site.

Tralee and Brandon bays, with more along the drive from Camp. Birdwatchers will want to turn left just before reaching the town to visit Lough Gill bird sanctuary, which attracts

such exotic species as the Bewick's swan from Siberia.

▶ *Turn back east on the **R560**, then right on to the unclassified road signposted 'Dingle, Connor Pass'.*

8 Connor Pass, Co Kerry
Climbing between the Brandon and central Dingle groups of mountains, this drive passes through some of Ireland's most spectacular scenery. On a fine day, there are vast panoramas of mountains, sea, lakes and valleys – on a not-so-fine day, mist and clouds can turn the narrow, winding road into a real driving challenge.

Just past the village of Stradbally, you cross the deep Glennahoo Valley and begin the climb to the 1,500-foot (460m) summit of the Connor Pass, with spectacular views of valleys strewn with boulders and, about a mile from the summit, tiny Pedlar's Lake. The road upwards winds along the base of great cliffs. From

the lay-by at the summit, there is a fine view of Dingle Bay and Dingle town to the south, with several small lakes in the deep valley to the left; the north aspect takes in the wide sweeping bays of Brandon and Tralee.

▶ *Continue southwest for 5 miles (8km), descending to An Daingean (Dingle).*

RECOMMENDED WALKS

The entire Dingle Peninsula invites walks off the one main road that circles westward from Dingle town. Details of the Dingle Peninsula Walking Route and The Kerry Way are available from the tourist office in Tralee.

The drive across the Connor Pass, in either direction, has some of the most magnificent mountain views in Ireland

4 An Daingean (Dingle),
Co Kerry

County Kerry's chief port in the old days of Spanish trading, and a walled town in the Elizabethan era, Dingle town today is a busy little market, fishing and tourism centre with a boat-building industry right on the harbour. Dingle is in the heart of a Gaeltacht district in which Irish is the everyday language, but, of course, everyone can speak English too.

Dingle is a centre for specialised tours, including riding, cycling and archaeological ones. The town itself is compact, with tiny streets that climb upward from the seafront with several excellent shops, and there are boat rides out into the bay to see Dingle's resident dolphin (see For Children).

On the western edge of town, the Ceardlann na Coille craft village is a cluster of small cottages housing shops and workshops that sell handcrafted leather goods, Uilleann pipes, knitted goods, and the work of weavers and a cabinetmaker.

One of the town's most impressive collections of Irish-interest publications and records can be found in the front shop section of An Café Liteartha in Dykegate Lane. For traditional music and song that stems from a long-time family tradition, look for the red-and-white pub on Bridge Street with the Irish name UaFlaibeartaig, which translates to O'Flaherty's. It is a warm, informal setting, as traditional as the music itself, its walls sporting the sort of haphazard collection of pictures, posters and other assorted items that have accumulated over the years. Most pubs have music on summer nights; try Mac Cárthaigh's, An Droichead Beag and John Benny Moriarty's.

[i] *The Pier*

▶ *Drive due west on the R559 for 6 miles (10km) through Baile an Mhuilinn (Milltown) to Ceann Trá (Ventry).*

Wonderful unspoilt beaches are dotted around the Dingle peninsula

---

FOR CHILDREN

What could be more fun for the younger ones than a boat ride out into Dingle Bay to watch Dingle's friendly Dolphin, Fungie. He playfully follows the boats that leave from the town quays to ferry visitors out to his watery home, cavorting with scuba divers, and sometimes taking a flying leap over a small boat. On dry land, near the harbour, Dingle Oceanworld is a state-of-the-art aquarium that includes an undersea tunnel.

---

5 Ceann Trá (Ventry),
Co Kerry

According to legend – and a 15th-century manuscript now in the Bodleian Library at Oxford, in England – Ventry beach was the scene of a fierce battle when the King of the World, Daire Doon, attempted to invade and conquer Ireland. He and his vassal monarchs, however, suffered a massive defeat at the hands of the King of Ireland, Fionn MacCumhaill, and his loyal Fianna band.

The village nestles at the head of Ventry Harbour, with the slopes of Mount Eagle and Croagh Marhin as a backdrop and a 5km (3-mile) safe, sandy beach.

The black, beetle-like boats you will see upturned on the beach are currachs, the traditional canvas-covered vessels painted with tar that have been used by fishermen in these waters for centuries.

▶ *Continue southwest on the R559 to Dunbeg.*

6 Dunbeg, Co Kerry

A relic of the Iron Age, Dunbeg Fort perches on a high promontory above Dingle Bay, its landward side surrounded by earthen trenches, and its 22-foot (7m) thick wall riddled with an elaborate souterrain (inner passage). Originally, there was an inner enclosure and a skilfully built inner house. But time has taken its toll, and some of its stones long ago tumbled into the sea. There's also a good visitors' centre with refreshments.

The beehive huts at Fahan are an evocative relic of prehistoric times

▶ Turn north, still on the *R559*, for 2 miles (3km) heading for *Dún Chaoin (Dunquin)*.

SCENIC ROUTES

The drive along the R559 from Ventry to Slea Head has a wide diversity of scenic pleasures, at times hugging the sides of sheer cliffs high above Dingle Bay, and at others passing through stony fields reaching up sloping mountains.

▶ Cross the *R559* to the Fahan archaeological grouping.

7 Fahan, Co Kerry

In farmyards on the southern slopes of Mount Eagle, across from Dunbeg, unmortared beehive cells, or clochans (huts), are reminders of the prehistoric people who made their homes here and, quite possibly, built the promontory fort. It is a revelation to stoop down and enter one of these unique structures that are as watertight today as when they were built.

From more recent history is the Famine Cottage, former home of a family that departed for the New World during the famine.

▶ Continue west on the *R559* for 2 miles (3km) to Ceann Sléibhe (Slea Head).

8 Ceann Sléibhe (Slea Head), Co Kerry

At the very tip of the Dingle Peninsula are the high cliffs of

Working and pleasure boats in the sheltered waters of Ventry harbour

---

FOR HISTORY BUFFS

About 3 miles (5km) above the main road (R559) at Fahan, an ancient road is lined with stone huts and other remains of ages past. The stone beehive huts, souterrains, standing and inscribed stones, earthen ring-forts, two sculptured crosses and two fortified headlands constitute Ireland's largest collection of antiquities.

Slea Head – the westernmost mainland point in Europe. It is from here that you get the most sweeping view of sheltered coves below and Na Blascaoidí (the Blasket Islands) across the water, sometimes called 'the last parish before America'.

An Bhlascaod Mhór (the Great Blasket), the largest of these seven offshore islands, was for many years home to a hardy band of islanders who inhabited the one small village. In 1953, when a living wage could no longer be wrested from fishing, its population was moved to the mainland and given government grants for small farm holdings on the peninsula. A day trip to the islands from Dún Chaoin is an experience of tranquillity and scenic beauty unequalled anywhere else in Ireland.

9 Dún Chaoin (Dunquin), Co Kerry

Dunquin Pottery, on the road between Slea Head and Dunquin, is one of the many excellent potteries on the Dingle Peninsula. Its speciality is hand-thrown, ovenproof stoneware in shades of sand, browns and blues. Boats from Dunquin harbour make intermittent trips out to the Blasket Islands (see Slea Head) during summer months, and arrangements can often be made with individual boatmen when there is no sailing scheduled.

The Blasket Centre at Dunquin has an art gallery and audiovisual presentation, and highlights the extraordinary literary contribution of island writers Tomás O Crohan, Maurice O'Sullivan and Peig Sayers.

▶ Follow the *R559* north, then east to Baile an Fhirtéaraigh (Ballyferriter).

10 Baile an Fhirtéaraigh (Ballyferriter), Co Kerry

The Ballyferriter Heritage Centre, with its interesting 'Treasures of the Dingle

Peninsula' exhibition, occupies the old schoolhouse in the centre of the village.

The West Kerry Co-op office, just off Main Street, issues an excellent illustrated guidebook to the Dingle Peninsula, with great detail on its many antiquities. The Co-op began in 1968 in an effort to stem the out-going tide of young people who could not be supported by the large areas of untillable ground, and to perpetuate the unique culture and heritage of the Gaelic-speaking region. The Co-op imported a special deep-ploughing machine to break up the layer of iron ore that lay just beneath the surface and turn it into productive acres. Vast areas have been reclaimed, and the Co-op's remit has widened to include upgrading tourist facilities, and administering the Gaelic summer-school programme, in which students of all ages lodge with local families to learn their language.

Louis Mulcahy has a pottery studio on the outskirts of town, turning out many unique items with special glazes. Giant jugs and vases, unusual lamp bases and beautiful wall plaques supplement the more practical dinner services and cookware.

Two miles (3km) southwest of Ballyferriter, turn north on to an unclassified, signposted road to reach the site of the 16th-century fortress Dún an Oir, the so-called 'Golden Fort', built within an ancient promontory fort at Smerwick. The harbour here was the disembarkation point for an expedition of Spanish and Irish, along with their families and other retinue, who arrived in September of 1580 and constructed a fort to support the cause of the Catholic Irish against the Protestant English. It was bombarded from land and sea by English forces until eventually the fort capitulated, but over 600 were slaughtered – men, women and children – once they were disarmed. Poet Edmund Spenser (most famous

for *The Faerie Queene*), and possibly Sir Walter Raleigh were participants in the battle, which came to be known as the 'Massacre of Smerwick Harbour'. There is an excellent safe beach here.

▶ Follow the **R559** northeast for 2 miles (3km) and turn right at the signpost to Gallarus Oratory.

⑪ Gallarus Oratory, Co Kerry

This marvellous example of early Irish architecture is perhaps the most impressive of the peninsula's antiquities. Built in an inverted boat shape, it has remained completely watertight for more than 1,000 years, its unmortared stones perfectly fitted. At the crossroads just above Gallarus, turn left for Cill Maoilchéadair (Kilmalkedar), a 12th-century ruined church. In the church is the famous Alphabet Stone, a standing pillar carved with both Roman and

Ogham characters. The east window of this medieval church is known locally as 'the Eye of the Needle' through which one must squeeze to achieve salvation.

▶ Proceed via an unclassified road to Baile na nÁith (Ballynana), turning southeast on to the **R559** to Baile an Mhuilinn (Milltown) and An Daingean (Dingle), then drive east for 10 miles (16km) on the **N86** to Anascaul.

FOR CHILDREN

The Freshwater Experience, 3 miles (5km) east of Dingle, is a 15-acre (6-hectare) park with lakes, a wildfowl reserve, nature trails and a reconstruction of an ancient Celtic lakeshore dwelling. This is also a working trout farm, with man-made ponds where you can catch your own dinner.

including kitchen middens. In summer, there is sometimes horse-back riding across the firm sand and through the gentle surf. From the cliffside drive, west of the village, views out over the Iveragh Peninsula across the water are nothing short of spectacular.

▶ Continue east along the R561 for 12 miles (19km) to the little town of Castlemaine.

14 Castlemaine, Co Kerry
In the town, immediately after turning left on to the Tralee road (N70), turn left again and look for the unclassified road signposted 'viewing park' less than a mile (1.5km) further on. There is a viewpoint about 2½ miles (4km) along this road, with splendid views of Castlemaine Harbour and beyond the Laune Valley to Killarney. A second viewpoint, a little further on, looks north to Tralee Bay, Tralee town, and the Stack's Mountains.

▶ Reach the N70 and drive north to return to Tralee.

12 Anascaul, Co Kerry
Look for the South Pole Inn as you enter the village. It is named in honour of the former proprietor, Tom Crean, a member of the Scott Antarctic expedition. Beautiful Anascaul Lake is well worth a short detour.

▶ Heading south, then east on the R561, pass through Red Cliff to reach Inch.

On Dingle's western extremity, Dunquin (and its sheep) looks out across Blasket Sound

13 Inch, Co Kerry
The wide, 4-mile (6km) long sandy beach on this spit at the head of Castlemaine Harbour is one of the best bathing beaches on the peninsula. The high dunes backing the beach have yielded archaeological evidence of ancient dwelling sites,

---

RECOMMENDED WALKS

On the Dingle road west of Anascaul, park the car for a short, easy walk north along a signposted road that leads to lovely Anascaul Lake set in a boulder-strewn hollow. Hardy walkers with two or three hours to spare can continue around the lake and strike out across the hills of the Beenoskee Mountains to Stradbally and Castlegregory.

SCENIC ROUTES

The drive from Anascaul to Castlemaine through Red Cliff and Aughils via the R561 follows a narrow, winding road with fantastic views south across Castlemaine Bay and north to the open sea and Dingle harbour. Stop to admire the view from one of the tiny lay-bys along the way – it is extremely dangerous to stop the car and block the road.

SPECIAL TO...

The Rose of Tralee International Festival, which is in full swing for six days and nights in late August, is a fierce, but entertaining competition to see which of the beauties of Irish lineage from around the world best fits the time-honoured description from the famous song '...lovely and fair as the rose of the summer.' This gathering is much more fun than other beauty contests, which are usually taken very seriously indeed. The Rose of Tralee is a festival of light-hearted fun and frolic that includes parades, pipe bands, street entertainment and inter-festival singing competitions for the Folk Festival of Ireland. The whole thing culminates at the end of the week in the crowning of the Rose.

Killarney &
The Ring of Kerry

An abundance of natural **2 DAYS • 107 MILES • 172KM** beauty has drawn visitors to Killarney and its lakes for centuries. The scenic network of Lough Leane, Muckross Lake and Upper Lake, in a broad valley west of Killarney, is the single most powerful magnet for visitors. Killarney was once a quiet little market town, but today its narrow, congested streets can make for nerve-racking driving – it is, however, a perfect town to explore on foot.

▶ *Take the N72 northwest for 13 miles (21km) to Killorglin.*

RECOMMENDED WALKS

Just around the road from the cathedral in Killarney, the wooded walks of Knockreer estate offer a welcome retreat from congested town streets. A short walk brings you to Knockreer House, with occasional exhibits of the flora, fauna and wildlife of the area. A longer walk takes you to the ruins of Ross Castle (about 1½ miles (2.5km) from the town centre) on a long peninsula out on to the Lower Lake. Built in the 14th century, it was a prominent fortification during the Cromwellian wars in the 17th century. You can hire a boat here, which is undoubtedly the best way to see the lakes.

RECOMMENDED WALKS

An exhilarating walk is that over Gap of Dunloe, for which you should allow a minimum of three hours.
The Kerry Way, a splendid walk of approximately 134 miles (214km), has been laid out for dedicated walkers. It begins at Killarney National Park and extends around the Iveragh Peninsula. The tourist office in Killarney has full details.

FOR HISTORY BUFFS

In ancient times, the Hill of Aghadoe just outside Killarney was the seat of the Celtic Archdruid. *The Annals of Innisfallen*, a chronicle of Irish history from the 11th to the 13th century, was recorded by dedicated monks on one of the Lower Lake's 30 islands.

The charming and peaceful town of Killorglin comes to life in August for its famous Puck Fair

❶ **Killorglin,** Co Kerry
Perched on hills above the River Laune, Killorglin is an ideal starting point for the Ring of Kerry drive, a 112-mile (180km) scenic drive with an ever-changing panorama of mountains, lakes, cliffs, sandy beaches and craggy offshore islands. The route skirts the edges of the Iveragh Peninsula to Kenmare, then circles back over the mountains via Moll's Gap and Ladies' View to Killarney. Make this a leisurely drive with an overnight stop in order to savour all the magnificent scenery along the way.

In mid-August, this rather quiet little town is abuzz with the three-day Puck (Poc) Fair. It dates from 1613, and things get off to a rousing start when a tremendous male (or puck) goat is crowned King of the Fair. In the somewhat rowdy atmosphere, pubs stay open around the clock, and every sort of street entertainment goes on non-stop. This is also a traditional gathering place for the country's travelling people, who come to engage in some hard-driving horse trading. The origin of the Puck Fair is a matter of dispute: some say a goat bleated to alert a shepherd boy of approaching enemy forces and he, in turn, alerted the town about impending attack. The argument that the festival dates back to the worship of the Celtic god, Lug, gains credence when linked to the Gaelic word for August – Lughnasa, or festival of Lug.

▶ *Turn southwest on to the* **N70** *to Glenbeigh.*

2 **Glenbeigh,** Co Kerry
Look for the Kerry Bog Village Museum adjoining the Red Fox Inn on the main street. Bogs have played an important role in Ireland, and this is an authentic depiction of the lives of the peatbog communities.

▶ *Follow the* **N70** *southwest to reach Cahersiveen.*

3 **Cahersiveen (Cahirciveen),** Co Kerry
The drive along the southern shore of Dingle Bay from

Glenbeigh to this small town at the foot of the Bentee Mountain is one of island-dotted coastal scenery and fields studded with prehistoric stone ringfort ruins, with clear views of the Dingle Peninsula across the water. At Cahersiveen, Valentia Island comes into view. There is a ferry service, and it is accessible by car via a causeway at Portmagee. The island is noted for its mixture of superb cliffs, mountains, seascapes and vividly coloured subtropical flowers.

Brooding mountains – and the weather – overwhelm the pretty village of Waterville

One mile (1.5km) northeast of Cahersiveen, on the N70, Carhan House was the birthplace of Daniel O'Connell (1775); Cahersiveen's Heritage Centre includes displays on Ireland's beloved 'Liberator'.

BACK TO NATURE

If the seas are calm and you are a birdwatcher, join one of the cruises that take you out to the rocky islands that make up the Skelligs. Landings are limited because of erosion and because this is a bird sanctuary. The smaller of the two, An Sceilg Bheag (Little Skellig), is a major breeding ground for gannets. More accessible is Puffin Island which has breeding puffins as well as Manx shearwaters. Boats go from Valentia Island. The Skellig Experience Heritage Centre focuses on monastic and birdlife on the Skelligs.

▶ *Drive 10 miles (16km) south on the N70 to Waterville.*

4 Waterville, Co Kerry
Set on a strip of land that separates Ballinskelligs Bay from the island-sprinkled Lough Currane, this popular resort and angling centre is also

SCENIC ROUTES

From Waterville, the N70 follows the coast, then rises some 700 feet (215m) above sea level at Coomakista Pass, with breathtaking views of the bay, the Skellig Islands, and the coastline. It was on Sceilg Mhichíl (Skellig Michael), a rocky hulk that rises 700 feet (215m) above the sea, that a colony of early Christian monks built a retreat of stone beehive huts. It is now a UNESCO World Heritage Site. From Castlegrove, the road turns inland through wild and gorgeous scenery before returning to the sea at Sneem.

internationally known for its superb golf course. Mountains rise from the lake's eastern and southern shores, and on Church Island there are ruins of a 12th-century church that was dedicated to the 6th-century holy man, St Fionan.

▶ *Continue south, then east on the N70 for 22 miles (35km) to reach Sneem.*

5 Sneem, Co Kerry
On the drive east on the N70 from Waterville to Sneem, just east of Caherdaniel, is Castlecove, where, about 1½ miles (2km) north of the road you will see Staigue Fort, one of the country's best-preserved Iron-Age stone forts. The circular stone walls, 13 feet (4km) wide and 18 feet (5.5km) high,

Sheltered by encircling hills, Sneem nestles at the head of an inlet of the Kenmare River

have held over the centuries without the benefit of mortar, and along their interior are several flights of stairs in near perfect condition.

Just beyond the Coomakista Pass, about 1 mile (1.5km) beyond Caherdaniel on the Derrynane road, is Derrynane House, set in the wooded Derrynane National Historic Park. This is where 'The Liberator', Daniel O'Connell, lived for most of his political life, and the house is now a museum containing all sorts of O'Connell memorabilia.

The park covers some 300 acres (120 hectares), incorporating semi-tropical plants and coastal trees and shrubs, as well as dramatic coastal scenery. There is a well-marked nature trail, and sea bathing is accessible to visitors.

The pretty little town of Sneem, where the Ardsheelaun River estuary joins the Kenmare River, is a popular angling centre for brown trout and salmon, and its fine sandy beaches provide safe swimming. George Bernard Shaw wrote part of his play *St Joan* here. Sneem is also the last resting place of Father Michael Walsh, who was a parish priest in the area for 38 years in the 1800s and has been

immortalised as 'Father O'Flynn' in an Irish ballad.

Two miles (3km) to the south in Parknasilla, the elegant Great Southern Hotel is famed for its rock gardens and colourful sub-tropical blooms.

▶ *Continue east on the N70 for 17 miles (27km) to Kenmare.*

6 Kenmare, Co Kerry
The drive from Sneem along the banks of the Kenmare River has lovely views of the Caha and Slieve Miskish mountains on the opposite shore. Kenmare

faces the broad Kenmare river estuary, with impressive mountains behind.

Known as Ceann Mara (Head of the Sea) by the ancients, today it is a lively resort and heritage town. It is also noted for its fine salmon, brown trout and sea fishing, safe swimming, local walks and climbs, homespun woollen industry and lace. (See Tour 6.)

i *Kenmare Heritage Centre (seasonal)*

▶ *Turn north on to the N71 to reach Moll's Gap.*

7 Moll's Gap, Co Kerry

The drive north to Moll's Gap is one of rugged mountains and stone-strewn valleys. The viewing point at this gap affords sweeping views of Macgillycuddy's Reeks and of Ireland's highest mountain, the 3,408-foot (1,039m) Carrauntoohill. The restaurant and craft shop make this a good refreshment stop.

▶ *Follow the N71 northeast for 3 miles (5km) to Ladies' View.*

8 Ladies' View, Co Kerry

This mountainside viewing point overlooks the broad valley of the Killarney lakes. Queen Victoria and her ladies-in-waiting so enthused about this view that it was promptly named in their honour.

Nine miles (14.5km) north on the return to Killarney, are the well-preserved ruins of Muckross Abbey. The abbey dates from 1448 and was built on the site of an earlier religious establishment. About a 10-minute walk from the abbey, Elizabethan-style Muckross House, Gardens and Traditional Farm is surrounded by landscaped gardens that slope down to the lake. Built by a wealthy Kerry MP in 1843, it was sold to Americans in 1911, and presented as a gift to the Irish people in 1932. The house is furnished in the manner of the great houses of Ireland, while the basement portrays the busy life of the servants.

Muckross Traditional Farm is a working museum which farms the land using methods that were used in the 1930s. There are three separate farms, complete with animals, fully equipped workshops, a forge and a furnished farm labourer's cottage.

The gardens include a Victorian Walled Garden with glasshouses, craft workshops, a restaurant and gift shop.

About 1 mile (1.5km) before Muckross House, a signpost on the N71 directs you to a scenic footpath up a mountain slope to the 60-foot (18m) Torc Waterfall in a beautiful wooded area. Continue upwards to the top of the falls for magnificent views.

▶ *Continue for 11 miles (18km) northeast on the N71 to Killarney.*

FOR CHILDREN

Most children love being on the water, so what better way for them to see the Lakes of Killarney than aboard one of the watercoaches that leave the Ross Castle slipway several times daily to cruise the Lower Lake. They are sure to be fascinated by the mystical legends of the lake related by the boatmen as they glide past Innisfallen Island, O'Sullivan's Cascade, Tomies Mountain, Darby's Garden, the old copper mines, Library Point and many other points of interest.

The lakes and woodland of the Killarney National Park stretch out below Ladies' View

Kenmare & The
Beara Peninsula

The attractive town of Kenmare, at the head of Kenmare Bay, is a thriving market town and tourist centre, and an excellent base for exploring the Iveragh and Beara peninsulas which extend westwards on either side of the bay.

Its own attractions include The Kenmare Heritage Centre, the Lace Centre and one of Ireland's most impressive stone circles, known locally as the Druid's circle, beside the River Finnehy.

1/2 DAYS • 96 MILES • 154KM

ITINERARY	
KENMARE	▶ **Glengarriff** (18m-29km)
GLENGARRIFF	▶ **Adrigole** (12m-19km)
ADRIGOLE	▶ **Castletown Bearhaven** (9m-14km)
CASTLETOWN BEAR-HAVEN	▶ **Allihies** (12m-19km)
ALLIHIES	▶ **Eyeries** (10m-16km)
EYERIES	▶ **Ardgroom** (14m-23km)
ARDGROOM	▶ **Kenmare** (21m-34km)

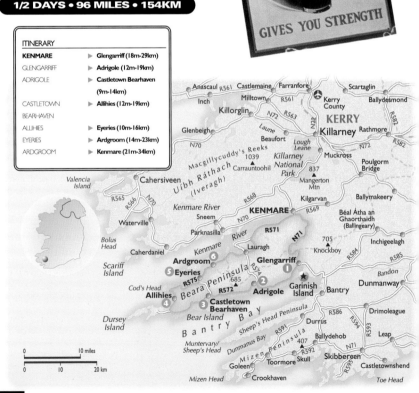

[i] *Heritage Centre, Kenmare (seasonal)*

RECOMMENDED WALKS

Walk out along the Glengarriff road (N71) from Kenmare and turn right at the signpost for the pier. Try to go when the tide is in, as the views of the Kenmare River are at their most impressive then. The river, with its backdrop of surrounding mountains and drifts of graceful swans, presents a view of tranquillity and natural beauty and is ample reward for the short walk.

FOR HISTORY BUFFS

Cross the bridge over the River Finnehy at Kenmare to find an impressive stone circle and dolmen. There are 15 stones in the circle, which measures about 50 feet (15m) across. In its centre is the dolmen, a megalithic tomb where upright stones support a large, flat capstone. Kenmare has been designated a Heritage Town as a 'planned estate town'. There is a visitor centre in the square which includes exhibitions of lacework and the story of the Nun of Kenmare.

Stormy skies add an extra touch of mystery to the ancient standing stones at Kenmare

Shaw, who came here to write much of his *St Joan*.

Only the strongest-willed visitor will be able to resist the entreaties of the bold boatmen who line the main street hawking a trip to the gardens; those who pass on by will be the poorer for it.

Glengarriff is also one of the few places in the country that preserves some specimens of the ancient mixed forests that once covered much of Ireland, best seen at Glengarriff Forest Park, on the northern edge of the village. A little more exotic is the Bamboo Park, impossible to miss behind its Japanese gateway. Delightful paths meander between plantings of bamboo, palms and other tropical species, which thrive in the balmy climate here, and there are some wonderful views over the bay.

Along with the boatmen advertising trips to Garinish Island, the main street is lined with shops selling Irish crafts.

Glengarriff lies at the head of the Beara Peninsula, a

▶ *Drive south for 18 miles (29km) on the N71 to reach Glengarriff.*

❶ Glengarriff, Co Cork
The 18-mile (29km) drive from Kenmare to Glengarriff (Rugged Glen) is known as the Tunnel Road. Two tunnels, one the longest in Ireland, bore through the Caha Mountains, and the road alternately climbs around mountain heights and dips into deep valleys.

Lying in the heart of a secluded valley surrounded by mountains, Glengarriff's sheltered position nurtures luxuriant Mediterranean flowers and plants such as fuchsia and arbutus. Its harbour is dotted with wooded islands. On Garinish Island you will find the world-famous Italian gardens, laid out between 1910 and 1913 by John Annan Bryce and Harold Peto. The lovely little island was a favourite of George Bernard

30-mile (48km) long finger of land between Bantry Bay and the Kenmare River. It is bisected by the Cork/Kerry county border running along the Caha mountain range that forms the backbone of the peninsula. A drive around this wild, sparsely populated peninsula constitutes the remainder of this tour.

FOR CHILDREN

A delightful bonus for children on the short boat ride from Glengarriff Pier to Garinish Island, about 1 mile (1.5km) offshore in Bantry Bay, is the sight of seals cavorting through the waters. The island's beautiful Italian gardens are a riot of colour in season, with subtropical plants in gorgeous bloom. Turn the children loose to wander along the woodland pathways, through the formal gardens, and down to the shores of the bay, or to explore the Grecian temple and old Martello tower.

RECOMMENDED WALKS

Scenic walks in Glengarriff include the Blue Pool, via a pathway west of the post office; Lady Bantry's Lookout, 2 miles (3km) southwest of the village on the Castletown Bearhaven road, returning by Shrove Hill viewpoint; or continue past Lady Bantry's Lookout to Eagle's Nest, and on to Biddy's Cove on the shores of the bay.

---

i *Town Centre (seasonal)*

▶ *Drive southwest on the R572 to Adrigole.*

2 **Adrigole,** Co Cork
From Glengarriff, the road follows the shoreline of Bantry

Lush vegetation cloaks the hillsides around Glengarriff

Bay, winding along the rocky coastal strip at the foot of the Caha Mountains, with 1,887-foot (575m) Sugarloaf Mountain on the right. At Adrigole Bridge, the spectacular Healy Pass (named after Tim Healy, the first Governor-General of the Irish Free State) crosses the mountains and is an alternative (and shorter) route to Kenmare and Killarney.

Some 3 miles (5km) west of Adrigole, Hungry Hill, highest of the Caha range, rises 2,251 feet (686m), with a rocky shelf halfway up its face with two lakes that feed a 700-foot (214m) cascade into the valley below – especially spectacular after rain.

SCENIC ROUTES

At Adrigole Bridge, turn right for the Healy Pass road. Begun during the famine, the road — after years of stopping and starting, and a high death-rate during its construction – was completed in 1931 and named after Tim Healy, the first Governor-General of the Irish Free State when it became a dominion in 1922. This spectacular drive, about 10 miles (16km), climbs right across the spine of the Caha mountain range and over the Cork/Kerry border, with magnificent views of Glanmore Lough, the forests of Tousist, Kenmare Bay and Macgillycuddy's Reeks. There is a viewing point and Crucifixion shrine at the top.

▶ *Continue southwest for another 9 miles (14km) on the R572 to Castletown Bearhaven.*

3 **Castletown Bearhaven,** Co Cork
Sheltered by the elongated Bere (Bear) Island just offshore, Castletown Bearhaven, now a fishing port, was once a British naval base. On North Street, the Call of the Sea offers an imagi-

---

native exploration of local maritime history, including the naval heritage, fishing, smuggling and Vikings, plus displays on the local copper mining industry.

There is a regular ferry service out to the island, where some forts still remain, manned from time to time by Irish forces. On a hillside near the old waterworks, look for a group of boulder burials and a fine stone circle, the latter on the western side of the hill.

Less than 2 miles (3km) west of town, facing Bere Island, are the remains of 16th-century Dunboy Castle, in spacious grounds overlooking the inlet. Its star-shaped fort was the stronghold of O'Sullivan Bere, the last Irish leader to hold out with Spanish allies against the British forces led by Sir George Carew in 1602. After a long siege, during which the garrison refused to surrender until the walls were completely shattered, the fort was all but destroyed. The ruins have been excavated for easy exploration.

Fifteen miles (24km) further west, Ireland's only cable car connects Dursey Island with the mainland. The beautiful, long, mountainous island is rimmed by high cliffs and is the site of a gannetry.

▶ *Continue southwest on the R572 to its junction with the R575, which turns north to Allihies.*

4 **Allihies,** Co Cork
The road from Castletown Bearhaven continues southwest to Black Ball Head before turning northwest to reach Allihies through a gap in the hills. This was once a rich copper-mining centre that formed the basis for the Puxley family fortunes. The 19th century was its most prosperous period, although some work continued right up to 1962. There are picturesque ruins on the scarred hillsides, but they should be explored with extreme caution, since the

Rejoining the main road, the R571, the drive into Kenmare follows Kenmare Bay, with scenic views along a striking section of the journey.

▶ Remain on the **R571** for 21 miles (34km) back to Kenmare.

old workings, with unguarded shafts, can be very dangerous.

Seascapes seen from the hills are breathtaking, the strand is safe for swimming, and just north of the village there is an old Mass rock.

▶ Follow the **R575** northeast to Eyeries.

5 Eyeries, Co Cork
From Allihies, the road leads northeast along the wide sea inlet of the Kenmare River through rugged scenery to the little village of Eyeries, set back from the sea on a pretty bay.

A little to the east, at Ballycrovane, there is an inscribed Ogham pillar stone thought to be the tallest in western Europe, at more than 17½ feet (5.18m) high. In general, Ogham stones served as gravestones and the script on them records details of the person who is buried.

One of Ireland's most striking wayside shrines looks south from the summit of the Healy Pass over the Caha Mountains

▶ Continue northeast on the **R571** for 14 miles (23km) to Ardgroom.

6 Ardgroom, Co Cork
Just beyond the little village of Ardgroom, you cross into Kerry, where there is yet another fine stone circle in Canfie, on the Lauragh road.

Lauragh, at the northern end of the Healy Pass, has a scenic ridge walk along a horseshoe of peaks surrounding the valley in which the village stands.

Near by is almost totally enclosed Kilmakilloge harbour, where boats can be hired to sail the safe waters. A little beyond Lauragh, signposts direct you inland to Cloonee Loughs, which is worth a detour.

Island City,
Magic Stone

Spreading out along a long valley, Cork is the Republic's second city, with an atmosphere and character all of its own. It has a lively arts scene, excellent shopping and such attractions as the Crawford Art Gallery, the Old Gaol and the famous St Anne's church at Shandon. (See also Tour 8)

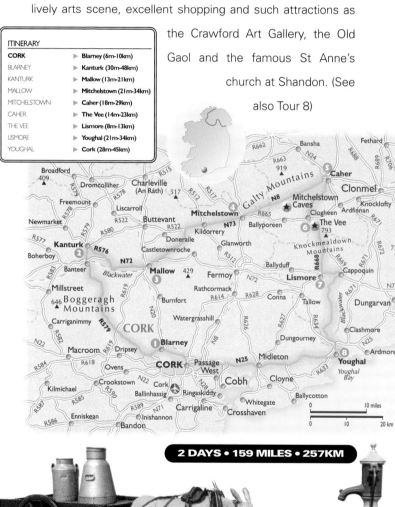

2 DAYS • 159 MILES • 257KM

ⓘ *Grand Parade, Cork*

FOR HISTORY BUFFS

Between 1848 and 1950 over six million people emigrated from Ireland; 2.5 million left through the port of Cobh, 15 miles (24km) east of Cork. The Queenstown Story, a multimedia exhibition, details the life of the port. Convict ships, transatlantic steamers and other ocean liners all departed from here, and the ill-fated *Titanic* called here before setting out across the Atlantic. The Titanic Trail is a daily walking tour of maritime history sites.

RECOMMENDED WALKS

There is a fine riverside walk in Cork which leads between rows of old trees, with seats and rustic shelters sprinkled along the way. The river widens into Cork Harbour, and on the opposite bank fine town houses climb up the hills of the Montenotte and Tivoli residential sections. The small fishing village suburb of Blackrock is at the end of the marina, with Blackrock Castle (now a restaurant) on a little promontory jutting out into the River Lee.

▶ *Cross Patrick Street bridge and turn left for a 6-mile (10km) drive northwest on the **N20**. Turn left onto the **R617** to reach Blarney.*

❶ Blarney, Co Cork
The well-preserved ruins of Blarney Castle, built in 1446, draw visitors not just for their history, but also for the magical powers attributed to the famous stone embedded in its parapet wall. The legend of its powers rose from Queen Elizabeth I's frustration in dealing with Cormac MacCarthy, Lord of

The climb to kiss the Blarney Stone renders many visitors speechless rather than eloquent

Blarney, and his smiling flattery that veiled wiliness with eloquence. Her declaration that 'This is nothing but Blarney – what he says, he never means!' added a new word to the English language and probably gave rise to the legend of the 'gift of eloquence' associated with the stone. Kissing the magical stone, however, involves climbing 120 steep steps to lie on your back and hang over an open space.

About 200 yards (180m) from the castle is the superb Scottish baronial mansion, Blarney Castle House, set amidst lovely 18th-century gardens.

Blarney Woollen Mills are also worth a visit.

ℹ️ *Town centre*

▶ *Go west from Blarney on the R617 and a few miles from the village turn northwest on to the R579 for the drive to Kanturk.*

2 Kanturk, Co Cork
One mile (1.5km) south of town, unfinished Kanturk Castle was begun in 1609 by Irish chieftain MacDonagh MacCarthy, who planned it as the largest mansion in Ireland, with a large quadrangle and four-storey towers at each corner. Alarmed at its size and strength, the English Privy Council ordered work to cease, declaring that it was 'much too large for a subject'. The roof-less, stout walls and towers have survived in remarkably good condition.

At Mealehara there is a fascinating farm museum.

▶ *Drive southeast on the R576 to its junction with the N72, then turn east for 9 miles (14km) to reach Mallow.*

3 Mallow, Co Cork
Set on the Blackwater River, Mallow was a popular spa town during the 18th and early 19th centuries; its lively social life gave rise to the famous song,

The Rakes of Mallow. The fine fortified house, built in the 16th century to replace 12th-century Mallow Castle, itself burned in 1689 on the orders of James II, now stands in fairly complete ruins in its own park by the river crossing.

From the Tourist Office in Cork or Youghal ask for the Blackwater Drive map, which shows a wealth of historic relics.

About 9 miles (14km) north of Mallow, via the N20, the little town of Buttevant was the venue for the world's first steeplechase in 1752, run between its church steeple and the one in Doneraile. Buttevant was the model for 'Mole' in Spenser's *The Faerie Queene*.

On the outskirts of town are the remains of Ballybeg, an Augustinian Canons' Regular House, enclosed by low stone walls, that date back to 1237. The ruins include a dovecot with ranks of stone nesting boxes inside.

▶ *Take the N72 northeast, then turn left on to the N73 for 21 miles (34km) to Mitchelstown.*

4 Mitchelstown, Co Cork
This is a tidy, attractive land-lord-planned town founded in the early 19th century. Ten miles (16km) northeast of town via the N8, are the signposted

Mitchelstown Caves are thought to be the largest system of river-formed caves in Ireland

Mitchelstown Caves, an under-ground wonderland of passages and high-ceilinged chambers, including the biggest chamber in the British Isles. The Old Caves were used as a refuge for the 16th-century Earl of Desmond, with a price on his head. There are escorted tours through 2 miles (3km) of the fantastic netherworld, with its fine stalactite formations.

▶ *Follow the N8 for 18 miles (29km) northeast to Caher.*

5 Caher, Co Tipperary
Caher Castle occupies a small islet in the River Suir, a natural site for fortifications as far back as the 3rd century. The present castle was built in the 13th century but was severely damaged during the 16th and 17th centuries. Oliver Cromwell besieged it in 1650 and sent in surrender terms. Historians argue as to whether or not the terms were accepted immediately but they did surrender before the walls were battered again, and the castle thus remained in sound condition. It has been restored almost to its original condition, and there is an excellent audiovisual show in the 1840 courtyard cottage.

On the southern edge of town, Caher Park is a lovely area of riverside woodland and shrubs, with a 2km (just over a mile) trail, fishing, a picnic site and walks to Swiss Cottage. This lovely building dates from the early 1880s, and its elegant interior contrasts with the rustic exterior and thatched roof. (See also Tour 10.)

▶ *Head south on the **R668** through Clogheen to begin The Vee mountain pass road en route to Lismore.*

6 The Vee, Co Tipperary and Waterford

The viewing points along this drive through a gap in the Knockmealdown Mountains provide spectacular panoramic views of Killballyboy Wood, Boernagore Wood, the Galty Mountains, the Golden Vale of Tipperary, Bay Lough and the Comeragh mountain range. (See also Tour 10.)

▶ *Continue south on the **R668** for 8 miles (13km) to Lismore.*

7 Lismore, Co Waterford

This historic little town, site of an ancient monastic centre of learning, is beautifully situated on the Blackwater River. Its most outstanding sightseeing attractions are Lismore Castle, whose gardens are open to the public, the Protestant cathedral, with grave slabs from the 9th and 11th centuries, and the modern Romanesque-style Catholic cathedral. An outstanding audiovisual show in The Heritage Centre depicts the town's history. The Centre has booklets detailing interesting town walks. (See also Tour 10.)

The fairy-tale appearance of Lismore Castle is second only to the fascinating facts of its history and illustrious occupants

[i] *Heritage Centre*

▶ *Take the **N72** east for 4 miles (6km) to the bridge on the outskirts of Cappoquin and turn right on to an unclassified road to a T-junction. Turn right on to the road signposted Youghal that follows the Blackwater River south to the sea, then turn right on to the **N25** south for the short drive into Youghal.*

8 Youghal, Co Cork

This picturesque fishing harbour and seaside resort is filled with mementoes of its past. Sir Walter Raleigh lived here, and legend has it that this is where he first smoked tobacco from the New World and planted the first potato in Irish soil. Myrtle Grove, his Elizabethan house, is at the top of Nelson Place.

A Tourist Trail booklet available from the Heritage Centre details a signposted walking tour of the town, which includes the historic Clock Tower in the town centre that was erected in 1771 as a gaol.

The Heritage Centre also contains displays on the history of the town. A short distance away, there are fragments of the old town walls, constructed in 1275 and added to up until 1603. During summer months there are harbour and river cruises as well as deep-sea fishing charters.

As the Blackwater River broadens near its entrance to the sea north of Youghal, look for the extensive ruins of 13th-century Molana Abbey, situated on what was once an islet. Although it has become rather overgrown, the site has the ruins of a church, cloisters and conventual buildings, as well as what is believed to be the burial place of the Norman knight Raymond le Gros.

Eight miles (13km) east of Youghal, via a signposted turnoff from the N25, the pretty little seaside village of Ardmore grew from the 7th-century settlement founded by St Declan. It has a fine group of ecclesiastical remains, including one of the most

perfectly preserved round towers in Ireland. There are also bracing cliff walks along the sea's edge.

i *Heritage Centre, Market Square*

▶ *Follow the **N25** west for 28 miles (45km) to return to Cork.*

Sunset over a deserted Youghal beach, on the south coast

BACK TO NATURE

About 5 miles (8km) west of Youghal on the N25, the entrance to Glenbower Wood is at the Thatch Inn in Killeagh village. Its nature trail is a 1½-mile (3km) loop that can be walked in about half an hour, or fully savoured for an hour or two. The wood is set in a glen through which the River Dissour rushes, and at one point an earthen dam was built to power the village corn mill, forming a lovely lake. Native trees include hazel (considered to have magical powers to ward off evil), sessile oak, alder, scrub oak, holly, birch and rowan. Tree plantations are mostly Norway spruce, Western hemlock and Sitka spruce. The profusion of ferns includes hard fern, bracken fern, hart's tongue and the male shield fern.

FOR CHILDREN

The Fota Wildlife Park, just to the east of Cork, is a child's paradise, inhabited by an engaging animal population that includes zebras, cheetahs, kangaroos, giraffes, ostriches, antelopes, gibbons and monkeys, as well as rare and endangered species. There are pools for flamingos and penguins, and swans float serenely on the lake. The tour train is great fun, and there is a children's corner and playground.

SPECIAL TO...

Cork's high-spirited Guinness Cork Jazz Festival in October attracts some of the world's most outstanding musicians, with concerts all around the town, as well as impromptu jam sessions breaking out in pubs, B&B drawing rooms, and wherever two jazz devotees happen to meet. The Cork Film Festival in late September or mid-October enjoys a worldwide reputation as a showcase for independent film-makers.

Cork's
Coastal Villages

Its great age and its location in a long, marshy valley have fashioned Cork City into what a native son once aptly described as 'an intimate higgledy-piggledy assemblage of steps, slopes, steeples and bridges'. Parallel to the Western Road is the Mardyke, a mile-long (1.5km) tree-shaded walk bordered by Fitzgerald Park, the site of the Cork Museum. (See also Tour 7.)

2 DAYS • 143 MILES • 229KM

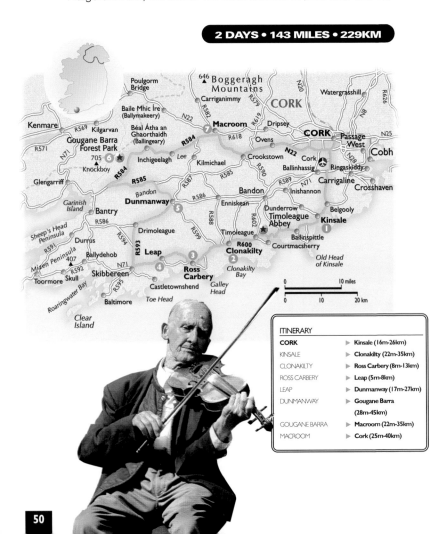

ITINERARY		
CORK	▶	Kinsale (16m-26km)
KINSALE	▶	Clonakilty (22m-35km)
CLONAKILTY	▶	Ross Carbery (8m-13km)
ROSS CARBERY	▶	Leap (5m-8km)
LEAP	▶	Dunmanway (17m-27km)
DUNMANWAY	▶	Gougane Barra (28m-45km)
GOUGANE BARRA	▶	Macroom (22m-35km)
MACROOM	▶	Cork (25m-40km)

RECOMMENDED WALK

Cork has a Tourist Trail marked out for visitors and a copy can be obtained from the Tourist Information Office.

FOR CHILDREN

Treat the children to a cruise of Cork harbour (tel: 021 4811485). Departing from Kennedy Pier in nearby Cobh (see Tour 7), the cruiser passes harbour forts, Spike Island, the naval base, and ships of all descriptions.

▶ *Take the **N27/R600** south for 16 miles (26km) to Kinsale.*

❶ Kinsale, Co Cork
The fishing and boating village of Kinsale has figured prominently in Ireland's history since it received its charter in 1334. A decisive British victory here in 1601 led to a mass exodus of Irish royalty known as the 'Flight of the Earls'. Twelfth-

century St Multose Church displays the old town stocks, and there are ruins of a 12th-century Carmelite friary and 15th-century Desmond Castle. The Seanachie Pub in Market Street has traditional music, and The Spaniard is a haunt of yachtsmen and local fishermen.

FOR HISTORY BUFFS

When Don Juan d'Agila arrived in Kinsale from Spain in 1601 with a large force to assist the Irish rebels against the English, an Irish victory seemed certain, even though the English Lord Deputy, Mountjoy, threw some 12,000 soldiers into the siege of the town. Irish chieftains O'Donnell and O'Neill marched their troops down from the north to mount a rear offensive against the English. This might well have succeeded had not word reached Mountjoy of their strategy, enabling him to successfully rout both Irish and Spanish. South of the town, you can visit the remains of King James Fort (or Old Fort), which housed the Spanish.

The narrow promontory of the Old Head of Kinsale shelters the popular yachting centre of Kinsale Harbour, to the east

Near Summer Cove, there are extensive, well-preserved remains of Charles Fort, built around 1677, with spectacular views of Kinsale harbour.

Seven miles (11km) south via the R600 and R604 is the Old Head of Kinsale, where a ruined clifftop castle overlooks the spot where the *Lusitania* was sunk in 1915 by a German submarine.

[i] *Pier Road*

SPECIAL TO...

The lively town of Kinsale is internationally known for its gourmet restaurants featuring cuisines from around the world, with local seafoods and meats in various guises on all the menus. Look for restaurants displaying the Kinsale Good Food Circle emblem. Or come for the Autumn Flavours Festival of Fine Food and Fun in October.

▶ *Continue on the **R600** for 22 miles (35km) southwest to Clonakilty.*

SCENIC ROUTES

For a scenic alternative route from Kinsale to Clonakilty, turn southeast at Timoleague on the R601 and drive along Courtmacsherry Bay. The fishing village of Courtmacsherry nestles between the bay and the thick woods behind.
Continue south to Butlerstown, where there are marvellous seascapes and views of the Seven Heads, a rugged peninsula with seven jutting headlands. Follow the unclassified road west to North Ring, then head north along the shores of Clonakilty Bay, to reach Clonakilty.

2 **Clonakilty,** Co Cork
Ten miles (16km) from Kinsale, on the Clonakilty road, Timoleague Castle Gardens were laid out more than one and a half centuries ago. Timoleague Abbey is a well-preserved ruined Franciscan friary, which in its day was an important religious centre.
At Clonakilty, castles dot the shores of the bay; the Catholic church is a fine example of Gothic architecture. The Michael Collins Centre is at the Irish resistance leader's birth-place, about 2 miles (3km) west at Woodfield.
You can also learn about Collins at the Arigideen Heritage Park, about 2 miles (3.5km) northeast of Clonakilty, which also includes an archaeology trail with full-size replicas of historical monuments, a maize maze and a cottage folklore theatre, plus guided walks, lectures and storytelling events.

ⓘ *25 Ashe Street*

FOR CHILDREN

A West Cork town of the 1930s to 1950s has been re-created at 1:24 scale at the West Cork Model Railway Village, and while kids can enjoy peering into the buildings and watching the trains, adults can appreciate the accurate historical content and workmanship.

▶ *Continue southwest on the N71 to Ross Carbery.*

3 **Ross Carbery,** Co Cork
At the head of Ross Carbery Bay, this picturesque little town

The gentle hills and tranquil waters of Ross Carbery

was the site of a medieval Benedictine monastery in the 6th century, founded by St Fachtna, and was famous for its school. A few remains of its foundation can be seen near the church, which stands on the site of an ancient cathedral.
One mile (1.5km) east of town are the ruins of Benduff Castle, and a little further on, the beautiful demesne of Castlefreke. Two miles (3km) west of town, the fine Drombeg stone circle can be seen from the Glandore road, R597, and near by is Fulacht Fiadh stone trough, an ancient Celtic cooking pot in which water was brought to the boil with stones heated in a fire.

▶ *Take the N71 west to Leap.*

4 **Leap,** Co Cork
This pretty little village sits at the head of a narrow inlet where the River Leap (pronounced 'lep') enters Glandore harbour. Stop in at the Leap Inn in the main street to experience an authentic Irish country inn that has been run by the same family for generations; the dining room serves good, solid, traditional Irish favourites.

Climb the hill above the village for beautiful harbour views, and drive to nearby Unionhall on a scenic road that follows the harbour as it widens to enter the sea.

▶ *Continue west on the **N71** until Skibereen, then turn north on the **R593** for Drimoleague and the **R586**. Turn north for Dunmanway, a total distance of 17 miles (27km).*

5 Dunmanway, Co Cork
The famous Gaelic Athletic Association figure, Sam Maguire, was born near this early 17th-century linen industry plantation town and is buried in St Mary's cemetery. The town pitch bears his name.
There are fine forest walks at Clashnacrona Woods, 3 miles (5km) southwest of the town on the R586, and at Aultagh Wood, which lies 4 miles (6km) north on the R587.

▶ *Take the unclassified Derrynacaheragh road northwest, then turn left on meeting the **R585** and continue to Kealkill. Turn northeast on the **R584** through the Pass of Keimaneigh to reach the Gougane Barra road.*

6 Gougane Barra Forest Park, Co Cork
Gougane Barra was Ireland's first forest park. The River Lee rises in Gougane Barra lake, a corrie lake surrounded by thickly wooded crags. Before moving on to the marshes of Cork, St Finbar had a hermitage in this remote spot. St Finbar's Holy Island, connected to the shore by a causeway, holds a tiny Romanesque chapel built in 1901. Pilgrimages are made to the hermitage each September.

▶ *Drive northeast on the **R584** to Macroom, turning left on to the **N22** to enter the town.*

The Gougane Barra Forest Park is a haven of peace and wildlife

---

BACK TO NATURE

Gougane Barra Forest Park is one of the few forest parks to have a drive-around trail, but the best way to experience it is to walk along the numerous signposted paths or the nature trail. Picnic tables are provided to make this an ideal day's outing. The 350-acre (140-hectare) park was virtually bare until the government planted it with lodgepole pine, Sitka spruce and Japanese larch. Along the nature trail there are specimens of trees native to the area, silver birch, ash, holly and hawthorn.

---

7 Macroom, Co Cork
This is the main market town for the Gaelic-speaking region to the west. Macroom Castle, off the square, dates from the 13th century and was a seat of the MacCarthys of Muskerry. Oliver Cromwell granted it to Admiral Sir William Penn, whose son William spent much of his childhood here and later founded the US state of Pennsylvania. Little now remains of the castle, although its impressive entrance has been restored.

i *Castle Gates (seasonal)*

▶ *Take the **N22** east for 25 miles (40km) and return to Cork.*

Unspoiled
Peninsulas

Bantry sits at the head of one of Ireland's most beautiful bays, with a sheltered harbour that reaches right into the town centre, where the narrow streets and lovely broad square are lined with shops and houses that have changed little over the centuries.

The beautiful landscaped grounds of Bantry House are open to the public, and the French Armada Interpretive Centre, holds items from the disastrous invasion of 1796.

1/2 DAYS • 96 MILES • 156KM

ITINERARY

BANTRY	▶ **Drimoleague** (11m-18km)
DRIMOLEAGUE	▶ **Skibbereen** (8m-13km)
SKIBBEREEN	▶ **Skull** (14m-23km)
SKULL	▶ **Mizen Head** (18m-29km)
MIZEN HEAD	▶ **Durrus** (21m-34km)
DURRUS	▶ **Bantry** (24m-39km)

Killarney National Park

Baile Mhic Íre

Kilgarvan

Kenmare

Béal Átha an Ghaorthaidh (Ballingeary)

Macroom

R569

R571

R618

R584

Parknasilla

Bolus Head

Caherdaniel

Kenmare River

Lauragh

705 ▲ Knockboy

Inchigeelagh

Lee

Crookstown

Kilmichael

Scariff Island

Ardgroom

Glengarriff

R585

R587

R585

Enniskean

Cod's Head

Beara Peninsula

685 ▲

R572

Adrigole

Garinish Island

BANTRY

Bandon

R586

Dunmanway

R586

Allihies

Castletown Bearhaven

Bear Island

R586

Drimoleague

R588

R602

Dursey Island

Bantry Bay

Sheep's Head Peninsula

Durrus

R594

R593

Leap

Ross Carbery

Timoleague

R600

Clonakilty

Muntervary/ Sheep's Head

Dunmanus Bay

R591

Mizen Peninsula

407 ▲

Ballydehob

N71

Skibbereen

Clonakilty Bay

Mizen Head

Toormore

Goleen

R592

Skull

Crookhaven

Roaringwater Bay

R595

Castletownshend

Baltimore

Toe Head

Galley Head

Clear Island

0 ———— 10 miles

0 —— 10 —— 20 km

Beautiful Bantry House Gardens enjoy an unparalleled setting on the shores of Bantry Bay

i   *The Old Courthouse, The Square, Bantry (seasonal)*

▶ *Take the N71 south and turn left for Drimoleague, east via the R586.*

❶ Drimoleague, Co Cork
The Roman Catholic church in this small town is noteworthy for its architecture, a modern box-like structure with a solid, unbroken wall on one side, and glass on the other. Castle Donovan, north of town and now in ruins, is a relic of the late 15th and early 16th centuries.

▶ *Turn south on to the R593 to Skibbereen.*

❷ Skibbereen, Co Cork
This progressive town sits on the River Ilen just where it broadens and then empties into

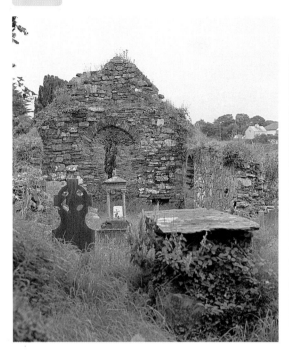

Baltimore Bay. Its long history of independence has produced two battling bishops – one who died fighting Elizabethan forces in 1602 and another who was hanged in 1650 during the Cromwellian conflicts. The Maid of Erin monument in the town square was erected in 1904 by the Young Ireland Society. The Pro-Cathedral, a fine Grecian-style edifice built in 1826, is well worth a visit. Surprisingly picturesque, the old gasworks building has been beautifully restored and converted into the Skibbereen Heritage Centre, which includes a Great Famine exhibition and information on nearby Lough Hyne. Guided walks are also available.

You can see garden design in progress at the superb Liss Ard Gardens, 200 acres of woods, meadows, lakes and waterfalls that will mature in 30 to 50 years. Pathways thread through scenic and tranquil areas dotted with art works.

Abbeystrewery Abbey, dating from the 14th century, lies in ruins 1 mile (1.5km) west

Abbeystrewery is a sad and atmospheric place, with its mass famine graves amidst the overgrown abbey ruins

of town, the setting for mass famine graves that bear silent witness to one of Ireland's most tragic eras.

Castletownshend, 5 miles (8km) southeast of Skibbereen via the R596, is a pretty little village with only one street that slopes rather steeply down to the sea. This was home to Edith Somerville and Violet Martin Ross, two Victorian ladies whose humorous *Experiences of an Irish RM* has kept the English-speaking world chuckling. They lay buried in the Church of Ireland grounds, their lively spirits no doubt still haunting the halls of their beloved Drishane House at the upper end of the village. Just outside town, on a ridge overlooking the sea, Knockdrum ringfort has an underground passage (souterrain) and a stone with megalithic cup marks.

Eight miles (13km) southwest of Skibbereen, the little

fishing village of Baltimore also has a stormy history, attested to by the ancient castle of the O'Driscolls, now in ruins on a rock overlooking the harbour. Despite the presence of that powerful clan, in 1631 Algerian pirates captured some 200 town residents for sale to North African slave traders and massacred most of those left behind. Poet Thomas Davis's *The Sack of Baltimore* gives a vivid account of the raid.

There are fine views of the bay and Sherkin Island from the tall whitewashed navigational beacon a short distance outside the village, and there is a regular boat service to Sherkin Island, which defines the westward side of Baltimore Bay. Silver Strand is typical of several good swimming spots among the island's many coves. Near the pier stand ruins of another castle of the O'Driscolls, destroyed in 1537, and on the

eastern end of the island are the remains of a friary founded by one of the O'Driscolls in the 15th century for the Franciscan Order of Strict Observance.

Southwest of Sherkin is Clear Island, one of the four Gaeltacht (Irish-speaking) areas in the Cork/Kerry region, with a regular boat service from Sherkin and mailboat service from Baltimore. You will be well rewarded by a visit to the Cape Clear Heritage Centre. There is also a small bird observatory that has tracked the migrations of a host of interesting species. Just south of the island, on the southernmost offshore point in Ireland, Fastnet Rock Lighthouse stands as a major navigational aid to mariners. It was built in Cornwall in 1906 from local granite, disassembled and refitted on to Fastnet Rock, each block dovetailed into the next to withstand the fierce seas.

BACK TO NATURE

About 4 miles (6km) southwest of Skibbereen is Lough Hyne, the country's most important marine nature reserve. Its pollution-free waters, 30°C (54°F) warmer than the sea, form a natural habitat for several thousand species of marine animals and plants. Many southern, or Lusitanian, species common to the Mediterranean and surrounding area thrive here, as do others peculiar to Ireland and Britain. At low tide, search the shore for intriguing marine creatures such as jewel anemones, sea squirts and gobies. From the lake shores, you can observe patches of different-coloured seabed, which change with the intensity of grazing by the fascinating marine population.

There is always activity on the water at Skull harbour

RECOMMENDED WALKS

At the head of Lough Hyne, look for the path that climbs up through woodlands to the hilltop. The panoramic view is breathtaking, looking down over the Hundred Isles, down the length of the peninsula to Mizen Head, and east as far as Kinsale.

[i] North Street

▶ Take the **N71** west to Ballydehob, then turn southwest on to the **R592** to reach Skull.

3 **Skull,** Co Cork
The scenic drive west from Skibbereen follows the River

Ilen and then the shore of Roaringwater Bay to Ballydehob, a picturesque little harbour that has attracted scores of crafts-people, whose workshops may well prompt a shopping stop. During World War II a German war plane crashed on the slopes of Mount Gabriel, which is now topped by a tracking station. Beautiful Cuss Strand, 2 miles (3km) from Ballydehob, offers excellent swimming.

Further on, Skull's virtually enclosed harbour is a haven for fishing and pleasure boats. This delightful little town usually has music in the pubs and a variety of special events during summer months. In the village, the Church of Ireland church (no longer in use) incorporates some interesting medieval remains, and in the grounds of the Community College, a 60-seat planetarium is the only one in the Republic of Ireland.

There is also a regular ferry service to Clear Island from Skull harbour.

▶ *Follow the **R592** to Toormore, then turn left on to the **R591** to Goleen. At Goleen take an unclassified road to Mizen Head.*

4 Mizen Head, Co Cork
This part of the peninsula route calls out for a leisurely drive as it sweeps around beautiful Toormore Bay to Goleen, where a lovely secluded beach invites a break for a swim. From Goleen, you can either drive straight out to Mizen Head via a minor road off the R591 or make a short side trip to the village of Crookhaven, where the charming harbour is a favourite with yachtsmen, before proceeding on to land's end.

The fine sandy beaches of Barley Cove are worth the side

trip to this popular resort spot. The drive on to Mizen Head is one of breathtaking seascapes and high vertical cliffs against which breaking white-foamed waves beat ceaselessly. Exercise extreme caution, however, as the clifftops end abruptly with a straight drop. Mizen Head Visitor Centre is housed in the former lighthouse-keeper's house and engine room and includes a Navigational Aids Simulator, automatic weather station and award-winning displays.

▶ *An unmarked road strikes north at Barley Cove, but is rough driving. The recommended route is to return to Goleen and rejoin the **R591** north to Toormore, then head*

The ever-changing seascapes of the Mizen Peninsula culminate in this spectacular headland

northeast for the scenic drive to Durrus, 21 miles (34km).

northeast for the scenic drive to Durrus, 21 miles (34km).

FOR CHILDREN

While most children will enjoy the coastal scenery and wooded stretches along the drive, they will welcome stops for a swim and romp on the fine beaches at Goleen, Barley Cove, Ahakista, and Kilcrohane. Surfers will find good waves at Barley Cove.

5 Durrus, Co Cork

Situated at the head of Dunmanus Bay, this village is the gateway to the narrow, 15-mile (24km) long Sheep's Head Peninsula. A minor, unnumbered road leads southwest along the coast to the wooded inlet of Ahakista, where there is good swimming at sandy beaches. You will see the Air India Memorial commemorating the loss of the passengers and crew of the plane that crashed off this coast in 1985. Then it's on to Kilcrohane, which also has a good beach. Adventurous souls may want to continue southwest to the car park from where you can walk out across the rocky headland to Sheep's Head.

▶ *From Durrus, take the unclassified road west to Kilcrohane, then take the road known as Goat's Path across Seefin Mountain for the drive along the southern shore of Bantry Bay. Just past the village of*

RECOMMENDED WALKS

It is an easy walk from the summit of the Goat's Path road up to the top of Seefin Mountain. The small effort will be rewarded by even more extensive views of the peninsula and coastline, since Seefin is almost twice the height of the road summit.

The Sheep's Head Peninsula has a wonderful rocky coastline, backed on its sheltered southern slopes by luxuriant hedgerows and gardens

Tedagh, turn left on to the N71 for the short drive back to Bantry.

SCENIC ROUTES

The drive from Durrus down Sheep's Head Peninsula – especially the Goat's Path road just outside Kilcrohane that leads across the mountains – is the most scenic part of the route. When you reach the summit, stop to enjoy the extensive panorama east over County Cork and west to the Beara Peninsula and parts of County Kerry. The narrow but well-surfaced road is especially beautiful in autumn when gorse (dwarf furze/whin) covers the mountains and countryside with golden yellow flowers.

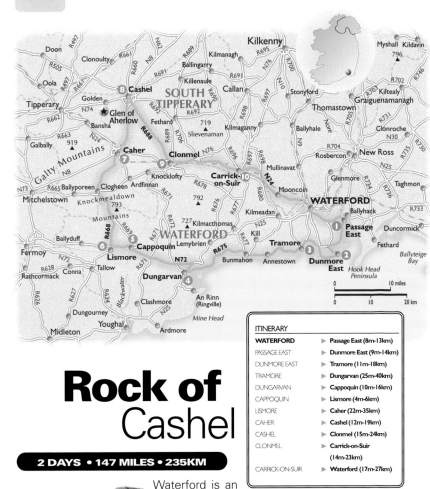

Kilkenny

ITINERARY

WATERFORD	▶	**Passage East (8m-13km)**
PASSAGE EAST	▶	Dunmore East (9m-14km)
DUNMORE EAST	▶	Tramore (11m-18km)
TRAMORE	▶	Dungarvan (25m-40km)
DUNGARVAN	▶	Cappoquin (10m-16km)
CAPPOQUIN	▶	Lismore (4m-6km)
LISMORE	▶	Caher (22m-35km)
CAHER	▶	Cashel (12m-19km)
CASHEL	▶	Clonmel (15m-24km)
CLONMEL	▶	Carrick-on-Suir (14m-23km)
CARRICK-ON-SUIR	▶	Waterford (17m-27km)

Rock of
Cashel

2 DAYS • 147 MILES • 235KM

Waterford is an important seaport and cultural centre and reflects much of Ireland's history. Reginald's Tower, on The Quay, dates back to 1003, and the Waterford Museum of Treasures is in the old Granary on Merchant's Quay. There are traces of the old Viking city walls, a fine cathedral and the famous Waterford Crystal Glass Factory, and summer river cruises are great attractions.

In September, a lighthearted gathering of amateur companies from around the world and from all parts of Ireland converges on Waterford for the annual International Festival of Light Opera. For 16 nights there are performances of such musicals as *Brigadoon* and *Showboat*, all to a very high standard.

▶ *From Waterford head east to Passage East.*

❶ **Passage East,** Co Waterford

This quaint riverside village with its whitewashed cottages, narrow, winding streets and a car-ferry service to Ballyhack, County Wexford, was the landing point for Henry II, who arrived in 1171 with 4,000 men in 400 ships to receive oaths of loyalty from Irish chieftains who wished to hold on to their lands. The hill just above the village provides splendid views of the head of Waterford harbour.

On the road to Dunmore East are the ruins of Geneva Barracks, relics of a colony of goldsmiths and silversmiths from Switzerland who sought refuge from religious persecution in 1782. Their planned town of New Geneva failed, and by 1785 was abandoned. The barracks became a prison for insurgents (or 'croppies') of the 1798 rising, subjects of the ballad 'The Croppy Boy'.

▶ *Follow an unclassified coastal road south, join the **R684** and turn left for Dunmore East.*

❷ **Dunmore East,** Co Waterford

Neat thatched cottages perch on steep hills above the harbour of this pretty little village that is a popular summer resort and sea-angling centre. Pleasure boats and fishing vessels fill the picturesque harbour. The bay is divided into cliffs and coves, with good walks to Creadan Head to the north, Black Knob promontory to the south, and Swines Head at the southern end of the peninsula. There are also several safe sandy beaches in the area.

Dunmore East offers the Irish idyll in pretty, traditional-style holiday homes

▶ *Take an unclassified coastal road to the junction with the **R685**, turn left, then left again at the junction with the **R675** and continue to Tramore.*

There are exciting diversions for children in Tramore. Splashworld has water-based fun, with slides, flumes and white-knuckle rides, while Laserworld provides a high-tech game with special effects, set in a Celtic maze.

❸ **Tramore,** Co Waterford

This lively seaside town is one of the southeast coast's most popular resorts, with a wide, 3-mile-long (5km) beach, its waters warmed by the Gulf Stream. Attractions include a 50-acre (20-hectare) amusement park, a race course, miniature golf, and an 18-hole golf course. Watersports, particularly surfing, are popular here, and there is good swimming at the pier,

Guillameen Cove and Newton Cove.

The giant clifftop 'Metal Man' statue at Great Newtown Head, was erected as a navigational landmark for sailors, and legend has it that any unmarried female who hops around it three times will hop down the aisle within 12 months.

On the coastal drive to Dungarvan, the little fishing village of Bunmahon has a good sandy beach surrounded by jagged cliffs that rise to about 200 feet (60m), with interesting rock formations at their base.

In Stradbally look for Stradbally Hall and its narrow gauge railway.

i *Town Centre (seasonal)*

▶ *From Tramore, follow the R675 coastal drive via Stradbally southwest to Dungarvan.*

Sand and rocks between Dungarvan and Tramore

4 **Dungarvan,** Co Waterford

A busy market town,
Dungarvan sits on the broad,
natural harbour where the
Colligan river meets the sea.
Along the quays you can see
remnants of Dungarvan Castle,
dating from 1186, surrounded
by fortified walls. On St
Augustine Street you'll find
the excellent and very active
Waterford County Museum,
with interesting local displays,
a splendid photographic collection and a space devoted to
visiting exhibitions from other
major museums.
    Five miles (8km) south of
town on the R674 is the village
of An Rinn (Ringville), where
Irish is the daily language and
is taught in an acclaimed
language college. Further east,

Helvick Head rises to 230 feet
(70m) and shelters a
picturesque small harbour.

[i] *The Courthouse*

▶ *Take the N72 west to
Cappoquin.*

5 **Cappoquin,** Co Waterford

The broad Blackwater River
makes a 90-degree turn to the
west at Cappoquin, and
provides scenic riverside drives
and some of the best salmon
fishing, trout angling and
coarse fishing in Ireland.
    Cappoquin House and
Gardens command fine views
over the River Blackwater. The
house, built in 1779, used to
face the town, but later the
entrance was turned round and
the façade is now enhanced
by informal gardens and handsome trees which extend
towards the river.

Ballysaggartmore Gatehouse is
a fitting entrance to romantic
Lismore Castle

▶ *Follow the N72 for 4 miles
(6km) to Lismore.*

6 **Lismore,** Co Waterford

Set on the Blackwater River,
Lismore is one of Ireland's
Heritage Towns, a definitive
example of an Estate town. It's
proud history is portrayed in
the Lismore Heritage Centre,
in the fine Courthouse building, where the story of the
town from AD636 is related
through an award-winning
multilingual audiovisual
presentation.
    The most prominent
feature is Lismore Castle,
which looms over the town and
river, looking for all the world
like a fairy-tale castle. It was
built by King John in 1185 on
the site of a 7th-century
monastery that was a renowned
seat of learning. The castle was
presented to Sir Walter
Raleigh, who sold it to Richard
Boyle, Earl of Cork, in 1602.
His son, Robert, the noted
chemist and author of Boyle's
Law, was born here. Since
1753 it has been the Irish seat
of the Dukes of Devonshire,
and the gardens are open to
the public.

The medieval Protestant cathedral dates from the 17th century. It has soaring Gothic vaulting and still retains in its west wall 9th- and 11th-century grave slabs from an earlier church. The modern (1888) Catholic cathedral is Romanesque in style. Lady Louise's Walk along the river and the interesting Town Walk are well signposted.

Five miles (8km) south of Lismore, via the N72, the little town of Tallow was the birthplace of famed 19th-century sculptor John Hogan. Panoramic views open up from 592-foot (180m) Tallow Hill, and there are ruins of an ancient fortified Fitzgerald keep located ½ mile (1km) west of Tallowbridge.

Six miles (10km) west of Lismore, via the R666, the village of Ballyduff is a popular angling centre.

☐ *Heritage Centre*

▶ *At the eastern end of the bridge in Lismore take the R668 which follows the Blackwater River northwards, and then climbs to the pass in the Knockmealdown Mountains known as The Vee and descends to Clogheen, then on to Caher.*

7 Caher, Co Tipperary
Caher Castle, with its massive great hall, grim dungeon, and thick protective enclosing walls, is a superb restoration of the 1142 castle set on a rocky islet in the River Suir. It is also one of Ireland's best-preserved castles. Furnishings in the residential apartments are authentic reproductions of the period. The Articles ending the long Cromwellian wars were signed here, and in modern times it has served as the setting for such films as *Excalibur* and *Barry Lyndon*.

Other interesting buildings include the 13th-century abbey, founded by a Norman knight, which is being restored, and the delightful little Swiss Cottage. Caher is also a centre for walking and climbing.

A few miles northwest of Caher, the N24 (the road to Tipperary town) leads to a left turnoff heading to the lush Glen of Aherlow, a secluded glen that was once a major route between the counties of Tipperary and Limerick and the scene of ancient battles. Later, Irish insurgents and outlaws took refuge in the thickly wooded valley that runs between the Galty Mountains and Slievenamuck Hills.

Even the myths, legends and history pale beside the actual sight of the Rock of Cashel

BACK TO NATURE

The mile-long (1.5km) nature trail in Glengarra Wood is a delight for those interested in rare and exotic trees and plants. To reach the wood, drive 8 miles (13km) southwest of Caher via the N8, and turn right on to the signposted and unclassified road, then continue 2 miles (3km) to the car-park. There are nature walks along the Burncourt river and through forest groves, where Douglas fir, ferns and native heathers, Western hemlock, rowan, holly, birch, arboreal rhododendron, Bhutan pine from the Inner Himalayas of eastern India, and many other plants and trees can be seen. Native birds such as the treecreeper, the tiny goldcrest, wren, robin, chaffinch, magpie, jay and the introduced pheasant make this their home, as do a herd of fallow deer.

☐ *Castle Car Park (seasonal)*

▶ *From Caher, follow the N8 due north to Cashel.*

8 **Cashel,** Co Tipperary
Dominating the landscape is the awe-inspiring Rock of Cashel which soars 200 feet (60m) above the surrounding plains. Since ancient Celtic times, its summit has been connected with royalty and mysticism. Cormac's Chapel, the Round Tower, St Patrick's Cathedral, and a replica of St Patrick's Cross, (the base of which may actually have been a pre-Christian sacrificial altar), are among the impressive ruins, all in good condition. At the foot of the Rock, the Bru Boru Heritage Centre presents traditional Irish entertainment.

i *Heritage Centre (seasonal)*

FOR HISTORY BUFFS

In the 5th century, a cashel, or stone fort, was erected on the lofty Rock of Cashel, and it was here, legend has it, that St Patrick came to preach to the King of Munster, using the humble shamrock as a symbol of the Christian Trinity. In 1101, Murtough O'Brien presented the Cashel of the Kings to the Church. In 1127, Cormac MacCarthaigh, King of Desmond, built the little chapel, a miniature gem of Romanesque style. King Henry II came here to receive homage from Irish princes; Edward the Bruce held a parliament here; and the first Protestant service was conducted here.

▶ *Take the R688 southeast for 15 miles (24km) to Clonmel.*

9 **Clonmel,** Co Tipperary
Set on the banks of the River Suir, Clonmel is the main town of County Tipperary, and is home to the South Tipperary County Museum, where lively exhibits span prehistoric to modern times.
It was in Clonmel that the world's first public transport system was established by

Charles Bianconi in 1815, based at Hearn's Hotel in Parnell Street. This aspect of Clonmel's history is reflected in the Museum of Transport in Gortnafleur Business Park.
Parts of the Franciscan church in Abbey Street date back to the 13th century, and 19th-century St Mary's Church near by has a fine high altar. The town's streets are lined with restored shopfronts.

i *Sarsfield Street*

RECOMMENDED WALKS

From Clonmel, you can walk the 12-mile (19km) towpath to Carrick-on-Suir.

One of Clonmel's charming streets is framed by the arch of the great West Gate

▶ *Take the N24 east to Carrick-on-Suir.*

10 **Carrick-on-Suir,** Co Tipperary
This scenic town is on the River Suir, and its Ormonde Castle is the only Elizabethan fortified mansion of its kind in Ireland. A principal seat of the Butlers, it is said to have been built by 'Black Tom', Earl of Ormonde, to host Elizabeth I, who subsequently cancelled her proposed visit.
The Heritage Centre, housed in the former Protestant Church, contains many memorials to various Ormonde earls, plus local artefacts and a collection of church plate.
The Tipperary Crystal workshop and showroom are on the N24.

i *Heritage Cente*

▶ *Take the N24 back to Waterford.*

LEINSTER

Leinster might well be called the 'Royal Province' of Ireland. Its 12 counties have harboured rulers from the days of the prehistoric clans who constructed the great burial mound at Newgrange to the High Kings of Ireland who ruled from the Hill of Tara, from Viking and Norman conquerors, to appointees of English kings and queens. Indeed, with Irish chieftains battling against invaders and each other, it seemed best to concentrate beleaguered Crown forces in 'The Pale', a heavily fortified area around Dublin.

At Clontarf, just outside Dublin, the great Irish High King Brian Boru defeated the Vikings in 1014. In 1649, Oliver Cromwell arrived with his dreaded 'Ironside' forces and proceeded to march from Dublin to Drogheda, where he slaughtered thousands of men, women and children. And in 1690, William of Orange's decisive victory at the Battle of the Boyne had a profound effect on Ireland's history that echoes down the centuries to the present day.

South of The Pale, County Wexford bears the scars of Viking occupation followed by Normans, who first landed in Ireland along this county's coast. Cromwell and the insurgents of 1798 left their imprint too. The lush countryside of Kilkenny lured the Normans, who dotted the landscape with castles and built a dignified town that soon rivalled Dublin as an administrative centre.

Inland, Athlone stands guard over County Westmeath's rural, lake-dotted landscape and the River Shannon that divides it from Connacht. Along the banks of that great waterway in County Offaly are the remains of one of Ireland's most awe-inspiring ecclesiastical settlements, Clonmacnoise. Kildare's Hill of Allen is thought to have been the winter quarters of Fionn MacCumhail's legendary Fianna warriors, but these days the county is known for its stud farms and Curragh race course.

Kilkenny Castle reflects the history and importance of this lovely town (Tour 14)

The lushness and variety of Leinster's landscape are as much a delight to today's visitors as they were to past conquerors, many of whom sprinkled it with great mansions and gardens. The lake-filled midland counties draw avid anglers and boating enthusiasts on the Shannon, and the peat bogs of counties Laois and Offaly form part of the most important bogland in Europe, with global significance. Along the coast are curving bays and sandy beaches, as well as nature reserves inhabited by a wide range of wildlife.

Tour 11
From the historically important Athlone and its modern-day riverboating, this tour takes you to the former garrison town of Mullingar, whose proximity to good trout lakes makes it an excellent angling centre. Then you travel to Tullamore, home of a world-famous distillery, and on to Birr, with its castle and garden. The monastic ruins of Clonmacnoise lend a spiritual aspect to your travels, as do the ruins at Clonfert.

Tour 12
This is a historic drive through Ireland's past, in pleasant countryside rich in megalithic and early Christian monuments, including the intriguing passage grave of Newgrange, exquisite high crosses at Monasterboice, Slane and its associations with St Patrick and the Hill of Tara, redolent of the heroic age of the High Kings of Ireland. The tour ends with the site of the Battle of the Boyne in 1690, where King William met King James to finish a conflict of national and European significance.

Tour 13
From Dublin, the tour visits bright coastal towns which owe much of their character to Victorian enthusiasm for the seaside. The route winds its way into the mountains, and visits Glendalough, one of Ireland's most captivating combinations of history and landscape. The scenery is a combination of bog, lake and mountaintop, and a highlight of this tour is the profusion of glorious gardens, justifying the claim that this area is 'the Garden of Ireland'.

Tour 14
Norman castles, ecclesiastical ruins and tales of medieval witches haunt Kilkenny, starting point for this tour. History and active river commerce meld happily in New Ross on the River Barrow. Further along the river, prehistory has left its mark

Mount Usher Gardens (Tour 13) on the River Vartry

just outside Carlow town in the form of an impressive dolmen. Kildare's horse country will appeal to followers of the sport of kings, and the gardens near Portlaoise have universal appeal. Celtic kings and St Patrick draw you on to Cashel.

Tour 15
Founded by Vikings, invaded by Normans, conquered by Cromwell's troops, and a hotbed of insurgence, Wexford is an excellent tour base: north to the country's famed beaches, then inland for more history, before turning south to the river town of New Ross. Continue south to Waterford, another Viking stronghold and the east coast's most important port, then a ferry ride takes you to the enchanting Hook peninsula through villages undisturbed by 'progress', and on to a noted bird refuge and a holy island.

Monastic Ruins
& The Midlands

Athlone is an important commercial and holiday centre, and a junction for road, rail and river traffic. Its marina on the Shannon has fleets of smart river cruisers for hire, and Athlone also has good facilities for anglers and golfers. Athlone Castle, over-looking the bridge, provides marvellous town views and has an interesting visitor centre. There is much to see in the vicinity.

1/2 DAYS • 141 MILES • 227KM

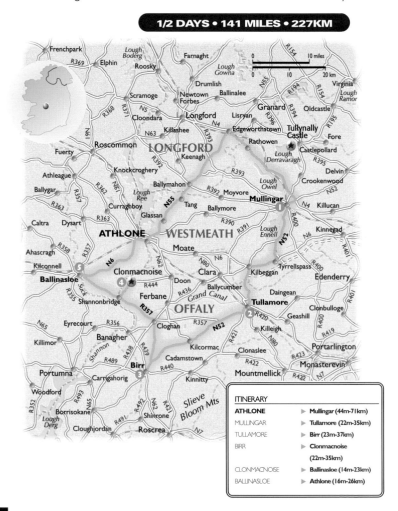

ITINERARY		
ATHLONE	▶	Mullingar (44m-71km)
MULLINGAR	▶	Tullamore (22m-35km)
TULLAMORE	▶	Birr (23m-37km)
BIRR	▶	Clonmacnoise
		(22m-35km)
CLONMACNOISE	▶	Ballinasloe (14m-23km)
BALLINASLOE	▶	Athlone (16m-26km)

SCENIC ROUTES

Leave Athlone on the N55 northeast, and about 2 miles (3km) outside town turn right on to the R390. At Ballymore, some 12 miles (19km) north-east of Athlone, look for the remains of a 14th-century Anglo-Norman fortress. Continue on the R390 for 4 miles (6km) to the 602-foot (183m) high Hill of Ushnagh. This was a place of religious importance during pagan times, as it was the accepted centre of the universe, and from the summit there are fine views of Ireland's vast central plain.
There are burial mounds and an earthen fort, and on the southwest side of the summit, Aill na Mireann (The Stone of Divisions) is thought to mark the boundaries of all five ancient provinces of Ireland.

RECOMMENDED WALKS

On Lough Ree's western shore, about 8 miles (13km) from Athlone, Rinndown Peninsula juts out into the lake just east of the village of Lecarrow. Follow the unnum-bered road from Lecarrow until it becomes a track leading to the lakeshore. The heavily wooded path passes ancient ruins from the 13th century that combine with the dense shade to create a somewhat spooky atmosphere. The walk takes in the remains of St John's Castle (so named for the Knights of St John who once occupied it) and a church with its outbuildings.

ℹ️ *Athlone Castle, St Peter's Square, Athlone (seasonal)*

▶ *Take the N55 northeast from Athlone to the town of Edgeworthstown, then turn southeast on to the N4 for the drive to Mullingar.*

Mullingar Cathedral is famous for its mosaics and its ecclesiastical museum

❶ Mullingar, Co Westmeath
En route to Mullingar, stop by in Edgeworthstown, the village named after the Edgeworth family. The father of the family was a noted inventor and author, and his daughter Maria became one of Ireland's leading women writers. She holds a special place in Irish affections for her work among the suffering during the famine years. A friend of Sir Walter Scott, her best known work was *Castle Rackrent*.

If you plan to eat steak in Ireland, Mullingar, the county town of Westmeath, is the place to do it, in the heart of Ireland's cattle-raising area. Mullingar's long history includes a position of prime importance as a barracks town for the British military. It was here, during the Williamite Wars, that British commander de Ginkel rallied his forces for the 1691 Siege of Athlone. The imprint of those years is stamped on the town's face even today in the form of large, grey, rather formidable buildings. The present-day personality of the town, however, in no way reflects

its somewhat grim past, and Mullingar is an excellent base for seeing the Westmeath lakes, most of which offer excellent brown trout fishing.

The Cathedral of Christ the King, designed by Ralph Byrne, has outstanding mosaics of St Patrick and St Anne near the high altar that are the work of Russian artist Boris Anrep. Permission must be obtained from the sacristan to see the ecclesiastical museum.

In July, Mullingar celebrates eligible bachelors from all over the world, with the International Bachelor Festival.

A little way south on the Tullamore road is Belvedere House, Gardens and Park. The 18th-century mansion is an architectural gem, and interpreters bring convincingly to life the stories and scandals from its history. The grounds, on the shore of Lough Ennell, include woodland, lakeshore walks, Ireland's largest folly, and walled gardens with a wonderful collection of rare and unusual plants. The stable block now houses exhibitions, a visitor centre and a

multimedia show, and there's an animal sanctuary and children's play area near by.

Travel in almost any direction from Mullingar and you will find the lakes that have made this region famous for trout. Lough Ennell is about 6 miles (10km) to the south, with a championship golf course overlooking the lake and the ruins of ancient Lynn Church on its northeastern shore.

Three miles (5km) north of town, Lough Owel is a sailing and sub-aqua centre, and there are good swimming facilities. About 6 miles (10km) north of town, Lough Derravaragh is a beautiful, irregular-shaped lake with thickly wooded shores. It plays a central part in one of Ireland's most tragic and beloved legends, since it was one of three lakes on which the Children of Lir were doomed to spend 300 years when their wicked stepmother turned them into swans. To this day, swans on Irish waters are under the protection granted to all swans by the grieving father.

Tullynally Castle's rather grim exterior belies its splendid interior and works of art

For good views of the lakes and plains, Rathconnell Hill is just 2 miles (3km) northeast of Mullingar off the N52. You can see Lough Owel from 499-foot (152m) Shanemore (Slanemore) Hill, 4 miles (6km) northwest of town.

Thirteen miles (21km) north of Mullingar via the R394, Tullynally Castle and Gardens, in Castlepollard, are one of County Westmeath's chief attractions. Seat of the Earls of Longford since the 17th century, the turreted and towered Gothic-revival manor house has a two-storey Great Hall with a vaulted ceiling and impressive collections of art, china and furnishings. Life 'downstairs' in such a great house is depicted in the museum housed in the courtyard, Victorian kitchens and laundries.

The village of Fore, about 3 miles (5km) east of Castlepollard, is the setting for an interesting group of antiquities and the legend of the 'Seven Wonders of Fore'. In summer the Fore Abbey Coffee Shop provides information as well as refreshment, including a 'Seven Wonders' video shown at weekends. At the Seven Wonders pub, you can pick up the key to Fore Abbey, the ancient ruins of St Feichin's Monastery which date back to the 7th century.

i *Market House*

▶ *Continue south for 22 miles (35km) on the N52/N6 for Tullamore.*

2 **Tullamore,** Co Offaly
On the drive from Mullingar, stop off at the village of Kilbeggan, 7 miles (11km) north of Tullamore, where a museum, antiques shop and café now occupy the restored 18th-century Locke's Distillery, once one of Europe's largest.

The chief town of County Offaly, Tullamore owes its development to the Grand Canal laid out in 1798 to connect Dublin to the

Shannon. The canal carried huge cargoes of yellow brick made in the town to Dublin during its expansion in the 19th century.

Tullamore is the home of Irish Mist liquer and Tullamore

Dew whiskey, and the Tullamore Dew Heritage Centre offers an excellent insight into the distillery and town history.

i *Bury Quay*

▶ *Follow the N52 for 23 miles (37km) southwest to Birr.*

3 **Birr,** Co Offaly
Plan a stop in the village of Kilcormac, about 12 miles (19km) south of Tullamore on the N52, for a look at the beautifully carved wooden pietà in the Catholic church, which is thought to be the work of a 16th-century artist.

Georgian buildings and a world-famous castle and garden are the main attractions in the small town of Birr, just above the confluence of the Little Bronsa and Camcor Rivers.

Birr Castle is an impressive fortified manor house set in extensive grounds, but the

---

BACK TO NATURE

About 7 miles (11km) northwest of Tullamore, Clara Bog is one of the largest intact bogs of its type in Ireland. Its well-developed 'soak' system is considered to be the best in western Europe. Increased water flow from surface run-off or underground springs allows the growth of many more plant species than are normally found in a bog environment. Among those that thrive here are bog mosses, sundews, heathers, cotton grass, and bog rosemary. There are hummock/hollow complexes, bog pools and moss lawns. The bog is easily seen from the road, but is considered unsafe for exploration on foot.

Tullamore is a favoured starting point for narrowboat cruises on the Grand Canal

building is not open to the public, since it has, for several centuries, been the residence of the Parsons family, Earls of Rosse. The 3rd Earl was a noted astronomer, whose giant 72-inch (180cm) reflecting telescope, built to his own design in 1845, was the largest in the world for an astounding 70 years. The telescope has been restored to full working order and the scientific museum at Birr Castle has become Ireland's Historic Science Centre. It covers the pioneering achievements of the Parsons family and other Irish scientists, covering astronomy, engineering, photography and horticulture. The castle gardens cover 100 acres (40 hectares), laid out on the banks of the two rivers and around a lake, with over 1,000 species of plants and trees including magnolia and cherry.

[i] *Castle Street*

▶ *Take the **N62** north to Cloghan, and turn west on to the **R357** to Shannonbridge. Turn right on the **R444** for 4 miles (6km) to Clonmacnoise.*

4 Clonmacnoise, Co Offaly

Set beside the River Shannon, this is one of Ireland's holiest places. St Ciaran's monastery, founded here in AD548, became the most famous of Ireland's monastic cities and was one of Europe's leading centres of learning for nearly 1,000 years. It enjoyed the patronage of many Irish Kings, and Rory O'Conor, the last High King, lies buried here. Its great fame

History and science combine at Birr Castle to provide a fascinating day out

and wealth attracted plunderers from home and abroad, and the final indignity came in 1552 when the English garrison at Athlone carried off the spoils. Even the glass from the windows was taken, and the site was finally abandoned. Restoration began in 1647, but Cromwellian forces carried out yet another raid that put paid to the revival of its former glory. Today, there is a cathedral on the site, one of eight church ruins, two round towers, three

---

FOR CHILDREN

At Shannonbridge, north of Birr on the N62, is a narrow-gauge railway trip across a stretch of bogland, with a guide giving a commentary. A slide show precedes the tour.

SPECIAL TO...

Each year on 9 September and the following Sunday, great throngs, drawn from around the world, make the pilgrimage to Clonmacnoise to commemorate St Ciaran's feast day.

---

sculptured high crosses (and parts of two others), over 200 monumental slabs and a ruined castle. St Ciaran's grave is said to be in the east end of 'The Little Church', a small 9th-century cell.

i Monastic site (seasonal)

▶ Return to Shannonbridge and turn northwest on to the R357 for the 8-mile (13km) drive to Ballinasloe.

5 Ballinasloe, Co Galway
In a strategic position of military importance in the past, Ballinasloe once centred around its castle, but today it is a thriving market town. Seven miles (11km) from town on the Athenry road is the Abbey of Kilconnell, founded in 1400. Its nave, choir, side aisles, south transept, and some of the cloisters are in perfect condition.

Clonfert, 13 miles (21km) southeast of Ballinasloe, was chosen by St Brendan in the 6th century for a monastic settlement, of which nothing remains today. The cathedral has superb Romanesque decoration, with various motifs, including animal and human heads and intricate carvings of foliage.

SPECIAL TO...

Ballinasloe's great October Fair carries on for eight days of fierce horse trading, street entertainment, and non-stop revelry. It is one of the few such fairs still held in Ireland.

▶ Take the **N6** northeast to return to Athlone, a distance of 16 miles (26km).

FOR CHILDREN

West of Athlone off the N6, Glendeer Open Farm has friendly farm animals, ostrich, emu and deer, a play area and nature trail. In December it becomes 'Lapland', with Christmas displays.

One of the three intact carved high crosses of Clonmacnoise

FOR HISTORY BUFFS

Following their defeat at the battle of the Boyne in 1690, Irish forces who supported King James withdrew to the town of Athlone to establish the Shannon as their last line of defence against the English. Their leader, Colonel Grace, held the castle for King James and withstood a week's siege from the pursuing Williamite army.
In 1691, however, the English commander laid siege to the town. The Irish, retreating across the Shannon, destroyed the bridge, but the English started rebuilding it immediately. A heroic Irish Sergeant, Custume, then called for volunteers and with a handful of men managed to break down the hastily thrown-up structure. As a result, the town held out for another ten days, after which Irish Jacobite forces withdrew.

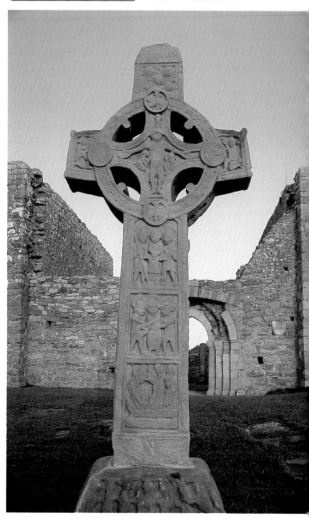

The Boyne
Valley

The great grassy mound of Millmount, which gives a panoramic view over Drogheda, was first a passage grave, then a Viking meeting place, a Norman motte, and an important military barracks in the 18th century, its history mirroring that of the town. Some of Millmount's buildings have been converted into a small museum. A view from any point of the town will show that Drogheda is a town of churches, including St Peter's which contains the head of martyred Oliver Plunkett.

2 DAYS • 84 MILES • 134KM

ITINERARY		
DROGHEDA	▶	**Monasterboice** (6m-10km)
MONASTERBOICE	▶	**Mellifont** (4m-6km)
MELLIFONT	▶	**Newgrange** (9m-14km)
NEWGRANGE	▶	**Slane** (6m-10km)
SLANE	▶	**Kells** (15m-24km)
KELLS	▶	**Navan** (10m-16km)
NAVAN	▶	**Hill of Tara** (7m-11km)
HILL OF TARA	▶	**Battle of the Boyne Site** (23m-37km)
BATTLE OF THE BOYNE SITE	▶	**Drogheda** (4m-6km)

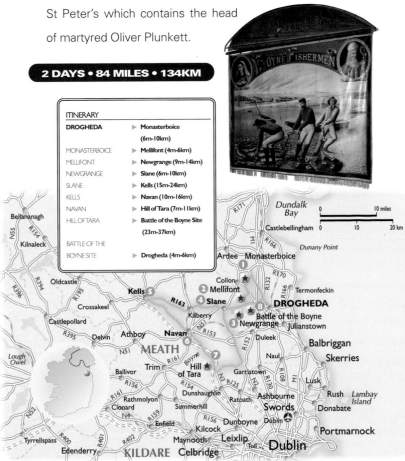

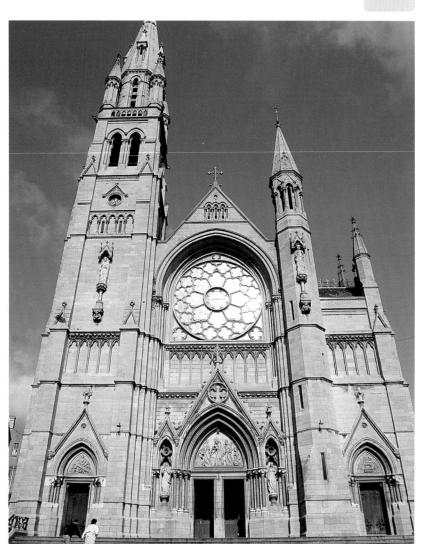

BACK TO NATURE

Visit Mornington sand dunes, which lie close to Drogheda on the coast. The dunes range from newly formed areas, colonised by marram grass close to the sea, to mature 'slacks' inland. The latter support a rich variety of plants including many orchids in the spring.

SCENIC ROUTES

This part of the eastern coast of Ireland may lack the grandeur of the north and west, but there is pleasant, gentle scenery with sandy beaches and shingle shores on the road from Drogheda to Mornington, Bettsytown, Laytown and Julianstown. The road follows the estuary of the Boyne, close to the great railway viaduct.

The superb frontage of St Peter's church in Drogheda

▶ *Take the R132 north. After 5 miles (8km) turn left, passing under the motorway and following signposts for Boyne Drive, Monasterboice. In ½ mile (1km) turn left again.*

❶ Monasterboice, Co Louth
Pick your way between ancient and modern graves to see two of the finest high crosses. These free-standing carvings in stone are of a quality unparalleled

anywhere in Europe at the time they were erected, yet the very high round tower is a reminder that these remarkable works of art were executed in the midst of Viking plunder. The West Cross stands close to the round tower, while the Cross of Muiredach – so called because of the inscription on the base, which says 'A prayer for Muiredach by whom this cross was made' – is smaller and more perfect in appearance. The messages on these crosses follow coherent themes of God's grace to man and the parallels between Old and New Testaments. On Muiredach's Cross look for the stories of Adam and Eve, Cain and Abel, the Last Judgement and the Crucifixion of Christ.

Pope John Paul II visited in 1979, and the point where he celebrated Mass is marked on the main Belfast–Dublin road.

▶ *Continue past Monasterboice. After a mile (2km), turn right at a T-junction for Mellifont. A mile (2km) further turn left on to the Drogheda road, R168, and after a further mile (2km) turn right to Mellifont.*

2 **Mellifont,** Co Louth
In a pleasant valley beside the River Mattock, Malachy, the former Archbishop of Armagh, founded the first Cistercian monastery in Ireland in 1142. A substantial square gate-house still stands, but only fragments of this great monastery now remain, including arches of a Romanesque cloister and a chapter house. An octagonal lavabo once equipped with water jets and basins is the most interesting structure.

▶ *Return to the crossroads just before Mellifont and turn right. After 2 miles (3km) turn right.*

Go straight over the cross-roads, following the signpost to King William's Glen. After 1 mile (1.5km) turn right on to the N51, then 2½ miles (4km) further on, turn left following signs for Newgrange.

3 **Newgrange,** Knowth and Dowth, Co Meath
Irish architecture may be said to have begun in the Boyne Valley, when, in about 3000BC, people who had only stone and wood for tools created the most impressive monuments of their kind in western Europe. Little is known of these people, or of those interred in these prehistoric tombs, but excavations have shown that they were cultivators of crops and had cleared areas of forest.

The mound at Newgrange, constructed with water-rolled pebbles, rises to a height of 36 feet (11m), its mass retained by a kerb of great stone blocks lying end to end, topped by white quartz and granite boulders. The passage is lined by huge stones, and the central cross-shaped chamber is roofed with a vault untouched in five millenia. Standing around the mound is an incomplete circle of stones.

Knowth has two passage-tombs surrounded by 18 smaller ones. It was used from the Stone Age, and in the early Christian era was a seat of the High Kings of Ireland. The Boyne Valley tombs are significant in that they combine art with the engineering feats of the passage-tombs of Ireland. Spirals, lozenges, zigzags, sunbursts – figures cut in stone with stone implements – decorate the monuments.

At Newgrange the sophisticated structure incorporates the unique phenomenon of a roof-box, which, only at the winter solstice, allows the rays of the rising sun to penetrate the chamber and flood it with light.

St Patrick's conversion of Ireland to Christianity took a leap forward at Slane in 433

Archaeological work continues, and important discoveries are still being made in the Boyne Valley which means that sites may be closed at times for excavation. Visits to Newgrange and Knowth are by guided tour only. These begin at the Brú na Boinne Visitor Centre – there is no direct access to the monuments – and in the busy summer months there will be delays; visits cannot be guaranteed. As well as issuing tickets, the centre has extensive interpretative displays and viewing areas.

i Visitor Centre

▶ *Return by minor roads to the N51 and turn left for Slane.*

4 Slane, Co Meath
Slane occupies an attractive curve on the River Boyne and is overlooked by the Hill of Slane, where, tradition has it, St Patrick lit his paschal fire in AD433 in defiance of the orders of King Laoghaire. In his persuasive speech to the King, Patrick used the shamrock as his illustration of the Trinity. He won his argument and permission to preach Christianity throughout the land. From the viewpoint on the hill, the pleasant village can be seen running steeply down to the banks of the river.

Just to the east is the cottage of the poet Francis Ledwidge, who died during World War I.

Slane Castle on the banks of the River Boyne is the home of the Mount Charles family. It

reopened to the public in 2001 following an extensive restoration project after a fire in 1991. The castle also hosts big open-air rock concerts.

▶ *Take the N51 for Navan, and after 1 mile (2km) turn right on to the R163 for Kells.*

5 Kells, Co Meath
Kells, or Ceanannus Mór, was one of the great religious centres of western Europe. You can pick out the circular ditch in the lie of the town, and see the round tower, an early church and the impressive Celtic crosses with their scriptural messages. The town is famous for the *Book of Kells*, the celebrated illuminated medieval manuscript, now on view in the library at Trinity College, Dublin. The restored courthouse now contains the Kells Heritage Centre, with a multimedia insight into the crafts and culture of the area.

▶ *Take the N3 to Navan.*

6 Navan, Co Meath
Once a walled town, Navan marks the meeting of the waters of the Boyne and the Blackwater. Look out for the stocks outside the town hall, and a very modern blue sculpture, which is dedicated to 'the Fifth Province, the ideal of the cultural integration of all the people of Ireland.'

i Ludlow Street (seasonal)

Tara, just a simple mound today, evokes a glorious past

FOR HISTORY BUFFS

Trim, south of Navan, is worth visiting for Trim Castle alone, the largest Norman castle in Ireland. It also has the Yellow Steeple, which was once part of an Augustinian monastery, a statue of the Duke of Wellington, who was educated here, and a small cathedral with a 15th-century tower. Richard, Duke of York, father of Edward IV, made Trim his Irish headquarters and initiated building projects in the town. Still magnificent, the castle has undergone extensive restoration work.

▶ *Take the N3 for Dublin, and after 6 miles (10km) turn right at the signpost for Hill of Tara.*

7 Hill of Tara, Co Meath
The seat of the High Kings of Ireland, the Hill of Tara commands majestic views over the fertile plains of Meath and beyond. This was the centre of Ireland's heroic age, a civilisation that had contact with the Roman Empire and was ruled by a king who was concerned with sacred rites and rituals as well as political matters. A *feis* at royal Tara was a renowned festivity, held at harvest, or for the crowning of a king, of which the dynastic O'Neills were the strongest.

Five chariot roads led here from all parts of Ireland. The Rath of the Synods is an elaborate trivallate earthwork. The Mound of the Hostages is an Iron-Age hillfort and encloses the Royal Seat, a ringfort. On Cormac's House is the Stone of Destiny, said to be the inauguration stone of the kings. Also here are the Banquet Hall, the Enclosure of King Laoghaire, the Sloping Trenches and Grainne's Enclosure.

A statue of St Patrick recalls his profound influence, but it was the coming of Christianity that led to the eventual decline of Tara. There's a good audio-visual presentation, and guided tours.

▶ *Return to the N3 and turn right. After 2 miles (3km) turn left following signs to Skreen Church and Cross, go straight over two sets of crossroads and follow a narrow, uneven road for 2 miles (3km) to a crossroads, then turn left towards Drogheda. After another 2 miles (3km) turn left towards Slane on the N2*

and follow the marked route for the Battle of the Boyne Site.

⑧ Battle of the Boyne Site, Co Louth and Meath

It does not take a great effort of the imagination to picture the field of battle in 1690, when the armies of William of Orange and James II met each other in a conflict that was significant for Ireland, Britain and Europe. A huge orange and green sign beside the deep

A cottage wall mural depicts Ireland's most famous battle

waters of the Boyne marks the main site of the conflict, while helpful signs along the way show where the opposing armies camped, where battle was joined and where the river was crossed. The route passes along the Boyne Navigation Canal, once a link in Ireland's waterways system.

▶ *Take the N51 to Drogheda.*

Dublin

1/2 DAYS • 89 MILES • 143KM

& Wicklow

Dublin is a lively and attractive city with a unique brand of Irishness. Easy to explore on foot, it has superb museums, galleries and shopping, elegant Georgian streets and the historic Temple Bar area, with its narrow lanes, pubs and restaurants. The River Liffey cuts the city in two, and the lovely Wicklow Mountains rise to the south.

i Suffolk Street, Dublin

▶ Take the **R118/N31** to Dun Laoghaire.

❶ Dun Laoghaire, Co Dublin

This is a place to promenade, along the extensive harbour piers, past the villas on the front, or through the parks. Savour the Victorian features of the place which was called Kingstown from the visit of George IV in 1821 until the establishment of the Irish Free State. When the granite piers were completed in 1859, the harbour was the biggest artificial haven in the world. Ships and ferries to England use the port and it is home to several yacht clubs, of which the Royal St George and the Royal Irish are the oldest. The town also boasts Ireland's National Maritime Museum, housed in the Mariners' Church.

Near by, at Sandycove, is a Martello tower, one of the distinctive squat round coastal defences erected in Napoleonic times. This one houses a James Joyce Museum (the writer stayed here briefly). The Martello tower and the nearby 'Forty foot' gentlemen's bathing place are vividly described in Joyce's novel *Ulysses*.

i Ferry Port

Elegant Georgian houses add an air of distinction to the resort and port of Dun Laoghaire

▶ Take the **R119** coastal road to Dalkey and Killiney.

❷ Killiney, Co Dublin

With the broad sweep of a steeply dropping bay, elegant villas among tree-filled gardens and the two Sugar Loaf mountains to complete the vista, Killiney has been likened to the Bay of Naples. A good place to take in the full extent of the panorama is Sorrento Point.

Another good viewpoint is Killiney Hill, some distance inland from the beach, where an attractive park on the summit gives superb views of the hills and sea. Its 18th-century stone obelisk was built as a famine relief project.

▶ Continue on the **R119**, then join the **R761** to Bray.

❸ Bray, Co Wicklow

A popular resort that retains much of its Victorian attraction, Bray's long beach stretches below the strong line of Bray Head, an extension of the Wicklow dome. From the promenade you can walk the outstanding cliff path for 3 miles (5km) to Greystones. Below the Head, fan-like fossils of the oldest known Irish animals have been found. In the town is an attractive Heritage Centre. The National Sea Life Centre in the town has 70 species of sea and freshwater creatures, including a Tropical Shark Lagoon exhibit.

Kilruddery, by contrast, was one of the great set-piece landscape gardens of the 17th century. Very few of these early formal gardens, designed on a large scale with geometric patterns of water, avenues and plants, now survive.

i Old Courthouse

▶ *Return to and take the M11/N11 for Wicklow, then turn right for Enniskerry.*

4 Enniskerry, Co Wicklow
The first Irish Roman Catholic Gothic revival church was built in this pretty village in 1843. Its spire is an attractive feature in the lovely glen of Glencullen.

The superb mountain setting enhances Powerscourt, one of Ireland's great gardens, extravagantly created by the 6th and 7th Viscounts Powerscourt, and extensively altered between 1843 and 1875. A formal landscape of water, terraces, statues, ironwork, plants, flowers and ancient trees is stunningly contrasted with the natural beauty of Sugar Loaf Mountain, combining to form one of the most photographed vistas in the country. The house, a magnificent Palladian mansion, was destroyed by fire in 1974, but has been partly restored. Also in the estate is Powerscourt Waterfall where the Dargle River plunges over a 400 feet (120m) high rockface.

▶ *Take the R760 south, turning left to join the R755 for 8 miles (13km) south to Roundwood.*

5 Roundwood, Co Wicklow
The highest village in Ireland, Roundwood sits amid lovely scenery. The Vartry Reservoir, which helps to serve Dublin, lies close to the village. To the northeast is the Glen of the Downs, a dry rocky gorge formed in the Ice Age, with an oak wood. The landscape gives an idea of what Ireland would have looked like in prehistoric times, before the clearance of the forests. Lough Dan and Lough Tay are dark loughs shadowed by granite.

Six miles (10km) southeast of Roundwood at Ashford is Mount Usher, one of the finest examples of the 'Wild Garden', an idea particularly suited to Irish gardens. In a sheltered valley, plants, which include many exotic species, grow

naturally and in abundance in perfect harmony with the gentle landscape. They spread along the banks of a winding stream with cascades that are spanned by unusual suspension bridges.

▶ *Continue on the R755 to Laragh, then turn right on to the R756 to Glendalough.*

Within the beautiful Powerscourt Demesne is this lovely waterfall, with woodland walks and picnic places near by

6 Glendalough, Co Wicklow

Glendalough, the glen of two loughs, is the loveliest and most historic of all its Wicklow rivals. Two beautiful loughs lie deep in a valley of granite escarpments and rocky outcrops. On its green slopes are the gentle contours of native trees, on its ridges the jagged outline of pines. Add to this picturesque scene a soaring round tower and ruined stone churches spreading through the valley, and you have a combination which makes Glendalough one of the most beautiful and historic places in Ireland. St Kevin came to Glendalough in the 6th century to escape worldly pleasures. He lived as a hermit, in a cell on a little shelf above the lake, but the settlement he founded flourished and grew to become a monastic city whose influence spread throughout Europe. The round tower was built when Viking raids troubled the serenity of Glendalough. Some of the little churches have fine stone carvings, and one has a good pitched stone roof. Guides will explain the full story of Glendalough, and a visitor

Glendalough's round tower is a prominent landmark in this very special valley

centre skilfully illustrates the life of a monastery.

To the south near Rathdrum is Avondale, the home of the great Irish leader Charles Stewart Parnell. The 18th-century house, now a museum, is set in a large beautiful forest park on the banks of the Avonmore River.

BACK TO NATURE

The wide open spaces of the Wicklow Mountains offer opportunities for seeing a variety of upland birds, including peregrines, merlins, hen harriers, ring ousels and red grouse. In the glens, wood warblers and the occasional redstart may be seen.

ℹ️ *Visitor Centre (seasonal)*

▶ *Follow the R756 through the Wicklow Gap, then turn right on to the R758 for Pollaphuca.*

FOR HISTORY BUFFS

Patrick Pearse, one of the leaders of the uprising in 1916, kept a school in St Enda's Park. The building has now been converted into a museum dedicated to his memory.

7 **Pollaphuca,** Co Wicklow
At Pollaphuca there are large lakes, now dammed to supply Dublin's water system and also forming part of the Liffey hydroelectric scheme. The proximity to the city and the abundance of lakeside roads make it a popular venue for Dubliners.

▶ *Follow the lakeside road by Lackan to Blessington.*

8 **Blessington,** Co Wicklow
An attractive village with a long main street, Blessington was an important coaching stop on the

main road south from Dublin.

Just south is Russborough House, serenely placed in a beautiful landscape before a fine lake. It was built in the middle of the 18th century, the work of architect Richard Castle, for Joseph Leeson, the Earl of Milltown. A Palladian house constructed of granite, it sweeps out elegantly along curving colonnades to flanking wings and pavilions. Features include superb plasterwork by the Francini brothers. Owing to a series of thefts, the famous Beit Art Collection may not be on show.

▶ *Take the N81 for Dublin. After 4½ miles (7km) turn right on to the R759 to the Sally Gap.*

FOR HISTORY BUFFS

Wicklow men played a large part in the 1798 rebellion, and in order to finally suppress the uprising and clear the mountains, the 'Military Road' was forged from Rathfarnham in the north through the Sally Gap to Aghavannagh in the south. Former barracks can be seen at Drumgoff and Aghavannagh.

9 **The Sally Gap,** Co Wicklow
The most complete stretch of blanket bog on the east of the country is the beautiful Sally Gap. There are many pools and

SCENIC ROUTES

The road from Sally Gap to Laragh rises and falls wonderfully, with views across the Cloghoge Valley to War Hill. The road goes south through rugged mountain land, into forest plantations and passes Glenmacnass, a deep glen formed by glaciers, with a magnificent waterfall.

streams here, as well as the characteristic bog rosemary.

▶ *Turn sharp left on to the R115 to Killakee.*

10 **Killakee,** Co Dublin
The view from Killakee gives an outstanding picture of Dublin, as George Moore put it, 'wandering between the hills and the sea'. It takes in the crescent of Dublin Bay, bounded by the twin bastions of Howth Head to the north and Killiney Head to the south. The River Liffey is clearly defined, and you can identify the green landmark of Phoenix Park.

South of Killakee is a sinister hilltop ruin, once a retreat of the Hell Fire Club which was formed by a group of rakes in 1735. There are colourful tales of their terrible wickedness, the worst involving a game of cards with the devil.

North of Killakee, towards Dublin, is Marlay Park, with recreational amenities, miniature railway, gardens and craft centre. In the same area is Rathfarnham Castle, which dates back to 1583. A national monument, it is presented to the public as a building undergoing active conservation.

▶ *Follow the R115 for 7 miles (11km) back to Dublin.*

RECOMMENDED WALKS

The Wicklow Way is a long-distance walk that follows a course from Marlay Park in the north to Shillelagh and then through into County Kilkenny, on high ground to the east of the Dublin and Wicklow Mountains. The route is mostly waymarked through forests, along old bog roads and up steep mountain tracks. It is best to come equipped for wet weather and wear strong walking shoes. In addition, there are dozens of forest walks through Wicklow.

Witches, Castles
& Horses

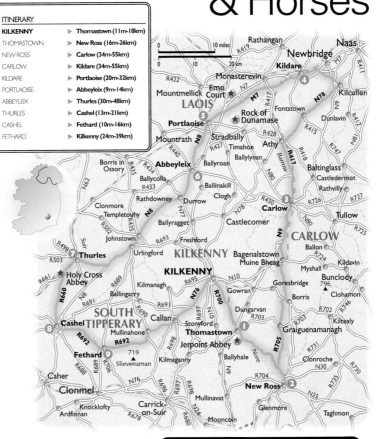

2/3 DAYS • 201 MILES • 324KM

Kilkenny is an ancient town that once rivalled Dublin in importance, and many of its historic buildings have been preserved, including the splendid 14th-century castle, perched above the river. Kilkenny is also the home of the Kilkenny Design Centre, promoting the best in Irish design and craftsmanship. The centre has craft workshops as well as a showroom.

Witches, Castles & Horses

SPECIAL TO...

Kilkenny was the home of Ireland's most famous witches. In 1324 Dame Alice Kyteler was the owner of Kyteler's Inn in St Kieran's Street. A beautiful woman who had become wealthy following the successive deaths of her four husbands, she was accused of witchcraft and condemned to a public whipping, followed by burning at the stake. She escaped, leaving her maid to be burnt in her place, and was never seen again. She is said to haunt the house still. Each August, Kilkenny Arts Festival takes place, when the town is host to world-class musicians and performers.

[i] *Shee Alms House, Rose Inn Street*

▶ *Take the* **R700** *southeast for 11 miles (18km) to Thomastown.*

❶ Thomastown, Co Kilkenny
This prosperous little market town on the banks of the River Nore is named after Thomas Fitz Anthony Walsh, Seneschal of Leinster, who built a castle and walled the town in the early 13th century. Grennan Castle, about 1½ miles (2km) to the southwest, is now in ruins. The most impressive remains of ancient buildings in the town are those of a large church dating from the 13th century.

Jerpoint Cistercian Abbey, some 2 miles (3km) southwest

Delightful formal gardens contrast with the forbidding stone walls of Kilkenny Castle

of Thomastown on the N9, is one of Ireland's finest monastic ruins. Founded in the 12th century, it was dissolved and its lands given to the Ormonde family in 1540. The extensive remains are awe-inspiring, with the original Romanesque pillars, a fine chancel and the most decorative cloister arcade of any Irish church. The detailed secular and religious carved figures are an accurate portrayal of the armour and clothing of 15th- and 16th-century Ireland. A visitor centre provides information on the abbey's long history. Mount Juliet, signposted from the town centre, was once one of Ireland's largest private

estates, covering 1,411 acres (570 hectares) of woodlands, pastures and landscaped lawns. Now a luxury hotel, the grounds provide an exceptionally beautiful drive off the main roads, and its public rooms are open to non-residents.

Though worn by time, this decoration on a tomb shows Jerpoint's artistic heritage

▶ Take the **R700** southeast for 14 miles (23m) to Mountgarret Bridge, where it joins the **N30** for the short drive to New Ross.

2 New Ross, Co Wexford
There is much evidence of its medieval origins in the narrow streets of New Ross, climbing the steep hill on which the town is built, overlooking the River Barrow. The town invites exploration on foot, as many of the streets are stepped and inaccessible to vehicles. The long bridge in the town centre connects New Ross to County

Jerpoint Abbey, once at the centre of its own small town, remains an impressive sight

Kilkenny. The original bridge was built around 1200 and the town was soon walled. In 1643, it held off a siege by the Duke of Ormonde, but fell to Cromwell just six years later.

The Tholsel (Town Hall), rebuilt in 1806, has a fine clock tower and holds the maces of Edward III and Charles II and ancient volumes of the minutes of the old town corporation. The 1798 memorial at the Tholsel depicts a 'croppy boy', typical of the insurgents who assaulted the town.

On the quay you can board and explore the *Dunbrody*, a seaworthy replica of one of the emigrant ships that carried so many Irish to the New World in the mid-19th century. River cruises depart from the quay during the summer months. (See also Tour 15.)

ⓘ *The Quay*

▶ Head north on the **N30**, turn left on to the **R700**, then right after a short distance on to the **R705** for 23 miles (37km) to join the **N9** at Leighlinbridge for the 7-mile (11km) drive into Carlow.

3 Carlow, Co Carlow
The village of Graiguena-managh ('the Granary of the Monks'), between New Ross and Carlow, was once a place of great ecclesiastical importance. Occupying the site was the

Abbey of Duiske, built between 1207 and 1240. It was suppressed in 1536, but determined monks stayed on for many years afterwards before abandoning the extensive settlement. By 1774 it stood in ruins and the tower collapsed. A large part of the church was roofed in 1813 and Catholic services were resumed. In the 1970s, a group of dedicated locals undertook a major restoration, and today the completely restored abbey serves as the parish church.

The county town of Ireland's second smallest county, Carlow was an Anglo-Norman stronghold, strategically placed on the border of the English 'Pale', a protected area around Dublin and its environs. The 640 insurgents who fell here during their 1798 attack on the town are remembered by a fine Celtic cross.

The west wall and the two flanking towers of 13th-century Carlow Castle can be seen near the bridge across the Barrow. This Norman castle was destroyed not by Cromwell, who captured it in 1650, but by one Dr Middleton in 1814. In his zeal to convert it into an asylum, he tried to reduce the thickness of the walls with explosives, rendering it no more than a dangerous shell, most of which had to be demolished.

The Cathedral of the Assumption, in Tullow Street, is a fine Gothic-style building erected between 1828 and 1833. Of special interest are its 151-foot (46m) high lantern tower and the marble monument by the sculptor John Hogan, of the 19th-century political writer Bishop Doyle. The Carlow Museum covers domestic and commercial life in the town, including some of the shop layouts, and Celtic finds. The museum is closed during its relocation to new premises on College Street.

RECOMMENDED WALKS

There is a pleasant walk in Carlow town along the banks of the River Barrow to the junction with its Burrin tributary. The meeting of the two rivers forms an attractive four-angled lake.

i *Tullow Street*

▶ *Follow the **R417** north to Athy. Turn northeast on to the **N78** for Kilcullen, then northwest on the **R413**, which takes you west to Kildare.*

4 Kildare, Co Kildare
En route to Kildare, stop in Athy to view the Dominican church, a striking example of modern

Ireland is dotted with prehistoric remains. This ancient dolmen is at Brown's Hill, near Carlow

SCENIC ROUTES

The Carlow/Stradbally road
(N8) takes you through Windy
Gap, one of eastern Ireland's
most famous scenic drives,
with wide vistas of the
surrounding countryside.

FOR CHILDREN

Take the children to see the
National Stud, 1 mile (2km)
east of Kildare off the N7.
Some of the world's most
renowned racehorses have
been bred and trained on
these grounds, and you can
visit the stables and watch the
thoroughbreds being exercised
and groomed. There is a museum depicting the history of the
horse in Ireland.

Collins was travelling when he
was ambushed in 1922.

The Hill of Allen, legendary
home of Irish folk hero Fionn
MacCumhail and the site of
three royal residences in ancient
Leinster, is northeast of town
and is crowned by a 19th-century
battlemented stone tower.

i | Market House

▶ *Take the M7 southwest to
reach Portlaoise.*

⑤ Portlaoise, Co Laois
Set at the junction of the
Dublin/Limerick and

*A climb up the round tower beside
the cathedral gives a wonderful
view over Kildare*

Dublin/Cork main roads,
Portlaoise is also the site of
Ireland's national prison.

There is a well-preserved
12th-century round tower in the
little village of Timahoe, about
7 miles (11km) southeast of
Portlaoise via the R426. Four
miles (6km) east of town, the
Rock of Dunamase rises 200
feet (60m) above the plain, with
the ruined 12th-century castle
of Dermot MacMurrough, one
time King of Leinster.

Emo Court, about 8 miles
(13km) northeast of Portlaoise
off the N7, is probably the
premier attraction of County
Laois. The grand house was
designed by the celebrated
architect James Gandon, and is
open to the public. The gardens

church architecture. Inside are
George Campbell's outstanding
Stations of the Cross. To the
southeast of Athy
Castledermot's ecclesiastical
ruins include a round tower, two
high crosses and the remains of
a Franciscan friary church.

Kildare's beautiful 18th-
century Church of Ireland St
Brigid's Cathedral incorporates
part of a 13th-century church.

In the heart of Ireland's
horse-breeding and training
country, Kildare sits on the edge
of the vast Curragh plain, and
the National Stud is near by. In
addition to its equine interest
(see For Children panel above),
the stud features a superb
Japanese garden and St
Fiachra's Garden, with monastic
cells, crystal garden and woodland walks.

East of town, horse racing
has reigned supreme for
centuries at The Curragh, where
all the Irish Classics are run.
The Curragh Camp, handed
over to the Irish army in 1922,
has been an important military
station for a century, and there
you can see the famous 1920
armoured car in which Michael

protect the crossing. Today it is a busy, well-laid-out marketing centre for the surrounding agricultural area. It is also the cathedral town of the archdiocese of Cashel and Emly.

▷ *Take the R660 south for 13 miles (21km) to reach Cashel.*

8 Cashel, Co Tipperary
Look above the ground floor of the shop opposite the city hall to see the crenellated battlements and gargoyles of what was 15th-century Quirke's Castle, named after a family who lived there in the 19th century. At the southwest end

are famous for their sweeping formal lawns, statuary and avenue of giant sequoia trees. The landscape of woodland and lake is undergoing restoration.

To the west of town the many roads crossing the Slieve Bloom Mountains offer interesting and scenic drives.

⌐i⌐ *James Fintan Lawlor Avenue*

▷ *Take the N8 for 9 miles (14km) south to Abbeyleix.*

6 Abbeyleix, Co Laois
This attractive town, with wide tree-lined streets and handsome buildings, is noted for the de Vesci Demesne, known as Abbeyleix House. The great house, which dates back to 1773, is not open to the public, but the splendid grounds are. They include formal terrace gardens to the west of the house, and a 'wild garden' that is carpeted

An eye-catching shopfront in Portlaoise leaves no doubt about the goods on offer

with bluebells in spring. In the walled garden of the old Brigidine Convent is the Abbey Sense Garden, created by and for people with disabilities.

The Heritage House in Abbeyleix is designed to be a focus for visitors to this historic town. Interactive multi-media displays tell the story of Abbeyleix and the surrounding area.

▷ *Take the N8 southwest to the N75 turnoff to Thurles.*

7 Thurles, Co Tipperary
In ancient times, the O'Fogartys fortified this site on the River Suir, and although the Norman Strongbow's army was soundly defeated here in 1174, Anglo-Normans returned later to build a castle that would

of Main Street, the ornamental fountain is in memory of Dean Kinane and his efforts in bringing an extension of the railway to Cashel in 1904. Cashel is best known for the Rock of Cashel, Folk Museum and Heritage Centre (see Tours 3 and 10.)

ℹ️ *Heritage Centre (seasonal)*

▶ *Take the **R692** southeast to Fethard.*

🥈 **Fethard,** Co Tipperary
Fethard was an important Anglo-Norman settlement in medieval times. Remnants of the old town walls and their towers can still be seen. In the town centre, there are keeps of three 15th-century castles, including that of Fethard Castle. Well-preserved remains of a priory contain several 16th- and 17th-century tombs. More than a thousand exhibits of rural life in this area are on display at the Folk, Farm and Transport Museum.

▶ *Take the **R692** northeast to Mullinahone. Turn right, staying on the **R692** until the **N76**. Turn left, through Callan, for the 11-mile (18km) drive back to Kilkenny.*

Perfectly proportioned 18th-century Abbeyleix House

By Hook or
By Crooke

Founded in the mid-9th century on the River Slaney, Wexford retains much of its old Viking layout, with tiny lanes leading down to the river. The narrow main street, lined with traditional shopfronts and pubs, is the heart of this lively and prosperous little agricultural and tourist town.

3 DAYS • 163 MILES • 262KM

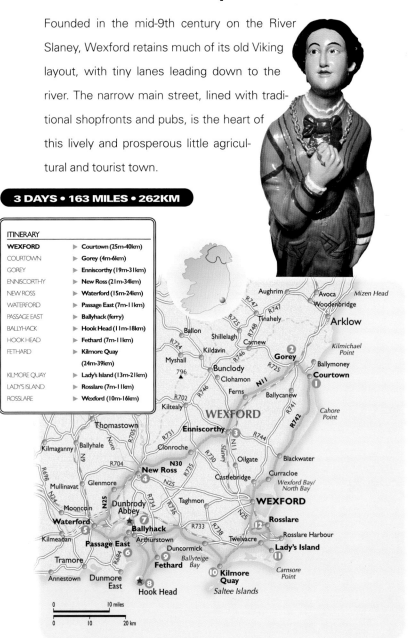

ITINERARY

WEXFORD	►	**Courtown (25m–40km)**
COURTOWN	►	**Gorey (4m–6km)**
GOREY	►	**Enniscorthy (19m–31km)**
ENNISCORTHY	►	**New Ross (21m–34km)**
NEW ROSS	►	**Waterford (15m–24km)**
WATERFORD	►	**Passage East (7m–11km)**
PASSAGE EAST	►	**Ballyhack (ferry)**
BALLYHACK	►	**Hook Head (11m–18km)**
HOOK HEAD	►	**Fethard (7m–11km)**
FETHARD	►	**Kilmore Quay**
		(24m–39km)
KILMORE QUAY	►	**Lady's Island (13m–21km)**
LADY'S ISLAND	►	**Rosslare (7m–11km)**
ROSSLARE	►	**Wexford (10m–16km)**

i *Crescent Quay, Wexford*

FOR CHILDREN

The Irish National Heritage Park, some 3 miles (5km) northeast of Wexford via the N25, has authentic reconstructions of Irish life including a campsite, farmstead and portal dolmen from the Stone Age; a stone circle from the Bronze Age; an Ogham stone, ringfort and souterrain, Viking boathouse and crannog from the Celtic and early Christian ages; and a Norman motte and bailey, the first Norman fortification in Ireland, and a round tower from the early Norman period. There is also a fine nature walk.

▶ *Take the **R741** north, then turn right on to the **R742** for Courtown.*

SCENIC ROUTES

The coastal drive via the R742 from Wexford to Courtown passes through charming little villages, countryside dotted with thatched cottages and stretches of wide sandy beaches.

❶ Courtown, Co Wexford
This pleasant harbour town set in the wide sweep of Courtown Bay is a popular family resort, with a fine, 2-mile (3km) long sandy beach, amusements and a picturesque golf course. Its harbour piers were a part of famine relief work sponsored by the Earl of Courtown in 1847.
  Ballymoney is a small resort with an excellent beach north of Courtown, and to the south, Ardamine and Pollshone are secluded coves with good swimming. At Ardamine, look for the little church by George Edmund Street, designer of the London Law Courts and restorer of Christ Church Cathedral in Dublin.

The wide sweep of Courtown Bay and its sandy beach make this one of the most popular resorts on the southeast coast

▶ *Follow the **R742** for 4 miles (6km) northwest to Gorey.*

❷ Gorey, Co Wexford
Against a backdrop of the Wicklow Mountains to the north, Gorey dates back to the 13th century. The wide Main Street and neat street plan give it a pleasant appearance. It figured prominently in the 1798 conflict, and insurgents camped at the western end of town at 418-foot (127m) high Gorey Hill before they marched on Arklow. A granite Celtic cross stands near the hill as a memorial to those who fell in battle. The Loreto convent, designed by Pugin, dates from 1839 to 1842.

i *Town Centre*

▶ *Take the **N11** southwest to Enniscorthy.*

RECOMMENDED WALKS

Northeast of Gorey, on an unclassified road to Castletown, Tara Hill (not to be confused with the more famous Hill of Tara) rises to 833 feet (254m). There are lovely forest walks, and the view from the summit is spectacular.

SPECIAL TO...

In late June/early July, Enniscorthy celebrates the Wexford Strawberry Fair, with tons of the luscious, locally grown fruit and non-stop street entertainment, art exhibitions and musical events.

❸ Enniscorthy, Co Wexford
Set on the steeply sloping banks of the River Slaney, Enniscorthy suffered several attacks following the arrival of

the Normans, and it was a veritable storm centre of the 1798 rebellion, when insurgents led by the revered Father John Murphy held the town for four weeks before being overthrown by Crown forces under General Lake. A bronze statue of Father Murphy and a pikeman stands in Market Square.

Wexford County Museum is housed in a Norman castle built in the 13th century by the Prendergast family, recalling the town's earliest history, while spectacular displays at the National 1798 Rebellion Centre interpret the momentous events of the 1798 Rebellion and place them in an international context. Lively presentation techniques are used to illustrate the rebellion and the subsequent journey to modern democracy in Ireland.

The 390-foot (120m) high Vinegar Hill at the eastern edge of town is where the Wexford pikemen made their last stand in June 1798. Their defeat marked the end of any effective resistance in the county. Today, it is a peaceful vantage point from which to view the town and surrounding countryside. The battles of 1916 are commemorated by a memorial to Commandant Seamus Rafter that stands in Abbey Square.

St Aidan's Cathedral is an impressive Gothic-revival structure designed by Pugin.

i The Castle (seasonal)

RECOMMENDED WALKS

At Dunamore Bridge, 3 miles (5km) south of Enniscorthy, Dunamore Forest Park is reached via an unclassified road to Killurin on the west side of the River Slaney. It is an ideal place to stop for a picnic, and has beautiful forest and riverside walks.

▶ Follow the **N30** to New Ross.

4 **New Ross**, Co Wexford
The busy port town of New Ross is on the River Barrow, which links up with Ireland's inland waterway system. On the quayside is the *Dunbrody*, a full-scale replica of a 19th-century three-masted famine ship, of the kind that took emigrants to the New World. You can explore above and below decks, and there are fascinating interactive displays.

Eight miles (13km) south of New Ross via the R733, the extensive ruins of Dunbrody Abbey, founded in 1182, are near the village of Campile. They are among the finest in Ireland, with a well-preserved nave, aisles, choir and transepts. Each transept is joined by three vaulted and groined chapels. (See also Tour 14.)

i The Quay

▶ Take the **N25** southwest for 15 miles (24km) to Waterford.

5 *Waterford**, Co Waterford
The most important seaport in the southeast, Waterford's face is lined with traces of its past. The French Church in

The massacre at nearby Vinegar Hill is among the displays in the museum at Enniscorthy Castle

Greyfriars Street was built in 1240 for the Franciscan order, but was later used by Huguenot refugees who fled religious persecution in France in the 17th century. Near the City Hall, St Olaf's Church dates from the 11th century. The impressive Church of Ireland Christ Church Cathedral sits on the elevated site, one street off the quay. The original structure was replaced in 1773, and the present building has been enlarged and renovated.

Waterford Museum of Treasures combines an extensive collection of rare and beautiful objects with the latest technology. A Viking Show, with music, song, dance and storytelling is staged on certain evenings in summer.

Waterford's lively cultural scene includes the Waterford Arts Centre in O'Connell Street, which has permanent and visiting exhibitions, and the Garter Lane Arts Centre, also in O'Connell Street, is the venue for special events and exhibitions. (See also Tour 10.)

[i] 41, The Quay

▶ *From Waterford take the R683 east to Passage East.*

6 **Passage East,** Co Waterford
This picturesque village at the foot of the steep hill overlooking the Waterford harbour estuary was fortified in years gone by to control shipping on the river. These days, it is the County Waterford terminal for the car ferry across to County Wexford. (See also Tour 10.)

▶ *Take the passenger ferry from Passage East across the estuary to Ballyhack.*

7 **Ballyhack,** Co Wexford
The ruined castle overlooking the estuary was part of the Preceptory of the Knights of St John, founded in the 11th century. Today, it is the County Wexford terminal for the car ferry from County Waterford

The Hook Head lighthouse is a distinctive landmark, night or day, for passing ships

SCENIC ROUTES

The road leading southeast out of Ballyhack gives extensive and beautiful views of Waterford harbour estuary as far as Hook Head on the Wexford side and the bulk of Creadan Head on the Waterford side.

and is noted for salmon fishing and boat building.

▶ *Turn southeast from Ballyhack on to the R733. Just past Arthurstown turn right for Duncannon. Shortly turn on to an unclassified signposted road south to Hook Head.*

8 **Hook Head,** Co Wexford
Perched on a craggy sea-carved peninsula, the striking black-and-white lighthouse called the Tower of Hook is thought to date from the 13th century. The tradition of a light to guide ships through the treacherous waters of this dangerous point began long before then. Legend has it

that it was the Welsh monk, St Dubhann, who first tended a cauldron of burning pitch, which he hoisted to the top of a high platform each night. The practice continued right through the 10th to 12th centuries as first the Vikings and then the Normans occupied the Hook area. Raymond le Gros, an important Norman leader, is believed to have built the tower some 700 years ago on the site of of St Dubhann's beacon, and it was this structure that was renovated in 1677, when an oil lamp was installed. Guided tours climb 115 steps to the parapet for superb views, passing through chambers with an audio show and displays about the history of the lighthouse. The former keeper's house has visitor facilities and a craft shop.

▶ *Return north on the unclassified road to the point where it branches right on to another unclassified road and take this road to Fethard.*

FOR HISTORY BUFFS

Hook Head gave to the English language one of its most frequently used expressions when the Norman leader Strongbow, Earl of Pembroke, declared in 1170 that 'I will take Waterford by Hook or by Crooke'. He was referring to the Tower of Hook on the Wexford side and to Crooke Castle on the Waterford shore near Passage East, both of which were heavily fortified. Strongbow made good his vow and thus changed the course of Irish history.

9 Fethard, Co Wexford

This pleasant little resort on the eastern shore of the Hook Peninsula has a fine sandy beach. In ancient times, there was woodland here, and traces of fossilised tree trunks have been found buried in the sands. The monument in the village centre is in memory of nine members of the Fethard lifeboat crew who drowned in 1914 as they made a gallant attempt to save the crew of a Norwegian vessel that had gone aground.

Fethard Castle, now in ruins but with its round tower still intact, was built in the mid-14th century. Tintern Abbey, 3½ miles (6km) north of Fethard between Wellington Bridge and Duncannon, dates from about 1200 and was built by the Earl of Pembroke in thanks for surviving a fierce storm at sea. The long drive into the wooded estate is signposted at the gate. In 1540, following the dissolution of the monasteries, the land and buildings passed into private hands, and parts of the church and tower were used as a residence until 1963. The domestic alterations have now been removed.

▶ *Take the R734 north for about 4 miles (6km), then turn east on the R733 to Wellington Bridge. Turn right on to the R736 to Duncormick, then right again via unclassified roads to Kilmore Quay.*

10 Kilmore Quay, Co Wexford

The charming little fishing village of Kilmore Quay is noted for its lobsters and deep-sea fishing, and is also the port of departure for the Saltee Islands to the south.

Between the Quay and the village of Kilmore, look for Brandy Close and the mound of wooden crosses at the roadside – tradition decrees that mourners place a small cross on the heap each time a funeral passes. The outstanding feature of the village of Kilmore, further along, is its concentration of fine thatched cottages.

▶ *Take the R739 northeast, through Kilmore, to the*

BACK TO NATURE

The Saltee Islands, 4 miles (6km) offshore from Kilmore Quay, harbour huge seabird colonies including razorbills, kittiwakes, puffins and thousands of gulls. Negotiate with local boatmen for a trip out, or arrange for one of the fishing trawlers to drop you on their way out to sea and pick you up on their return.

BACK TO NATURE

Lady's Island Lake is itself an important habitat for many bird species. However, on the lake's two islands all five species of terns have established the largest breeding colonies of these birds in Ireland. It is also the only known site where all species breed together. The islands and terns are easily viewed from the pathway around Lady's Island Lake, but during late spring and summer, access to the islands themselves is restricted to prevent disturbance.
---

resort with a fine 6-mile (10km) curving beach and good restaurants and accommodation.

i *Rosslare Harbour, Kilrane*

▶ *From Rosslare take the **R740** to the **N25** and turn right to return to Wexford.*

SPECIAL TO...

The Wexford Opera Festival is a gala October/November event of music and festivity, where local and international opera companies present lesser-known operas as well as standard classics. There are three performances during each week, along with music recitals, workshops, art exhibitions, and many other related activities. Throughout the town, there are peripheral events, competitions and street performances.
---

*junction with the **N25**. Turn right to reach Rosslare Harbour, and drive straight across to reach Rosslare.*

⑫ Rosslare, Co Wexford
Car and passenger ferries arrive daily at Rosslare Harbour, from Wales and northern France. Five miles (8km) to the north, Rosslare is a popular seaside

Kilmore Quay is at the heart of an area where traditional thatched roofs are still maintained

Fethard, now a quiet little resort, is close to the place where the first Anglo-Normans landed

*junction with the **R736**. Turn right on to this road and proceed to its junction with a signposted, unclassified road south (at Twelveacre Cross Roads) to Lady's Island.*

⑪ Lady's Island, Co Wexford
Lady's Island is at the head of a saltwater lagoon, Lady's Island Lake. Its ancient name translates to 'Meadow of the Women', and it may well have been inhabited by druidesses. With the coming of Christianity, it became one of the first shrines of the Blessed Virgin and an important place of pilgrimage. The church was destroyed and the holy men of the island were savagely butchered by Cromwellian forces in 1649, but pilgrimages began again at the end of the Cromwellian era and continue to this day.

▶ *Return to Twelveacre Cross Roads via the unclassified road north, then turn north-east on to the **R736** to its*

CONNACHT

The counties that make up the province of Connacht seem to fit the popular image of Ireland more than any other region. It is a land of stony fields, brooding mountains, windswept cliffs along a rugged coastline dotted with offshore islands, and wide skies alive with the shifting light and shadow of clouds moving inland from the Atlantic.

County Galway's eastern landscape stretches along flat, fertile plains from Lough Derg and the Shannon Valley north to Roscommon. The streets and lanes of Galway town are filled with medieval architecture and a lively creative arts-and-crafts culture. Poet William Butler Yeats drew inspiration from the surroundings of his beloved Thoor Ballylee tower home near Gort, and Lady Gregory, the moving force behind Dublin's Abbey Theatre, gathered some of Ireland's most distinguished writers around her hearth at nearby Coole Park. In western Galway, peaks of the Twelve Pins (Bens) face the misty heights of the Maumturk range across a lake-filled valley in rock-strewn Connemara, whose jagged coastline has a stark, silent beauty punctuated with rocky fields and tiny hamlets. The three Aran Islands, some 30 miles (48km) offshore, are a repository of antiquities left by prehistoric peoples and the language, customs and dress of a Celtic Twilight heritage.

County Mayo holds reminders of a great prehistoric battle on the plain of Southern Moytura near Cong. Christianity came with St Patrick, and pilgrims still follow his footsteps to the summit of Croagh Patrick on the shores of island-studded Clew Bay. Achill Island, connected to the mainland by a bridge, is ringed by mighty cliffs and tiny coves, with a flat, boggy interior.

Boyhood visits to his uncle's home in Sligo nurtured W B Yeats's deep love for the west, and some of his best works celebrate Sligo landmarks. Lough Ree was the haunt of early Christians, who had churches and monasteries on many of its islands. Lough Key lies in a luxurious forest park, with the remains of a great abbey at Boyle.

A long, narrow inlet, Killary Harbour, cuts into the hills of Connemara at Leenane (Tour 19)

Dominated by inland lakes and the River Shannon, County Leitrim has its fair share of mountains and hills. Carrick-on-Shannon, which grew up at one of the traditional fords of the Shannon, is home to a vast flotilla of cruisers for exploring the river and lakes.

Tour 16

This tour, which starts in the bright town of Sligo, is steeped in echoes of Ireland's greatest poet, William Butler Yeats, passing his grave beneath the majestic profile of the mountain, Benbulben, and visiting places which inspired some of his finest lyric poetry. This corner of Ireland is a happy unison of wooded lakes, bare mountaintops and Atlantic seascapes, and abounds in history from prehistoric times.

Tour 17

The majestic ruins of its 12th-century abbey and the beauties of its riverside setting and nearby Lough Key Forest Park make Boyle an attractive touring base. The Shannon, with its cruiser-filled marina at Carrick-on-Shannon, lures you onward, with perhaps a stop or two along the way for fishing in the trout-filled waters of this region. Roscommon's ruined castle speaks of the town's turbulent history, while Clonalis, the 'great house' of Castlerea, is a relic of more gracious times.

Tour 18

The ghost of Grace O'Malley will follow you on this tour after a visit to magnificent Westport House, with its museum and zoo. After a side trip to her Clare Island home, the route travels to Newport and one of her numerous strongholds before heading for Achill Island, Ireland's largest and most scenic, with yet another castle of the sea queen. At Knock, a huge basilica honouring a miraculous vision of the Blessed Virgin dominates the town. Monastic ruins and impressive Ashford Castle lie

Typical Connemara landscape near Roundstone (Tour 19)

along the route as you make your way back to Westport through the county town of Castlebar.

Tour 19

Galway town's many historic and cultural attractions may tempt you to tarry before setting out on this tour. A trip out to the very special Aran Islands beckons before embarking on the swing through Connemara's starkly beautiful landscape. This Gaeltacht (Irish-speaking) region is one of rocky, untillable fields, where the Twelve Bens mountain range faces the Maumturk range across a lake–filled valley. The jagged coastline is a solitary place of rocks and tiny hamlets and stark, silent beauty.

Sligo &
Yeats Country

The busy town of Sligo has good shops, traditional public houses, thriving art galleries and a theatre. There are fine 18th- and 19th-century buildings and 13th-century abbey ruins, all set against the distinctive backdrop of Benbulbin, an extraordinary flat-topped and rugged-faced mountain profile.

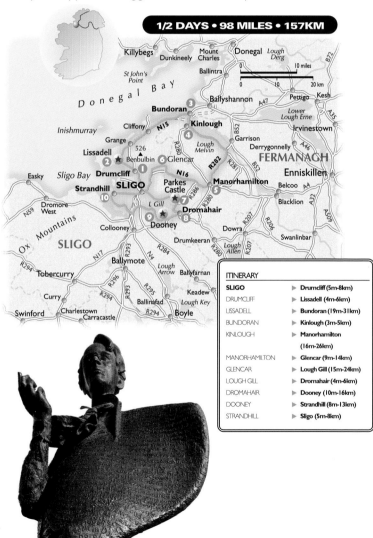

1/2 DAYS • 98 MILES • 157KM

ITINERARY		
SLIGO	▶	Drumcliff (5m-8km)
DRUMCLIFF	▶	Lissadell (4m-6km)
LISSADELL	▶	Bundoran (19m-31km)
BUNDORAN	▶	Kinlough (3m-5km)
KINLOUGH	▶	Manorhamilton (16m-26km)
MANORHAMILTON	▶	Glencar (9m-14km)
GLENCAR	▶	Lough Gill (15m-24km)
LOUGH GILL	▶	Dromahair (4m-6km)
DROMAHAIR	▶	Dooney (10m-16km)
DOONEY	▶	Strandhill (8m-13km)
STRANDHILL	▶	Sligo (5m-8km)

ⓘ *Temple Street, Sligo*

FOR HISTORY BUFFS

Carrowmore, 2 miles (3km) from Sligo, is the largest group of megalithic tombs in Ireland. Over 60 tombs have been found by archaeologists – the oldest predate Newgrange (see Tour 12) by 700 years.

▶ *Take the N15 for 5 miles (8km) to Drumcliff.*

❶ **Drumcliff,** Co Sligo
*'Under bare Ben Bulben's head
In Drumcliff churchyard Yeats is laid*

*An ancestor was rector there
Long years ago; a church stands near,
By the road an ancient cross,
No marble, no conventional phrase;
On limestone quarried near the spot,
By his command these words are cut:
Cast a cold eye
On life, on death,
Horseman, pass by!'*

Yeats's poem describes Drumcliff completely, and his grave can be found easily in the Protestant churchyard. The visitor centre at the church includes an audiovisual presentation on Yeats and Early Christianity.

▶ *Continue on the N15 and almost immediately take a left turn for 4 miles (6km) to Lissadell.*

❷ **Lissadell,** Co Sligo
The slightly forbidding classical façade of Lissadell hides the romantic background of the Gore-Booths. Yeats was a regular visitor here and his poem in memory of the two sisters, Eva and Constance, begins:
*'The light of evening, Lissadell,
Great windows open to the south,
Two girls in silk kimonos, both
Beautiful, one a gazelle.'*

Lissadell House would ring to the romanticism of poetry and patriotic fervour

Constance became the Countess Markievicz, a leader in the Easter Rising of 1916, and the first woman to be elected to Westminster, although she never took her seat. The 1830s mansion is made of Ballisodare limestone, and has a charming music room and a dining room with interesting murals. The house is set in fine parkland with small car parks beside the sea, supposedly the warmest bathing water in the country. It certainly seems to suit the seals, which can be spotted basking on the sandbanks. In the estate is the Goose Field, where Ireland's largest mainland colony of barnacle geese winter.

▶ *Drive through the parkland to rejoin the road and turn left, then right at the fork. Shortly turn right and continue to Grange. Turn left, to rejoin the N15 for Bundoran.*

BACK TO NATURE

At Streedagh, there is a dune system based on a shingle ridge, which is of international importance and which supports the plant, insect and bird life associated with dunes. The limestone rocks are laced with varieties of fossil coral. Bunduff Lake, near Creevykeel, is a salt-water marsh, where whooper and Bewick swans, Greenland white-fronted geese and many species of duck spend the winter.

SCENIC ROUTES

From the main Sligo-Donegal road, the Gleniff Horseshoe is a signposted loop that passes the jagged summits of Benwisken and Truskmore.

FOR HISTORY BUFFS

Creevykeel Court Tomb, southwest of Bundoran, is regarded as the finest example of a classic court tomb in Ireland. The cairn has a kerb of large stones surrounding a ritual court, with a boundary of upright stones. In the two burial chambers, which were originally roofed, a Harvard archaeological expedition found four cremated burials, as well as decorated neolithic pottery and stone weapons. These are now held in the National Museum in Dublin.

---

8 Bundoran, Co Donegal
Bundoran is a busy seaside resort, and presents quite a contrast to the placid towns and coastal villages of the northwest, offering a wide variety of attractions, as well as a 'blue flag' beach and cliff walks.

Glencar Waterfall plunges 30 feet (10m) through a ferny chasm into Glencar Lough

To the southwest of Bundoran, at Streedagh, is a small park that commemorates the place where three vessels of the Spanish Armada foundered in 1588. Members of the crew who struggled ashore from the overladen ships found little succour on land.

ⓘ The Bridge

▶ *Take the **R280** for 3 miles (5km) to Kinlough.*

❹ Kinlough, Co Leitrim

Sitting at the north end of Lough Melvin, this attractive village is a good place for coarse and salmon fishing. The ruins of Rossclogher Abbey stand on the shore, and on an artificial island are the remains of the MacClancy Castle (known as Rossclogher Castle), where nine survivors of the Armada were given refuge.

▶ *Follow the **R281** along the shore of Lough Melvin for 8 miles (13km), then turn right on to the **R282** for Manorhamilton.*

❺ Manorhamilton, Co Leitrim

This unassuming village stands in an area of untouched mountain valleys and grey cliff walls. Lush fertile slopes, steep clefts and lofty peaks characterise this part of Leitrim. Glenade Lough and the valley where the River Bonet rises have a special quality. The ruined castle that overlooks the town was built at the meeting of four mountain valleys by the Scottish 17th-century planter Sir Frederick Hamilton, who gave his name to the village.

▶ *Take the **N16** west for Sligo. After 7 miles (11km) turn right on to an unclassified road for Glencar Lough.*

❻ Glencar, Co Leitrim

Glencar is a beautiful lake; the steep slopes of the valley are generously clothed with mixed woodland and topped with cliffs. Plants grow here in profusion, including rare species, while the mountaintops are luxuriantly covered with heather. Glencar waterfall

Parke's Castle, built in 1609, looks out over the tranquil waters of Lough Gill

cascades down from a rocky headland to a deep pool, white with spray. Yeats immortalised the waterfall in his poem *The Stolen Child*.

RECOMMENDED WALKS

This is a region well provided with walks, many of them way-marked. Two good town trails can be found in Sligo and Dromahair. There are fine walks from the picnic site beside the village of Kinlough through Kinlough Forest, by Lough Melvin. A spectacular walk takes you from the Glencar Lake up a mountain road into Swiss Valley, a steep-sided cleft surrounded by peaks. The route then returns to the point where the waterfall cascades into the lake below.

> Follow the lakeside road to
> rejoin the **N16** and turn right
> towards Sligo, then turn left on
> the **R286** to Parkes Castle
> Visitor Centre.

7 Lough Gill, Co Leitrim
From Parkes Castle there is a
superb view of Lough Gill, one
of Ireland's loveliest loughs,
dotted with islands and wooded
with native trees like yew, arbutus, white beam, oak and birch.
The bare mountain reaches
down deep ferny glens to the
lake below.

Parkes Castle is an impres-
sively reconstructed fortified
manor house, originally a
stronghold of the O'Rourkes,
but owing its present name to
the English family who were

Echoes of England are still in
evidence in the purpose-built
village of Dromahair

FOR CHILDREN

Although they were not
conceived with children in
mind, the Hazelwood Park
wooden sculptures have
proved to be a delight to
young visitors. Along paths in
the woods by Lough Gill are
huge works of art, hewn, constructed and carved in wood.
A walk here is a voyage of dis-
covery, to meet 'Fergus rules
the Brazen Car', 'The Old
Woman' or 'The Fisherman'
among many.

'planted' here. An audiovisual
show and tea-room will enhance
a visit. If you explore the lake
you will find a sweat-house,
medieval Ireland's answer to
the sauna.

> Continue on the **R286**, then
> turn right on to the **R288** for
> Dromahair.

8 Dromahair, Co Leitrim
This area is O'Rourke country,
overlooked by a rock plateau
called O'Rourke's Table.
Dromahair hosts gatherings of
the O'Rourke family, as well as
a Wild Rose Festival, but it was
an English family, the Lane-
Foxes, who laid out the pretty
village around the River Bonet
based on a plan of a Somerset
village. In Thomas Moore's
song *The Valley Lay Smiling
Before Me*, the tale is told of the
elopement from Dromahair in
1152 of Dervorgilla O'Rourke
and the King of Leinster
(her husband was away on a
pilgrimage of penitence for
beating her).

To the west is the Isle of
Innisfree. You can take a cruise
from Parkes Castle aboard the
Wild Rose Water Bus, with an
entertaining commentary of
poetry, folklore and history.

> Take the **R288** for Carrick-on-
> Shannon, then turn right on to
> the **R287** for Sligo. After 2½
> miles (4km) turn right again
> on the **R287**, and follow the
> road past the sign for
> Innisfree to Dooney Rock
> Forest, before rejoining
> the **N4**.

9 Dooney, Co Sligo
This beautiful corner of Lough
Gill has forests and paths to
satisfy any enthusiastic walker,
offering great views of the
lough. Dooney Rock Forest
bears the vestiges of a once
important oak forest. You can
see the 'twining branches', two
linked oaks. Yeats wrote of 'the
Fiddler of Dooney', who made
folk 'dance like the waves of the
sea'. The poem has inspired a
Fiddler of Dooney competition

for the champion fiddler of Ireland, held in Sligo in July.

Slish Wood, or Sleuth Wood as Yeats knew it, has a lovely stream. Cairns Hill Forest Park marks the two cairns on Belvoir and Cairns peaks. A legend tells of two warriors, Omra and Romra. Romra had a daughter, Gille, meaning beauty, and Omra fell in love with her. When a mortal battle ensued after the lovers were discovered by Romra, Gille drowned herself, and Lough Gill was formed from the tears of her nursemaid. The legend holds that the two cairns are the burial places of the warriors.

Cashelore stone fort is a large oval stone enclosure, once the settlement of an important Celt. The tranquil Tobernalt is a holy well where Mass was said in penal times. A stone altar was erected in thanksgiving when the town was spared the worst ravages of a fever at the turn of the century.

▶ *Travel south on the **N4**, then turn right on to the **R292** for Rathcarrick and Strandhill.*

10 Strandhill, Co Sligo
Great Atlantic breakers crash on to the beach at Strandhill, making the small seaside village a favoured place for surfing championships. Lifeguards watch bathers, but if you prefer calmer waters, drive round to the beach at Culleenamore, which is safer and quiet. Culleenamore nestles under the mountain of Knocknarea, which is capped by a cairn visible for miles round. It is known locally as the grave of Queen Maeve, the warrior queen of Connacht.

If you climb to the summit of Knocknarea, Sligo tradition suggests that you add a stone to the cairn, as a protection against the fairies.

Among the fields below Knocknarea at Carrowmore is Ireland's largest group of megalithic tombs; more than 60 can be found here, mostly passage graves and dolmens. The best place to start to discover Carrowmore is from the Interpretive Centre, where a map is on display.

▶ *Take the **R292** for 5 miles (8km) back to Sligo.*

Firm sand and rolling waves attract bathers and surfers to the resort of Strandhill

Boyle &
The Lake Country

Lakes dotted with small wooded islands are the main characteristic of County Roscommon. Beautifully situated on the
bank of the River Boyle at the foot of the Curlew Hills, the town
of Boyle offers excellent fishing. Close to the river at the north
end of town are impressive ruins of the Cistercian abbey, and
the King House has excellent displays and presentations.

1 DAY • 87 MILES • 140KM

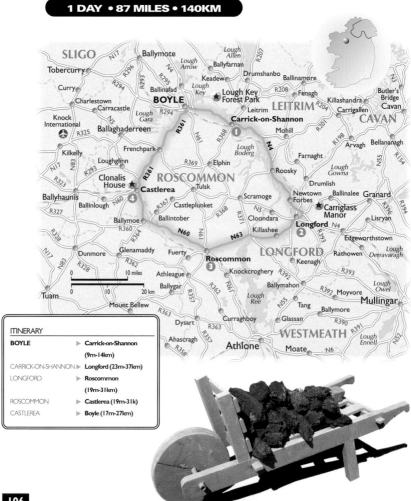

ITINERARY	
BOYLE	► **Carrick-on-Shannon**
	(9m-14km)
CARRICK-ON-SHANNON	► **Longford (23m-37km)**
LONGFORD	► **Roscommon**
	(19m-31km)
ROSCOMMON	► **Castlerea (19m-31k)**
CASTLEREA	► **Boyle (17m-27km)**

i King House, Boyle (seasonal)

▶ *Take the N4 for 9 miles (14km) southeast to Carrick-on-Shannon.*

❶ Carrick-on-Shannon, Co Leitrim

Chief town of Ireland's most sparsely populated county, Carrick-on-Shannon is also the smallest county town in the country, and was first given its charter by James I. When river traffic was superseded by road and rail, it hit the town hard, but

the growing demand for pleasure boating gave it a reprieve. Its situation on Shannon's navigational system makes this attractive town a major river-cruising and fishing centre.

Among the best preserved buildings in the town are the 19th-century Court House and the Protestant church.

i The Marina

▶ *Follow the N4 southeast for 23 miles (37km) to Longford.*

❷ Longford, Co Longford

Set on the south bank of the River Camlin, the market town of Longford dates back to 1400, when a Dominican priory was founded here. Nothing remains of that ancient establishment, but the slight ruins of a castle built in 1627 are incorporated into the old military barracks. In the town centre is the grey limestone, Renaissance-style St Mel's Cathedral, a classical building of the 19th century by

The riverside abbey ruins are a peaceful haven right in the centre of Boyle

SCENIC ROUTES

Heading south from Carrick-on-Shannon on the N4, leave the main road to divert to Jamestown on the Shannon and visit Drumsna, a small town in an exceptionally scenic setting. As you continue southeast to Longford, the landscape is dotted with many small lakes that are part of the Shannon system. Two miles (3km) beyond Aghamore, an unclassified road to the right leads to the wooded Derrycarne promontory, which projects into Lough Boderg.

J B Keane. Near by is Carriglass Manor, a romantic Gothic revival house, still occupied by the Lefroy family. A Palladian stable yard, a costume museum and delightful woodland walks add to the charm of Carriglas.

Longford was a terminal of a branch of the Royal Canal, called the 'Shoemaker's Canal'.

[i] *Dublin Street (seasonal)*

▶ *Take the* **N63** *southwest to Roscommon.*

FOR HISTORY BUFFS

Ireland's last hangwoman, the legendary 'Lady Betty', is commemorated by a plaque on the 18th-century gaol where she worked, and which was disused after 1822. A former prisoner, her own death sentence had been commuted when she agreed to take on the unwanted job of the hangman.

3 **Roscommon,** Co Roscommon

Situated at an important road junction, Roscommon is the county's chief town, named after St Coman, founder of an early 8th-century Christian monastery here. The ruin of the Dominican friary is mainly 15th-century and includes the 137-foot (42m) long, 23-foot (7m) wide church. A tomb in a burial niche in the north wall of the chancel is thought to be that of Felim O'Conor, King of Connacht, who founded the abbey in 1253. His effigy is perhaps the most interesting figure within the ruins. The eight gallowglasses (figures of mail-clad warriors) who support the tomb belonged originally to a much later tomb dating from around 1500.

Built in 1269 by Robert d'Ufford, the English Justiciar, but much altered since, Roscommon Castle was captured by the Irish four years later and razed to the ground. It was rebuilt in about 1280 and was besieged many times until the English Civil War, when it was held for the King by Sir Michael Earnley. It was surrendered to Cromwellian forces in 1652, who promptly dismantled it. The ruins form a large quadrangular area, with a round bastion tower at each corner. The gateway is protected by two similar towers that project from the eastern wall. Roscommon County Museum has a facinating collection, including early Christian relics, folk items, crafts, farm machinery and a display on the Old Jail and Lady Betty, Ireland's last hangwoman (see box).

[i] *Harrison Hall (seasonal)*

▶ *Take the* **N60** *to Castlerea.*

4 **Castlerea,** Co Roscommon

This pretty little town was the birthplace, in 1815, of Oscar Wilde's father, Sir William Wilde, who was an antiquarian and oculist. Just west of town the fine 'great house' of Clonalis, rebuilt in the 19th century, was the seat of the O'Conor Don, a direct descendant of the last High King of Ireland, who abdicated after the Anglo-Norman invasion of 1169. Ownership of such a manor house by a Gaelic family is unique, and Clonalis's furnishings reflect a more informal elegance than many other houses. The drawing room, for example, although beautifully furnished with Victoriana, is also a warm, comfortable room. Nineteenth-century portraits hang in the library, which also holds many fine books. There is a private chapel, and the highlight of the museum is the harp of Ireland's last great bard, Turlough O'Carolan (1670–1738), whose portrait is displayed. Among his many compositions was the tune to which the Star Spangled Banner is now sung.

Priceless Gaelic manuscripts, Victorian costumes, Sheraton furniture, porcelain and glass are also featured in the museum.

▶ *Take the* **R361** *back to Boyle.*

FOR CHILDREN

Swimming, boating and other water sports are on offer at Lough Key Forest Park, 2 miles (3km) east of Boyle on the N4. It is one of the largest and most picturesque forest parks in Ireland, with 865 acres (350 hectares) of woods, lakes and islands. There are nature walks, an observation tower, undergrond tunnels, a bog garden and various ruins to explore.

SPECIAL TO...

In August, the little town of Keadew (northeast of Boyle and Lough Key) buzzes with musical and sports events during the ten-day O'Carolan Festival, in memory of the last of the Irish bards, Turlough O'Carolan, who is buried in Kilronan Church cemetery, just northwest of the village.

The modest proportions of Clonalis House give no hint of the fascinating items within

Achill Island &
County Mayo

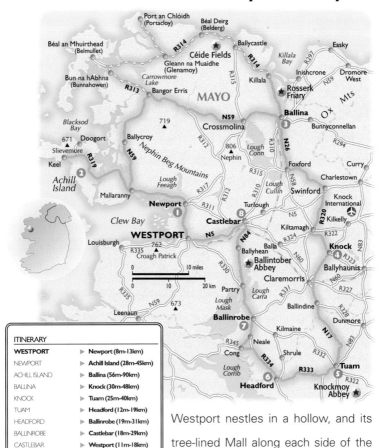

Westport nestles in a hollow, and its tree-lined Mall along each side of the Carrowbeg river is an attractive main artery. The town has splendid Georgian houses, a fine Heritage Centre, and lovely Westport House, a castle of the O'Malley clan, which dates back to the 1730s and is a major attraction.

2 DAYS • 207 MILES • 333KM

ⓘ James Street, Westport

RECOMMENDED WALKS

Croagh Patrick, 5 miles (8km) west of Westport via the R335, rises some 2,500 feet (762m) above the shore of Clew Bay near the little town of Murrisk. This is Ireland's Holy Mountain, on which St Patrick is said to have spent the 40 days of Lent in 441, and where legend says he lured all the snakes in Ireland to the summit, then rang his bell as a signal for all to throw themselves over a precipice. It is an easy climb that takes only about an hour by way of a path from Murrisk.

▶ Take the **N59** north for 8 miles (13km) to Newport.

❶ Newport, Co Mayo
This picturesque little town, which dates from the 17th century, faces Clew Bay and is sheltered by mountains. It is a

---

FOR CHILDREN

While you explore the glories of Westport House and browse through its museum and shops, the children can spend time in the playground, where play equipment is guaranteed to keep them occupied. You may, however, want to accompany them on a walk through the zoo.

---

noted angling centre, with fishing on loughs Furnace, Beltra and Feeagh as well as in the rivers Burrishoole and Newport. Its neo-Romanesque Catholic church was built in 1914 and features a superb stained-glass window of the Last Judgement designed by Harry Clarke.

Four miles (6km) west of town, off the N59, Rockfleet Castle, sometimes called Carrigahowley Castle, is another of Grace O'Malley's strongholds. Dating from the 15th and 16th centuries, the tower dwelling has four storeys with a

---

Westport is a lively and attractive town, with some splendid Georgian houses and colourful gardens

corner turret. The indomitable pirate queen came to live here permanently after her second husband died in 1583.

▶ Follow the **N59** west to Mallaranny, then the **R319** to Achill Island, a distance of 28 miles (45km).

❷ Achill Island, Co Mayo
The largest of Ireland's islands, Achill Island is connected to the mainland by a bridge. Only 15 miles (24km) long and 12 miles (19km) wide, its landscape is one of dramatic cliffs and seascapes, with a boggy, heather-covered interior. Fishing for shark and other big-game fish is excellent, with boats and guides for hire. There are also very good bathing beaches, and the beautiful Atlantic Drive around the island climbs from gently rolling mountain foothills, past stretches of sandy beaches, and

through tiny picturesque villages with excellent views of the sea, Clew Bay and the mainland. At Kildownet, another Grace O'Malley castle is well preserved, and ruins of a small 12th-century church are near by. At the centre of holiday activities is Keel, which has a fine sandy beach and a small harbour with fishing and sightseeing boats for hire.

Seen from a boat, the sea-carved rocks below the Menawn cliffs at the eastern end of the beach take on fanciful shapes. At Doogort, nestled at the foot of Slievemore, boatmen take visitors to the fascinating Seal Caves cut far into the cliffs of Slievemore.

i Cashel (seasonal)

▶ Take the **R319** back to Mallaranny, then turn north on the **N59** for the drive to Ballina, passing through Ballycroy and Bangor (where the **N59** turns sharply east).

❸ Ballina, Co Mayo
An important angling centre on the River Moy near Lough Conn, Ballina is County Mayo's largest town. Founded in 1730, it is also a cathedral town, and near its 19th-century Cathedral of St Muiredach, which has a fine stained-glass window, are ruins of a 15th-century Augustinian friary.

About 3 miles (5km) north of Ballina, the 15th-century Rosserk Friary sits peacefully on the shore of Killala Bay. The ruins include a tower, a small cloister, nave, chancel, a fine

Beautiful Achill Island is remote yet easily accessible

SCENIC ROUTES

An alternative route from Achill Island to Ballina takes you on a 48-mile (77km) loop around the north coast of County Mayo, through some of the finest scenery in Ireland (see map). Follow the N59 north to Bangor Erris, then take the Belmullet road, the R313, and just past Bunnahowen turn east on the R314 to Glenamoy, where an unclassified road turns left to reach the harbour of Portacloy. Returning to Glenamoy, proceed northeast on the R314 through Belderg and Ballycastle. Following the R314 south, you reach Killala, and 2 miles (3km) southeast of town, on a road to your left, is 15th-century Moyne Abbey. The R314 south takes you straight into Ballina.

A tangible representation of the vision that made Knock famous over 100 years ago

arched doorway and east window.

Eight miles (13km) north of Ballina via the R314, Killala, the small harbour where General Humbert and his French forces landed in 1798, has a wealth of antiquities in the immediate vicinity, as well as one of the finest round towers in the country. Nearby Franciscan Moyne Abbey was founded in the mid-15th century. Although burned in 1590, the well-preserved ruins include a six-storey square tower, vaulted chapter room, and a partially vaulted sacristy.

i Cathedral Road (seasonal)

▶ Take the N26 south, then southeast through Foxford to Swinford. Follow the R320 south to Kiltimagh, then turn southeast on the R323 for 5 miles (8km) to reach Knock.

4 Knock, Co Mayo
This small town was the scene of an apparition in 1879, the central figure of which was the Blessed Virgin. After intensive investigation by Catholic authorities, it was declared authentic and named a Marian shrine. A large, circular church was built to accommodate the huge number of pilgrims, with 32 pillars in the ambulatory contributed by all counties in the country, and four windows in medieval style that represent the four provinces of Ireland. In 1979 Knock was visited by Pope John Paul II.

The Knock Folk Museum exhibits relics of rural and small-town life in this part of Ireland.

i Town centre (seasonal)

▶ Take the N17 south to Tuam.

5 Tuam, Co Galway
A thriving commercial and agricultural centre under James I's charter of 1613, the layout of Tuam was altered to include a diamond-shaped town 'square' on which all roads converged. St Mary's Cathedral, founded in 1130 and rebuilt largely in the 19th century, is a fine example of Gothic-revival architecture and incorporates a 12th-century chancel with magnificent windows. The town's 12th-century High Cross, well adorned but incomplete, now stands in its grounds. A slightly earlier Roman Catholic Cathedral of the Assumption is a marvellous neo-Gothic building with fine window and tower carvings. Tuam can claim Ireland's first industrial museum, the Mill Museum, an operational corn mill with millwheel and other interesting industrial exhibits.

Just outside the town, on the Ryehill road, there is an interesting medieval lake dwelling, known as Loughpark Crannóg. Seven miles (11km) to the southeast, on the shores of a small lake, is the 12th-century Knockmoy Abbey. The tomb of its founder, Cathal O'Connor, King of Connacht, can be found within the ruins, as well as traces of ancient murals.

i Mill Museum (seasonal)

▶ Leave Tuam on the N17 southwest, and about 3 miles (5km) from town turn west on the R333 for 9 miles (14km) to reach Headford.

6 Headford, Co Galway
This popular angling and market centre is very close to Lough Corrib, and there are boats for hire at nearby Greenfield. Two miles (3km) northwest of town, Ross Errilly Friary is a large 1498 Franciscan friary that fell victim to Cromwellian forces in 1656. Its original size can be judged by its two courtyards, around which

are the domestic buildings, including a refectory, dormitories, and a kitchen with a surprising forerunner of modern fish tanks.

At the heart of Castlebar, the courthouse overlooks this delightful leafy green

▶ Take the **R334** northwest for just over 6 miles (10km), then turn left to Cong via the **R346**. From Cong take the **R345** northeast to rejoin the **R334** and turn left to reach Ballinrobe.

7 Ballinrobe, Co Mayo
In a beautiful spot, near three good fishing lakes (loughs Corrib, Mask and Carra), this small town is surrounded by mountains and woodlands. At the north end of town are the ruins of a 1313 Augustinian friary, and about 3 miles (5km) to the southwest is Killower Cairn, one of the most impressive in Connacht.

Just 7 miles (11km) south of Ballinrobe (take the R334 and turn west on the R345), the little town of Cong was the setting for most of the popular film *The Quiet Man*. That, however, is the least of its claims to fame. More notable are the ruins of the Royal Abbey of Cong, built by Turlough Mor O'Conor, High King of Ireland in the 12th century, on the site of a 7th-century monastic community, and burial place of Ireland's last High King, Rory

O'Conor, who died in 1198. The impressive Ashford Castle is now a luxury hotel. Its rather eccentric architecture incorporates several styles and periods.

[i] *Cornmarket (seasonal)*

▶ *Follow the **N84** to Castlebar.*

8 Castlebar, Co Mayo
The county town of Mayo, Castlebar has figured in several major Irish insurrections, most notable in 1798, when Irish–French forces routed British cavalry, causing such a hasty retreat to Hollymount, Tuam and Athlone that the campaign gained the nickname 'The Race of Castlebar'.

Four miles (6km) east of Castlebar in the village of Turlough, is Ireland's only National Museum outside Dublin, the National Museum of Country Life. The national folklife collection, set in the spectacular grounds and gardens of Turlough Park House, portrays all aspects of rural life – hunting, agriculture, religion, education and leisure pursuits – between 1850 and 1950.

[i] *Town centre*

▶ *Take the **N5** southwest back to Westport.*

SPECIAL TO...

Westport's Street Festival in July features street performers and folk singers from all over Ireland.

BACK TO NATURE

Ten miles (16km) west of Westport, 2 miles (3km) east of Louisburgh and ½ mile (1km) on a signposted road off the R335, the National Forest Old Head Wood is a welcome stop. There is a car park and also picnic grounds, with well-marked pathways through the small reserve. Oak is the dominant species, but shares the territory with native birch, willow and rowan. Beech and sycamore trees, not native to the area, have also been introduced. There are fine views over Clew Bay.

Ashford Castle at Cong is now a sumptuous hotel

Region of
Stony Beauty

Galway is a thriving commercial and university city with a particularly lively cultural scene. The heart of the city is a maze of colourful medieval streets and the famous Spanish Arch is a relic of the old city walls. Attractions include the impressive modern cathedral and, on a much smaller scale, Nora Barnacle's House.

2/3 DAYS • 136 MILES • 218KM

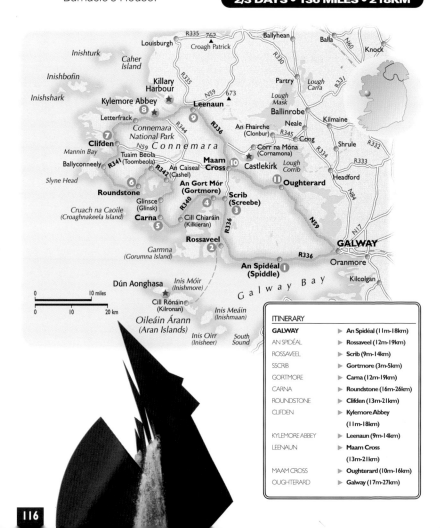

i *Forster Street, Galway*

FOR HISTORY BUFFS

Take a look at the Lynch Memorial Window in Galway's Market Street, and the inscription above the doorway. The story goes that Lord Mayor James Lynch FitzStephen's popular 19-year-old son murdered one of his closest friends, who he thought paid undue attention to a young lady they both admired. Overcome with remorse, the son turned himself in, and his father sat as magistrate in the case, returning a death-by-hanging sentence. The executioner refused to perform his duty, so the father carried out the sentence himself.

▶ *Take the coast road, the R336, west to An Spidéal.*

❶ An Spidéal (Spiddle), Co Galway

This charming little resort town has a marvellous beach, the Silver Strand, and shore

FOR CHILDREN

West of Galway, Salthill is a children's paradise. In addition to a good beach and pedal buggies for riding along the promenade, attractions at Leisureland Amusement Park are guaranteed to please. The town is also home to Atlantiquaria, the National Aquarium of Ireland, including touch tanks and a model sub.

fishing is especially good here. Roman Catholic St Eanna's Church, completed in 1904 in Celtic Romanesque style by William A Scott, is an architectural delight. A popular pastime in summer are races between local curraghs (lightweight wood and canvas boats). The Spiddle Craft Centre, a complex of craft workshops and showrooms, is well worth a visit.

▶ *Continue west on the R336 for 12 miles (19km) to Rossaveel, which lies just off this road.*

The lovely Eyre Square in the centre of Galway has many interesting monuments

❷ Rossaveel, Co Galway

There are still thatched cottages scattered about this small harbour village, from which peat for fuel is shipped by barge to the Aran Islands. The passenger boat trip out to the islands takes just 40 minutes from Rossaveel, rather than the 1½-hour voyage from Galway.

The Aran Islands group consists of three inhabited islands: Inishmore, with the only safe harbour for steamers; Inishmaan and Inisheer, where curraghs meet incoming boats to take passengers or freight to the docks.

Prehistory has left its mark on the faces of all three islands – promontory forts, ringforts and beehive huts speak of the 'Celtic Twilight' era – while lofty round towers, oratories and tiny churches are reminders of the early days of Christianity in Ireland.

A visit to Aran is an easy, delightful day-trip from Rossaveel, and accommodation

can be arranged in advance for those who want to stay longer. Steamers to Inishmore, the largest of the islands, dock at the main port of Kilronan, and jaunting cars are waiting to take visitors exploring. Rented bicycles are also available, and walkers will delight in following the one main road around the island, with an occasional stop to chat with its local inhabitants. Dún Aonghasa is an 11-acre (4.5-hectare) stone fort perched on a cliff some 300 feet (91m) above the sea, one of the finest prehistoric monuments in western Europe. Its three concentric enclosures are surrounded by drystone walls, and from the innermost rampart there are outstanding views of the islands and across the sea to the Connemara coast.

Near the village of Cowrugh, the grounds of a small 15th-century church hold four great flagstones marking the graves of saints, and south of the church there is a holy well. The area surrounding this village is littered with ancient monuments. But, then, it is literally impossible to go very far on this large island or the two smaller ones without encountering a vivid reminder of centuries past in one form or another.

Among the remains on Inisheer are the medieval tower of O'Brien's Castle which is situated on a prominent rocky hill, St Gobnet's Church and the Church of St Cavan.

The oval fort of Dun Conor rises from a steep-sided hill on Inishmaan; there is also a fine dolmen. Visits to Inishmaan and Inisheer can be arranged with boatmen in Kilronan.

▶ *Turn north on the R336 for 9 miles (14km) to Scrib.*

8 Scrib (Screeb), Co Galway
There is excellent game fishing from the small town of Scrib,

The Twelve Pins (or Bens) are rarely out of view on the Connemara horizon

and one of Ireland's peat-burning electricity generating stations is also in the vicinity.

▶ *Turn west on to the R340 to An Gort Mór (Gortmore).*

4 An Gort Mór (Gortmore), Co Galway
From this village, a left turn will take you to Ros Muc, site of Padraig Pearse's cottage. It was here that the great Irish leader, who was executed in 1916, spent his holidays and wrote his most important works.

▶ *Follow the R340 southwest to Carna.*

5 Carna, Co Galway
Lobster fishing is still the main occupation in this picturesque village. Three miles (5km) to the south, a bridge connects Mweenish Island to the mainland. The beautiful beaches and interesting University College Galway marine biology station make this a worthwhile detour from the route.

A boat trip is available from Carna to St Macdara's Island, named after the 6th-century saint who lived here.

▶ *Take the R340 north for about 7 miles (11km), then turn west on to the R342 (signposted Cashel) and at Tuaim Beola turn south on to the R341 for the 4-mile (6km) drive to Roundstone.*

6 Roundstone, Co Galway
This pretty village on the west side of Roundstone Bay is a quiet holiday resort that in recent years has attracted a host of artists and craftspeople as permanent residents, with workshops and showrooms. The settlement here was originally established in the early 19th century for Scottish fishermen.

About 2 miles (3km) out on the Ballyconneely road is a fine sandy beach at Dog's Bay (Portna-Feadog).

▶ *Continue on the R341 northwest to Clifden.*

7 Clifden, Co Galway
Nestled between the mountains and the Atlantic, with the Twelve Pins (or Bens) rising to the east, Clifden is often called 'The Capital of Connemara'. It lies at the head of Clifden Bay. Built in the 19th century, the town has managed to keep its Georgian character. Its two churches dominate the skyline, and the 1830 Catholic church is built on the site of an ancient monastic beehive stone hut, a clochan, which gave the town its name. The 1820 Protestant church is also a fine structure and holds a silver copy of the Cross of Cong. Clifden Castle was built by John d'Arcy in 1815. Its grounds give a fine marine view.

Clifden is at the heart of Connemara pony-breeding country, and you are in luck if you arrive in August during the annual Connemara Pony Show. The sturdy little Connemara ponies are native to the area, and are much in demand. It is great fun to watch the trading, and the festivities also include many exhibitions of Irish arts and crafts.

About 4 miles (6km) south of Clifden (1½ miles/2.5km north of Ballyconneely), look for signposts to the Alcock and Brown Memorial, the spot in

Derrygimlagh Bog where intrepid aviators Alcock and Brown crash-landed at the end of the first non-stop flight across the Atlantic from St John's, Newfoundland, in 1919. About 1½ miles (2.5km) away a limestone aeroplane commemorates the event. Near by are masts and foundations of the first transatlantic wireless transmitting station, set up here by Marconi, the Italian pioneer of radio.

i Galway Road (seasonal)

SCENIC ROUTES

Almost every mile of this tour can be described as scenic, but without doubt one of the most striking stretches is Clifden's Sky Drive. The 9-mile (14km) narrow cliff road circles the peninsula to the west of the town and opens up vast seascapes. The drive is well signposted from Clifden.

▶ *Take the **N59** northeast for 11 miles (18km) to Kylemore Abbey.*

❽ **Kylemore Abbey,** Co Galway

Situated in the scenic Pass of Kylemore, palatial Kylemore Abbey looks less like an ecclesiastical institution than any other in Ireland. Not surprising, since this magnificent gleaming white castellated mansion was built in the late 1800s as a private residence for millionaire MP Mitchell Henry. Its setting is enhanced by the castle's shimmering image reflected in the waters of one of the three Kylemore lakes. Now a convent of the Benedictine nuns of Ypres, it also houses a pottery and a restaurant run by the nuns. Visitors are welcomed to both, as well as to the lovely grounds and the Gothic chapel.

The gleaming fairy-tale towers of Kylemore Abbey are reflected in the lake

BACK TO NATURE

The Connemara National Park covers some 4,940 acres (2,000 hectares) that encompass virtually all varieties of this unique region's geology, flora and fauna. Four peaks of the Twelve Pins mountain range are here, surrounded by boglands, heaths and grasslands. The bogs are dotted with clumps of purple moor-grass, bog asphodel, bog myrtle and bog cotton. Insect-eating sundews and butterworts, milkwort, orchids and a variety of lichens and mosses are grown here. Birds of prey such as sparrowhawks, merlins, peregrines and kestrels are seen from time to time. Red deer, once native to the hills of Connemara, are being reintroduced, and there is a well-established herd of Connemara ponies. Detailed literature on the park is available at the visitor centre.

En route to Leenaun, the Maamturk mountain range comes into view, with loughs Fee and Nacarrigeen on your left. Further on, the road follows the southern shore of Killary harbour, a 10-mile (16km) long fiord-like inlet from the sea that runs between steep mountains.

► *Continue northeast on the* *N59 for 9 miles (14km) to* *Leenaun.*

9 **Leenaun,** Co Galway
Set near the head of Killary harbour, Leenaun is a popular angling centre and mountain-climbing base. This is the western end of the Partry Mountains, and the 2,131-foot (650m) Devil's Mother is the most striking feature of the landscape around this lovely village, location of the film, *The Field*. Close to Leenaun (on the road to Louisburgh) is the beautiful Aasleagh waterfall, which is well worth a short detour.

► *Turn southeast on to the* *R336 to Maam Cross.*

10 **Maam Cross,** Co Galway
This crossroads between north and south Connemara lies amid some of the region's most beautiful scenery. Local mountain peaks are relatively easy to climb and provide marvellous views. For good views of Lough Corrib and its fabled Castlekirk (the Hen's Castle), a 13th-century keep built by Rory O'Connor, take the road north signposted Maum and turn right at the T-junction. According to legend, Castlekirk was built overnight by a witch and her hen.

► *Continue southeast on the* *N59 to Oughterard.*

Aughnanure Castle is a fine ruin on Lough Corrib's shores

impressive, and local boatmen take visitors on excursions to the many islands. You can see the beautiful Hill of Doon by following the loughside road north. Aughnanure Castle, built by the O'Flahertys in about 1500, is a six-storey tower house by the shores of Lough Corrib.

Ross Lake and Ross Castle lie southeast of Oughterard. Here Violet Martin collaborated with her cousin Edith Somerville on *Experiences of an Irish RM* and other novels.

$\boxed{i}$ *Main Street*

► *Follow the N59 southeast for* *17 miles (27km) to Galway.*

SCENIC ROUTES

The 10-mile (16km) drive from Maam Cross to Oughterard passes through a landscape of amazing variety, encompassing lakes, moorland, mountain scenery and bogland.

---

11 **Oughterard,** Co Galway
This lively town on the upper shores of Lough Corrib is also a popular salmon- and trout-angling resort. Views along the loughside road are especially

---

SPECIAL TO...

Galway town seems always to be celebrating one thing or another with a festival. Among the most important are the Race Week in late July or early August, six days of horse racing, music and feasting; and the International Oyster Festival in late September, which attracts people from around the world to participate in oyster-opening competitions and non-stop feasting on these bivalves.

ULSTER

Ulster is a beautiful place, rich in history, rare in scenery, a province of mountains, loughs, coast and countryside, with tranquil villages and friendly people. The ancient province of Ulster had nine counties: Antrim, Down, Londonderry, Fermanagh, Tyrone and Armagh, which now form Northern Ireland; and Donegal, Cavan and Monaghan, which are part of the Republic of Ireland.

When Patrick came to Celtic Ireland, he chose Armagh for his ecclesiastical capital, because of the strength of Emain Macha, the Palace of the Red Branch Knights. Ulster made a contribution to Ireland's claim to be a land of saints and scholars. Great monasteries and educational establishments were founded, like that at Bangor, in County Down, which sent out missionaries to light up the Dark Age of Europe.

Since Patrick's time the province, like the rest of Ireland, has had successive waves of invaders. Vikings, Normans, English, Scots, Huguenots and refugees have settled here. However, in Ulster it was the number of Scots and Celts, but mostly Presbyterians, that created the special blend of Planter and Gael in Ulster. The hardy race of Scots-Ulster had a temperament tough enough to cope with the frontiers of the New World of America, and enterprising enough to leave a land where nonconformists were at a disadvantage. A dozen American presidents came from this stock. These were the men who defended Derry in the siege, fought with William at the Boyne, won glory for their bravery at the Somme and rejected an independent Ireland in the 1920s.

The lovely Mourne Mountains include great forests, remote lakes and scenic coast (Tour 25)

There is evidence of the two distinctive traditions in Ulster – fife and drum, uillean pipes and bodhran, paintings of King Billy or Mother Ireland on gable walls (most likely drawn by the same man). However, you may be surprised at how little difference there is between the two. Ulster people are delighted to see visitors and very anxious to show them the best of their province. Local councils have worked hard to provide fine amenities in even the most out-of-the-way places. Small villages are festooned with hanging baskets, and window boxes and flower-filled carts give the best impression. When Ulster people are really enjoying themselves – and they do, often – they say 'It's a great craic'. 'Craic' is fun, music, laughter and story-telling, often washed down with a drink or two, and they will be happy to share 'the craic' with visitors.

Tour 20

From historic walled Derry, a proud city rich in song and humour, the tour enters Donegal, whose incomparable scenery is world-renowned – empty beaches stretching for miles are commonplace, amid a landscape of rugged hills, stone walls and white cottages crouching against the Atlantic. The tour passes through fishing and farming communities where the Irish language and traditions are cherished, and ends with Donegal's treasure, Glenveagh National Park.

Tour 21

The Antrim Coast road, which clings to the shore between glens and mountains, headlands and villages, begins a drive of stunning variety. The Giant's Causeway is an essential destination, but the tour takes in lesser-known delights, as well as dramatic castles and historic landscapes, returning to Larne through pleasant countryside.

Tour 22

Belfast, a city of character, is the starting point for a tour that is full of interest for those who love history and wildlife or who simply enjoy discovering quiet villages in beautiful settings. The route takes in the Ulster Folk and Transport Museum, the two fine country houses of Mount Stewart and Castle Ward, and important early Christian sites. The tour focuses on Strangford Lough, rich in marine biology and no less important to ornithologists.

Tour 23

Fermanagh is a very distinctive Ulster county, more water than land it seems, and the land is sparsely populated. The combination of water, woodland and ancient buildings is nowhere so varied as in Fermanagh. The tranquil waters of Lough Erne are a fisherman's paradise. The route begins in the historic town of Enniskillen and includes the haunting beauty of the monastic round tower at Devenish and the neoclassical splendour of Castle Coole. Belleek pottery and Marble Arch caves provide additional interest.

Tour 24

Armagh, the ecclesiastical capital of Ireland, is the starting point for a tour that climbs from the gentle pastures and orchards of County Armagh to the rugged mountains of County Tyrone. This is a journey through Ulster's history, from the heroic era of the Red Branch Knights and the coming of Saint Patrick to the Irish emigrants' new world of America. Country houses, glens and forests, peatlands and parkland come together to form a picture of mid-Ulster.

Tour 25

County Down's distinctive landscape is that of the drumlins, small rounded hills that roll and roll, sheltering quiet green valleys and offering sudden views of sea or lough. The route leaves Newry and goes by way of the charming village of Hillsborough, and then winds through hills again until they give way to the Mountains of Mourne. The Kingdom of Mourne has its own identity, from the small fishing harbours of the rocky coast, through farmland crisscrossed by stone walls to the heights of the mountains. The end of the journey takes in beautiful Carlingford Lough, abundant in forests, castles and pleasant resorts.

The magnificent Palm House of Belfast's famous Botanic Garden, near the city centre (Tour 22)

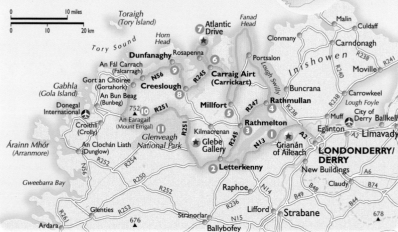

Seascapes &
Mountain Passes

History is in evidence all around Londonderry (or Derry), not least in the famous Walls of Derry, which form the most complete network of walls, gates and bastons in the British Isles. This town on the River Foyle is also a lively centre for the performing arts, and has craft shops, an art gallery and a museum.

2/3 DAYS • 172 MILES • 276KM

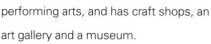

ITINERARY		
LONDONDERRY	▶	**Grianán of Aileach** (7m-11km)
GRIANÁN OF AILEACH	▶	**Letterkenny** (18m-29km)
LETTERKENNY	▶	**Rathmelton** (8m-13km)
RATHMELTON	▶	**Rathmullan** (7m-11km)
RATHMULLAN	▶	**Millford** (31m-50km)
MILLFORD	▶	**Carraig Airt** (10m-16km)
ATLANTIC DRIVE	▶	(10m-16km)
CARRAIG AIRT	▶	**Creeslough** (7m-11km)
CREESLOUGH	▶	**Dunfanaghy** (7m-11km)
DUNFANAGHY	▶	**Errigal** (16m-26km)
ERRIGAL	▶	**Glenveagh** (13m-21km)
GLENVEAGH	▶	**Londonderry** (38m-61km)

▶ Take the **A2** for Buncrana,
then the **N13** Letterkenny
road to the sign for Grianán
of Aileach.

1 The Grianán of Aileach,
Co Donegal
This massive stone fort can be
seen for miles around, and the
climb to Grianán Mountain
gives majestic views over
Lough Foyle and Lough Swilly.
It is easy to see why this
commanding site should have
been chosen for the royal residence of the O'Neills, Kings of
Ulster. It was enthusiastically
restored by Dr Bernard of Derry
in 1870, and his work has left us
with a complete picture of walls
17 feet (5.25m) high and 13 feet
(4m) thick, with steps rising to
four levels. The fine modern
church at Burt has architectural
echoes of Grianan.

▶ Return to the **N13** and turn
left to follow it to Letterkenny.

2 Letterkenny, Co Donegal
An administrative and commercial centre in the northwest,
Letterkenny sits at the southwest end of Lough Swilly on a
fertile plain. In the 19th century
it was spoken of as 'fast becom-
ing a place of importance and
wealth' and had a steamer

communication with Glasgow.
It gained the richly Gothic St
Eunan's Cathedral at the end of
the last century.

i Blaney Road

RECOMMENDED
WALKS

Pick any deserted beach for a
bracing walk, take a town trail
in Letterkenny, or try one of
the forest and woodland paths.

▶ Take the **R245** for 8 miles
(13km) to Rathmelton.

3 Rathmelton, Co Donegal
The long curve of the River
Leannan, steep hills, tree-lined
streets and handsome ware-
houses on the riverfront all
combine to make Rathmelton a
place of great charm. It was a
Planters' town ('planters' were
Presbyterian Scots and Anglican
English settlers loyal to the
English crown who were
encouraged to settle in Ireland
and replace the rebellious
Catholic Irish landowners).
Prosperity gained by the easy
navigation from the river mouth
brought fine Georgian houses,
as well as corn mills, a brewery,
bleach greens and linenworks in
the early 19th century. The first

The purpose of Grianán of Aileach
may lie in its name – 'stone palace
of the sun'

Presbyterian church in America
was formed in 1706 by
Reverend Francis Makemie,
who emigrated from
Rathmelton. Anglers come here
to fish, and 'The Pool', near by,
is a well-known salmon beat.
  Killydonnell Friary, founded
by the Franciscans in the 16th
century, is 2½ miles (4km) to the
south in the grounds of Fort
Stewart. There are excellent
views of the surrounding countryside from Cam Hill.

▶ Take the **R247** for 7 miles
(11km) to Rathmullan.

4 Rathmullan, Co Donegal
Rathmullan is a pretty village,
fringed with trees, on a beautiful beach on Lough Swilly,
looking over to the hills of the
Inishowen peninsula, with the
ruin of a 16th-century priory at
the water's edge. Large fishing
ships come into its pier, without
upsetting the tranquillity.
Despite its present peaceful-
ness, Rathmullan has witnessed
two major historical events. In
1587, Red Hugh O'Donnell was
treacherously lured on board a
disguised merchant ship and
carried as prisoner to Dublin
Castle; and that evocative

moment in Irish history, the Flight of the Earls, took place from here in 1607. The O'Neill, Earl of Tyrone, and the O'Donnell, Earl of Tyrconnell, with about 100 lesser chieftains, finally gave up their resistance to English law and authority in Ulster, and went into exile in Europe, leaving their estates to be forfeited and colonised by English and Scottish settlers. A Heritage Centre in Rathmullan tells the story.

Rathmullan is at the start of the Fanad Drive, with its beaches, streams, lakes and mountain ridges.

▶ *Follow the signposts for the Fanad Drive by Portsalon and Carrowkeel to Millford.*

5 Millford, Co Donegal

Millford is a leafy contrast to the grand headlands and magnificent bays of Donegal. It stands at the end of the narrow, islanded inlet of Mulroy Bay, and among its wooded hills are two lovely glens with waterfalls, named Golan Loop and Grey Mare's Tail.

▶ *Take the R245 to Carraig Airt.*

6 Carraig Airt (Carrickart), Co Donegal

This busy little town is tucked in an inlet of Mulroy Bay. To the north is Rosapenna, which boasts a championship golf course that is as scenic as it is challenging.

Nature challenged man and won in the 18th century, when a massive sandstorm engulfed houses and gradually overtook Rosapenna House, finally forcing the occupant, the Reverend Porter, from the top floor in 1808. From Rosapenna beach you can see the Muslac caves, cut by the sea into quartzite folds. The Downings is a small resort, particularly popular with families with small children, and has an important tweed factory and shop.

▶ *Follow the signs for the Atlantic Drive.*

7 The Atlantic Drive, Co Donegal

It is believed that the feast of scenery along the road around the Rosguill Peninsula, called the Atlantic Drive, is Donegal's best. The spectacular circuit passes both Sheep Haven and Mulroy bays; Horn Head and Melmore Head are in focus, with Muckish and Errigal mountains more distant to the south. The road passes little shingly bays, and hillsides dotted with white cottages, then opens out to the incomparable sight of Tranarossan Strand. Here the Youth Hostel is in a slightly idiosyncratic building designed by the English architect Edwin Lutyens.

▶ *Return to Carraig Airt and follow the R245 to turn right for Creeslough.*

8 Creeslough, Co Donegal

Overlooking Sheep Haven Bay is the little village of Creeslough. Doe Castle stands on a low, narrow promontory, bounded by the sea on three sides and a rock-cut ditch on the fourth. It is fortified with corbelled bartizans or turrets, firing platforms and musket loops, a round tower and a great square keep. It has had a colourful and turbulent history. It became the stronghold of the MacSweeneys, who were 'gallowglasses' (foreign warriors), a professional fighting force invited by the O'Donnells from Scotland. It was a refuge for Spanish Armada sailors, taken by the Cromwellians and

comandeered as a garrison for William of Orange. Finally it came into the hands of an English family, the Harts. The initials of General George Vaughan Hart are over the door.

▶ *Follow the signs for Dunglow, then take the N56 for 7 miles (11km) to Dunfanaghy.*

9 Dunfanaghy, Co Donegal

This is a good point from which to explore Horn Head. Thought by many to be the finest of all Irish headlands, this wall of quartzite rises from the sea, its ledges alive with gulls, puffins, guillemots and razorbills. You can appreciate the full majesty of Horn from Traghlisk Point to the east.

To the northwest is Toraigh (Tory) Island, still inhabited by people who make their living from the sea. The art world has considerable respect for the naïve paintings of the island's artists. To the southwest is An Fál Carrach (Falcarragh), the best point from which to climb the flat-topped mountain, Muckish.

▶ Continue on the **N56** to An Fál Carrach, then to Gort an Choiree (Gortahork). Turn left for Errigal Mountain.

Dunfanaghy and its superb beach lie sheltered behind Horn Head

⑩ Errigal Mountain, Co Donegal

Errigal Mountain is a distinctive peak, and once recognised you will see it from many parts of Donegal. Its cone-shaped summit rises 2,466 feet (752m) with silver-grey scree spilling around the slopes. Avoid the scree and, if you can, climb to the top for a panorama that can stretch from Scotland to Knocklayd in County Antrim, wide over the Donegal coastline and south to Sligo's Benbulben – on a clear day, of course. Below lies Dunlewy Lough, and the Poisoned Glen, a sinister name for so pretty a place, but proba-bly deriving from the toxic Irish spurge which used to grow there.

▶ *Take a sharp left onto the R251, and follow the signs for Glenveagh*

① Glenveagh, Co Donegal
Glenveagh is a beautiful place, and unusually for Donegal, the beauty here owes something to human hands. Henry McIlhenny, an American who acquired Glenveagh after it had been owned by several other Americans, developed a garden landscape of outstanding planting that never jars with the superb natural setting of water, mountain and bogland. He then gave the property to the nation to become a National Park. His 'garden rooms' are sensitively enclosed, and a walk through the garden follows the route he enjoyed showing to his visitors.

The castle is redolent of the house parties for which Glenveagh became famous, when film stars mixed with aristocracy. It bears witness throughout to Mr McIlhenny's fascination with deer.

Glenveagh's origins lie in its use as a hunting lodge, and Ireland's largest herd of red deer still roams the hills in a very important wilderness area.

Close by at Church Hill is the Regency Glebe House and Gallery, which has been exquisitely furnished and decorated by Derek Hill, the painter. The art gallery displays selections from the Derek

Glenveagh Castle and its lovely gardens are at the heart of a spectacular national park

Hill collection and beautiful gardens run down to the lakeside. The Columcille Heritage Centre at nearby Gartan celebrates the life and influence of the saint who is also known as St Columba.

FOR HISTORY BUFFS

Eviction and emigration are recurrent nightmares that stalked the troubled history of land tenure in Ireland. At Derryveagh, one of the most notorious mass evictions took place and was the cause of contemporary outrage. In 1861, John George Adair, landlord of Glenveagh, evicted 244 people from their homes to face the workhouse or emigration after a bitter feud with his tenants and the murder of his land steward. The eviction cottage is marked by a plaque put up by An Taisce, the National Trust, at a spot 1 mile (1.5km) from the Glebe Gallery.

BACK TO NATURE

The peat bog, a familiar feature of the Irish landscape, is a natural habitat not to be taken for granted and is now increasingly protected. A lowland blanket bog lies at Lough Barra in a broad valley below Slieve Snaght, and contains pools and rivers. It is an important site for Greenland white-fronted geese, a protected species. There is a raised peat bog in the glacial valley of Glenveagh National Park. Here, a rich variety of ferns and mosses grow in the woodland, while red grouse and red deer can be seen on the moorland.

▶ *From Glenveagh, turn right on to the R251 for Glebe Gallery, then follow this road before returning left on to the R250 for Letterkenny. Take the N13 back to Londonderry.*

The Causeway
Coast

2/3 DAYS • 163 MILES • 263KM

Larne is a busy port, the terminus for the shortest sea-crossing between Ireland and Britain. To the north is Carnfunnock Park, which has a maze in the shape of Northern Ireland. Larne marks the start of the scenic Antrim Coast Road, which was constructed in the 1830s to link the remote Glens of Antrim to the rest of Ulster.

i *Narrow Gauge Road, Larne*

▶ *Take the **A2** coastal road north for 12 miles (19km) to Glenarm.*

❶ Glenarm, Co Antrim
The Antrim Coast Road is so attractive that it is difficult to resist its magnetic lure, but leave it for a moment to sample the charm of Glenarm, a village that clings to the glen rather than to the coast. The neo-Tudor Glenarm Castle is the seat of the Earls of Antrim; its barbican and battlemented, buttressed walls of 1825 rise above the river just as it approaches the sea. The village has twisting streets (Thackeray apparently enjoyed their names), pavements patterned in limestone and basalt, a market house with an Italianate campanile and good, modest Georgian houses and shops.

The forest, through the gateway at the top of the village, gives the first opportunity to walk up an Antrim glen. This one is narrow, leafy and dense with pathways and waterfalls.

▶ *Take the **A2** to Carnlough.*

❷ Carnlough, Co Antrim
Carnlough, at the foot of Glencloy, the least dramatic of the glens, has a good, safe beach. A railway used to carry lime from the kilns above the village to the harbour, over the bridge that spans the coast road. The bridge, the clock tower and the former town hall are made from great chunks of limestone. Frances Anne Vane Tempest Stewart, Countess of Antrim and Marchioness of Londonderry, was responsible for many major works, including Garron Tower, built in 1848, once a family home, now a boarding school. She is remembered in the town's main hotel, the Londonderry Arms, which was built in 1854 and has the feel of a coaching inn.

▶ *Take the **A2**, following sign-posts for Cushendall for 9 miles (14km) to Waterfoot. Turn left on to the **A43** for 5 miles (8km) to Glenariff Forest Park.*

❸ Glenariff, Co Antrim
The road obligingly provides a perfect route along this magnificent glen. The bay at its foot is 1 mile (1.5km) long and the chiselled sides draw in the fertile valley symmetrically to the head of the glen. There, the Forest Park allows easy exploration of the deep, wooded gorge with its cascades, 'Ess-na-crub' (Fall of the Hoof), 'Ess-na-laragh' (Fall of the Mare) and Tears of the Mountain.

Waterfoot, the little village at the foot of the glen, hosts The Glens of Antrim Feis (pronounced 'fesh') in July, a major festival of traditional music and dancing.

All along the Antrim Coast Road, wonderful views unfold

Between Red Bay and the pier are three caves. Nanny's Cave was inhabited by Ann Murray until her death, aged 100, in 1847. She supported herself by knitting and by selling poteen (an illicit distillation, pronounced potcheen), or 'the natural' as she called it.

▶ *Turn right to follow the B14 to Cushendall.*

4 Cushendall, Co Antrim
'The Capital of the Glens', Cushendall sits on a pleasant, sandy bay below Glenballyemon, Glenaan and Glencorp and in the curve of the River Dall. The rugged peak of Lurigethan broods over the village, while the softer Tieveragh Hill is supposedly the capital of the fairies. Cushendall owes much to an East Indian nabob, Francis Turnley, who built the Curfew Tower in the centre as a 'place for the confinement of idlers and rioters'.

In a tranquil valley by the sea just north of the village is the 13th-century church of Layde. The MacDonnells of Antrim are buried here, as are Englishmen stationed in these lonely posts as coastguards, and one memorial stone mourns an emigré killed in the American Civil War in 1865 when he was only 18.

▶ *Continue on the A2 for 3 miles (5km), then turn right on to the B92 for Cushendun.*

5 Cushendun, Co Antrim
The very decided character of Cushendun is a surprise. This is a black-and-white village, with an orderly square and terraces of houses that were designed to look Cornish. Lord Cushendun married a Cornish wife, Maud, and commissioned the distinguished architect Clough Williams-Ellis to create a streetscape with style.

A little salmon fishery stands at the mouth of the River Dun, the 'dark brown water'. To the south is Cave House, locked in cliffs and approachable only through a long, natural cave. Castle Carra is to the north, the place where the clan quarrel between the O'Neills and the MacDonnells caused the treacherous murder of the great Shane O'Neill during a banquet in 1567.

▶ *At the north end of the village turn on to the road sign-*

Cushendun is famous for its unusual architecture

posted 'scenic route' for Ballycastle by Torr Head. After 9 miles (14km) turn right to Murlough Bay.

6 Fair Head and Murlough Bay, Co Antrim
Paths from the cluster of houses known as Coolanlough cross the barren headland broken by three dark lakes – Lough Doo, Lough Fadden and Lough na Cranagh, which has a crannóg or lake dwelling. Fair Head itself is exposed and barren, a place inhabited by wild goats and choughs (red-legged crows). The careful walker can descend the cliff using the Grey Man's Path, which follows a dramatic plunging fissure.

By contrast, Murlough Bay is green and fertile, generous in contours and abundantly wooded. Tradition has it that the Children of Lir were transformed into swans to spend 300 years here. At the top of the road is a monument to the Republican leader Sir Roger Casement, and a row of lime kilns, which would have burned the stone for use in fertiliser, whitewash or mortar.

▶ *After 1 mile (2km) turn right for Ballycastle, then right again on to the A2 to Ballycastle.*

BACK TO NATURE

For bird-lovers, a trip on the boat to Rathlin Island is not to be missed. Up to 20,000 guillemots, razorbills, fulmars, kittiwakes and puffins can be seen on the sheer rock stacks close to the West Lighthouse. Shearwaters can sometimes be seen offshore. Early summer is the best time to see them.

SPECIAL TO...

The Oul' Lammas Fair in Ballycastle, held every August Bank Holiday, is a real horse fair with a lot more besides. The streets of Ballycastle are crammed with stalls, including traditional games of chance, and the town is alive with music and fun. Horse-trading lives up to its reputation, and you are likely to hear the refrain:
Did you take your Mary Ann For some dulse and yellow man. At the oul' Lammas Fair in Ballycastle-O.
Dulse is edible dried seaweed and yellow man is a chewy sweet confection.

7 **Ballycastle,** Co Antrim

There are two parts to Ballycastle – the winding main street which carries you up to the heart of the town, and Ballycastle by the sea, with its fine beach and tennis courts.

At the foot of the Margy River is Bonamargy Friary, founded by the Franciscans as late as 1500. The notorious Sorley Boy MacDonald is buried here. Elizabeth I found that he eluded all her attempts at capture, but in 1575, when he had sent his children to Rathlin Island for safety, he had to stand on the mainland helpless while they were murdered.

Ballycastle's museum illustrates the folk and social history of the Glens of Antrim.

At the harbour is a memorial to Gugliemo Marconi, who carried out the first practical test on radio signals between White Lodge, on the clifftop at Ballycastle, and Rathlin Island in 1898. You can travel by boat to Rathlin and savour the life of the 30 or so families who live and farm here. The island is a mecca for divers and birdwatchers. Robert the Bruce hid in a cave on Rathlin after his defeat in 1306. Watching a spider repeatedly trying to climb a thread to the roof, he was encouraged to 'try, and try again'. He returned to Scotland to fight on, and was successful at the Battle of Bannockburn.

▶ *From the shore follow the B15 coastal route west for Ballintoy, then turn right, following the signpost to Carrick-a-Rede and Larry Bane.*

8 **Carrick-a-Rede,** Co Antrim

A swinging rope bridge spans the deep chasm between the mainland and the rocky island of Carrick-a-Rede, and if you have a very strong heart and a good head, you can cross it. The bridge is put up each year by salmon fishermen, who use Carrick-a-Rede, 'the Rock in the Road', as a good place to net the fish in their path to the Bush and Bann rivers. The rope bridge is approached from Larry Bane, a limestone head which had once been quarried. Some of the quarry workings remain, and the quarry access to the magnificent seascape provides some guaranteed birdwatching. It is possible to sit in your car and spot kittiwakes, cormorants, guillemots, fulmars and razorbills, though you might have to use binoculars to catch sight of the puffins on Sheep Island further out to sea.

Just to the west is Ballintoy,

a very pretty little limestone harbour, at the foot of a corkscrew road. A little further west is the breathtaking sandy sweep of White Park Bay, accessible only on foot, and worth every step. Among the few houses that fringe the west end of the beach, tucked into the cliff, is Ireland's smallest church, dedicated to St Gobhan, patron saint of builders.

▶ *Take the B15 to join the A2 for Portrush, then turn right on to the B146 for the Giant's Causeway.*

9 **Giant's Causeway,** Co Antrim

Sixty million years ago, or thereabouts, intensely hot volcanic lava erupted through narrow vents and, in cooling rapidly over the white chalk, formed into about 37,000 extraordinary geometric columns and shapes – mostly hexagonal, but also with four, five, seven or eight sides. That is one story. The other is that the giant, Finn MacCool, fashioned it so that he could cross dry-shod to Scotland.

Generations of fanciful guides have embroidered stories and created names for the remarkable formations – the Giant's Organ, the Giant's Harp, the Wishing Chair, and Lord Antrim's Parlour. The Visitor Centre tells the full story of the fact and fiction, the folklore and traditions, and provides a bus service down the steep road to the Causeway.

One story absolutely based on fact is of the *Girona*, a fleeing Spanish Armada galleon, wrecked in a storm on the night of 26 October 1588. A diving team retrieved a treasure hoard from the wreck in 1967, now on display in the Ulster Museum in Belfast. The wreck still lies under cliffs in Port na Spaniagh, one of a magnificent march of bays and headlands on the Causeway.

The most famous sight in Ireland, the Giant's Causeway never fails to amaze and delight

Near the Visitor Centre is the Causeway School Museum, a reconstructed 1920s schoolroom, complete with learning aids and toys of the era.

ℹ️ *Visitor Centre, Bushmills*

RECOMMENDED WALKS

There can be few more spectacular walks than the 10-mile (16km) coastal path between the Giant's Causeway and White Park Bay. Magnificent amphitheatres of rocky cliffs, dramatic clefted inlets, basalt sea stacks, an abundance of wild flowers and the company of seabirds add to the pleasure of this walk. A guide will help identify the evocative names for each bay and the historic features, including the remains of tiny Dunseverick Castle.

▶ *Take the A2 to Bushmills.*

10 Bushmills, Co Antrim
This neat village is the home of the world's oldest legal distillery, which was granted its licence in 1608. The water from St Columb's rill, or stream, is said to give the whiskey its special quality, and visitors can discover something of its flavour on tours of the distillery.

The River Bush is rich in trout and salmon, and its fast-flowing waters not only supported the mills that gave the town its name, but generated electricity for the world's first hydroelectric tramway, which carried passengers to the Giant's Causeway between 1893 and 1949.

The 'water of life', patiently maturing in oak barrels at the Bushmills Distillery

▶ *Follow the A2 west to Portrush.*

11 Portrush, Co Antrim
Portrush is a typical seaside resort, which flourished with the rise of the railways. It has three good bays, with broad stretches of sand, ranges of dunes, rock pools, white cliffs and a busy harbour.

Nearby Dunluce is one of the most romantic of castles, where a sprawling ruin clings perilously to the clifftop, presenting a splendid profile. The castle was a MacDonnell stronghold until half the kitchen fell into the sea on a stormy night in 1639. The Dunluce Centre is a high-tech entertainment complex.

ℹ️ *Dunluce Centre*

▶ *Take the A29 for Coleraine, then follow the A2 for Castlerock, then on to Downhill, a distance of 12 miles (19km).*

12 Downhill, Co Londonderry
The feast of magnificent coastal scenery is given a different face at Downhill. Here Frederick Hervey, who was Earl of Bristol and Bishop of Derry, decided to adorn nature with man's art, by creating a landscape with eyecatching buildings, artificial ponds and cascades, in keeping with the taste of the time. He was a great 18th-century eccentric, collector and traveller, who gave his name to the Bristol hotels throughout Europe. Although nature has won back much of the Earl Bishop's ambitious scheme, the spirit of the place is strongly felt, and Mussenden Temple, a perfect classical rotunda, sits on a wonderful headland.

Near by is 20th-century

man's idea of seaside recreation, at Benone Tourist Complex, beside the 7 mile (11km) Benone Strand, one of the cleanest beaches in Europe, backed by a duneland park.

SCENIC ROUTES

The Bishop's Road runs over Eagle Hill and Binevanagh Mountain, rising steeply from Downhill. The Earl Bishop had it built to provide local employment in the 18th century. From Gortmore viewpoint the panorama stretches from Donegal to Fair Head, above the fertile shores of Lough Foyle and beyond to Scotland. The AA has placed a chart here showing directions and distances of the views, and another plaque recalls that this was the site chosen in 1824 by surveyors for the most accurate measurement ever then achieved between two places.

▶ *From the* **A2** *turn left on Bishop's Road for Gortmore, then after 8 miles (13km) turn right on to the* **B201**, *then left on to the* **A2** *for Limavady.*

13 Limavady, Co Londonderry

The Roe Valley was the territory of the O'Cahans, and O'Cahan's Rock is one of the landmarks of the nearby Roe Valley Country Park. One story says that it was here a dog made a mighty leap with a message to help relieve a besieged castle, giving this pleasant market town its name, 'The Leap of the Dog'.

The *Londonderry Air* was first written down here by Jane Ross, when she heard it being played by a street fiddler. Limavady was the birthplace of William Massey (1856–1925), Prime Minister of New Zealand from 1912 to 1925.

i *7 Connell Street*

▶ *Take the* **A37** *for Coleraine, then turn right on to the* **B66**; *follow signs for the* **B66** *to Ballymoney.*

14 Ballymoney, Co Antrim
A bustling town, Ballymoney recalls its farming past at Leslie Hill Open Farm, where visitors can travel through the park by horse and trap. Drumaheglis Marina provides access to the River Bann, elsewhere a fairly secluded river, and offers water-

bus cruises. Three miles (5km) northeast, in Conagher, off the road to Dervock, is the birthplace of the 25th President of the US, William McKinley.

▶ *Take the* **A26** *to Ballymena.*

15 Ballymena, Co Antrim
Ballymena, the county town of Antrim, boasts as one of its sons Timothy Eaton, who founded the now defunct Eaton's Stores in Canada. To the east the hump of Slemish Mountain rises abruptly from the ground. It was here that St Patrick worked when he was first brought to Ireland as a slave. In the southen suburbs is the 40-foot (12m) high Harryville motte and bailey – one of the finest surviving Anglo-Norman earthworks in Ulster.

Just to the west is 17th-century Galgorm Castle, a Plantation castle built by Sir Faithful Fortescue in 1618. Beyond is the charming village of Gracehill, founded by the Moravians in the 18th century.

▶ *Take the* **A36** *for 21 miles (34km) and return to Larne.*

Farming the old-fashioned way at the Leslie Hill Open Farm in northern County Antrim

Strangford
Lough

From the centre of Belfast, the rolling hills which cradle the city catch the eye at the end of many streets. Belfast is an industrial city with a strong ship-building tradition and the skyline is dominated by two huge cranes in the dockyard. Near by the Waterfront Concert Hall is a splendid venue for international events. The city is rich in Victorian and Edwardian architecture, from the magnificent City Hall to the atmospheric Crown Liquor Saloon. A peaceful haven are the Botanic Gardens, which also contain the superb Ulster Museum.

2 DAYS • 87 MILES • 138KM

ℹ️ *Belfast Welcome Centre, 59 North Street*

▶ *Leave Belfast via the **A2**, following signposts for Bangor, and after 7 miles (11km) turn off for the Ulster Folk and Transport Museum.*

❶ Cultra, Co Down

The Ulster Folk and Transport Museum, in the grounds of Cultra Manor (also open), tells the story of the province's past through buildings that have been saved and meticulously reconstructed at this site.

Visitors can wander through former Ulster homes, which include a thatched cottage, a rectory and a terraced house, and watch demonstrations of traditional crafts. A church, schoolhouse, water-powered mills and many other buildings give a vivid picture of the past.

In the transport section, the collection spans the history of transport, from creels used by a donkey carrying turf, through the grand ocean-going liners built in Belfast, to ultra-modern aircraft from the Belfast firm Short Brothers and Harland.

This is undoubtedly one of the best museums in Ireland.

▶ *Turn left and follow the **A2** for 4 miles (6km). Turn right following the signpost for Newtownards, 3 miles (5km) further.*

❷ Newtownards, Co Down

This thriving town lies among some of the richest arable land in Ulster. St Finnian founded Movilla Abbey in AD540, and the Dominican priory was established by the Normans in the 13th century. The hollow, octagonal, 17th-century market cross also served as the town watch and gaol. The impressive town hall was built around 1770, by the Londonderry family who also built Scrabo Tower, on the hill overlooking the town.

This dominant landmark, standing 135 feet (41m) high, was erected in memory of the third Marquess of Londonderry.

The surrounding country park has woodland walks, sandstone quarries and panoramic views.

Bustling shopping streets surround Donegall Square in the heart of Belfast

SPECIAL TO...

The area around Newtownards is home to some of the world's most famous roses. The Dickson family first opened a nursery here in 1836 and have been international prize-winning rose breeders since 1887, bringing much-loved favourites like 'Grandpa Dickson' and 'Iceberg' to a worldwide market. The dynastic chain has continued unbroken, and Dickson's are still perfecting new varieties at their nurseries at Newtownards.

ℹ️ *31, Regent Street*

▶ *Take the **A20**, following signs for Portaferry, to Greyabbey.*

❸ Greyabbey, Co Down

The village derives its name from the 12th-century

Cistercian abbey founded by Affreca, wife of the Norman lord John de Courcy.

North of the village is Mount Stewart, a magnificent garden where many exotic plants flourish in formal terraces and parterres or in natural settings, enjoying the mild climate of the peninsula.

Lady Londonderry, the renowned hostess and leader of London society, created it after World War I, and this unique garden is considered one of the finest in these islands. Each garden is given a name – 'Tir n'an Og' (the Land of Eternal Youth), the Mairi Garden, Peace Garden, the Dodo Terrace and the Italian Garden. The lake is particularly beautiful.

The house, the early home of Lord Castlereagh, contains the 22 chairs used at the Congress of Vienna and a masterpiece by the painter George Stubbs among its treasures. Designed as a banqueting house, the Temple of the Winds is an exquisite piece of 18th-century landscape architecture.

The shoreline is an excellent place for viewing birds, including thousands of Brent geese that winter on the lough.

▶ *Follow the **A20** for 4 miles (6km) to Kircubbin. Take a left turn on to the **B173** for*

The Mount Stewart estate is one of the finest National Trust properties in Ireland

3 miles (5km), then turn left for Portavogie.

4 **Portavogie,** Co Down
Up to 40 boats fill the attractive harbour of Portavogie when the fleet is in. Shellfish are plentiful and hotels serve a good variety of fresh fish. Seals regularly follow the boats into the harbour to scavenge for food while the catch is being unloaded, and auctioned in the harbour.

▶ *Take the **A2** south for 2 miles (3km). At Cloughey turn left*

for and follow signposts to Kearney. After 1 mile (1.5km) turn left for Kearney and follow signposts at two left turns for Kearney, about 3 miles (5km).

5 **Kearney,** Co Down
Kearney is a tiny village of whitewashed houses in the care of the National Trust. Once a fishing village, it now offers fine walks along a rocky shoreline that looks out across the Irish Sea to the Isle of Man, Scotland and the north of England. Close

by is the sandy beach of Knockinelder, and south is Millin Bay cairn, a neolithic burial site with ancient decorated stones.

At Temple Cowey and St Cowey's Wells, on a remote and peaceful shore, are a penance stone and holy well at a site founded in the 7th century, and later used for worship in penal times. Mass is still held here from time to time.

▶ *Turn left and left again to follow the road around the tip of the peninsula by Barr Hall and Quintin Bay to Portaferry.*

6 **Portaferry,** Co Down

One of Ulster's most beautifully sited villages, Portaferry's attractive waterfront of colourful terraced cottages, pubs and shops is framed by green meadows and wooded slopes. No fewer than five defensive tower houses guard the narrow neck of the lough. The Marine Biology Station, part of Queen's University, Belfast, is situated opposite the ferry jetty. Close to the tower house is the Northern Ireland Aquarium, Exploris, set beside a pleasant park, which explains the unique nature of the marine life of Strangford Lough. Over 2,000 species of

marine animal thrive in the waters of Strangford, including large colonies of corals and sponges in the fast-flowing tides of the Narrows, and sea anemones, sea cucumbers and brittle stars in the quieter waters. The lough is home to large fish, including tope and skate. A regular, 5-minute car-ferry service to Strangford, gives stunning views of the lough.

i *The Stables, Castle Street*

▶ *Take the car ferry to Strangford. Boats leave at half-hourly intervals.*

7 **Strangford,** Co Down

Strangford is a small village with two bays, pretty houses and a castle. Close by is Castle Ward, set in fine parkland with excellent views over the lough. The 18th-century house is exactly divided into Gothic and classical architectural styles, the result of disputed tastes between Lord and Lady Bangor. Restored estate buildings demonstrate the elaborate organisation which once supported a country house. A small theatre is used for many events, including a midsummer opera festival.

One mile (1.5km) south, on the A2 to Ardglass, a lay-by at Cloughy Rocks is a great place for viewing seals when the tide is right. Further south is Kilclief Castle and Killard Point, at the narrowest point of the neck to the lough. This lovely grassland

area with low cliffs and a small beach is rich in wild flowers.

▶ *Take the **A25** to Downpatrick.*

8 **Downpatrick,** Co Down

Down Cathedral stands on the hill above the town, while English Street, Irish Street and Scotch Street jostle together below. There has been a church on the site of the cathedral since AD520, but the present building dates largely from the 18th century. Ireland's patron saint is reputed to be buried in the churchyard with the bones of St Brigid and St Columba. The Norman John de Courcy ordered their reinterment:
In Down three saints one grave do fill
Brigid, Patrick and Columcille.

The supposed grave is marked by a granite stone erected in 1900. Down

County Museum relates the story of St Patrick.

Quoile Pondage is an area of meandering freshwater wetland between wooded shores, with fine walks. Just north is 12th-century Inch Abbey, and to the southwest is the popular Downpatrick race course.

i The St Patrick Centre, 53A Market Street

▶ Follow the **A22** to Killyleagh.

9 **Killyleagh,** Co Down
A fairy-tale castle with towers and battlements overlooks this quiet loughside village. The Hamilton family has lived there for 300 years, and although the original castle was built by the Normans, its present appear- ance owes more to the 19th century. Sir Hans Sloane, the physician and naturalist whose collection formed the nucleus of the British Museum, was born in Killyleagh in 1660 and educated in the castle. It is said that the famous Emigrant's Lament – 'I'm sitting on the stile, Mary', written by Lady Dufferin, a guest at the castle during the Famine – was inspired by the stile at Killowen Old Churchyard.

▶ Follow the **A22** for 5 miles (8km) to Balloo crossroads. Turn right at the sign for

FOR HISTORY BUFFS

Driving through the centre of Comber, you cannot fail to see the statue of Major General Rollo Gillespie. Born in this square in 1766, he became a cavalryman at 17, eloped, fought a duel, was acquitted of murder, shipwrecked off Jamaica and attacked by pirates, of whom he killed six. He then settled down to an army life, and the list of his battles in Java, Bengal and elsewhere is recorded at the foot of the col- umn, together with his famous last words – 'One shot more for the honour of Down' – uttered after he had been shot through the heart attacking the fort of Kalunga.

Killinchy, and continue for 4 miles (6km), turning right three times for Comber. After 2½ miles (4km) turn right, following the sign for Nendrum Monastic Site.

10 **Nendrum Monastic Site,** Co Down
A place of great tranquillity, Nendrum monastic site was established on one of the many islands that are sprinkled along Strangford's calm middle waters, and is now reached by a causeway. The site is one of the

The graveyard of Downpatrick's cathedral is said to contain the burial place of St Patrick

most complete examples of a very early monastery in Ireland, and the ruins, in three concen- tric rings, include the stump of a round tower, monks' cells and a church with a stone sundial.

BACK TO NATURE

A short distance from Nendrum is Castle Espie Wildfowl and Wetlands Centre. When disued clay pits began to fill with water, a sensitive owner quickly realised that this was an important habitat for wildfowl. The careful manage- ment that followed has made Castle Espie a haven for birds and an attractive place to visit. Birds which use Strangford Lough can be seen here, as well as endangered species from exotic places. In particu- lar, look for Brent geese, wigeon, sanderling, knot and grey plovers. There is also an art gallery, and the tea-room has views over the lough.

▶ *Return across the causeway and after 3 miles (5km) turn right for 3 miles (5km) to join the A22 to Comber, and on to Belfast.*

Fermanagh
Lakeland

At Enniskillen, 'the Island Town', water greets you at every turn – from Lower and Upper Lough Erne and the River Erne, which flows through the town. Places of interest include the museums housed in the Watergate, a former castle, and the fine, neo-classical Castle Coole.

1/2 DAYS • 84 MILES • 133KM

i Fermanagh Information Centre,
Wellington Road, Enniskillen

▶ Take the **A32** towards Omagh
for 2 miles (3km) until you
reach the signpost for the
ferries to Devenish.

❶ Devenish, Co Fermanagh
Take a ferry from Trory to get to
Devenish Island. Across the
silvery water is one of the most
important monastic sites in
Ulster, founded by St Molaise
in the 6th century, although the
remarkable group of buildings
dates mostly from the 12th
century. The round tower was
repaired in the 19th century,
and is regarded as one of the
finest in Ireland, beautifully
proportioned, with finely cut
stone and precision of line. The
towers, famous symbols of
Christianity in Ireland, acted as
signposts, bell towers and places
of refuge and retreat in attack,
and a safe storage place for treasures during Viking raids. The
great treasure of Devenish, the
book shrine of Molaise, which is
a masterpiece of early Christian
art, is kept at the National
Museum in Dublin.

On a hill, with uninter-
rupted views over both loughs,
Devenish was such a favoured
place for parleys in disputes
between Ulster and Connacht
that it was sometimes called
'Devenish of the Assemblies'.

▶ Take the **B82** for 7 miles
(11km) for Kesh and Castle
Archdale.

❷ Castle Archdale, Co
Fermanagh
With a marina, caravan sites, a
youth hostel and recreational
activities, Castle Archdale is
one of the busiest places
around Lough Erne, but it is
still very easy to find a quiet
place in this country park. In
the old estate of the Archdale
family is an arboretum, butterfly park and farm with rare
breeds. The ruins of the old
castle, burnt in the Williamite
wars of 1689, can be seen in the
forest, and the stable block of
the 18th-century house is an
important part of the park. The
focus of Castle Archdale is the
marina, where concrete jetties
and slipways, built for flying
boats taking off for the Battle
of the Atlantic in 1941, have
been turned to more peaceful
use. You can hire a boat with a
'gillie' (a man to help you with
the fishing). It is possible to
reach White Island from here
to see the enigmatic carved

Round towers are an evocative
symbol of ecclesiastical sites. This
one is on Devenish Island

stones that for centuries have puzzled experts and fascinated visitors. Set in the little 12th-century church, they seem to represent biblical figures, with the exception of 'Sheil-na-gig', a female fertility figure, a strange meeting of Celtic pagan art and Christianity.

▶ *Turn left on to the **B82**. After 2 miles (3km), turn left for Kesh via the scenic route for 4 miles (6km). At Kesh turn left for Belleek, on to the **A35**, then after 1 mile (1.5km) turn on to the **A47** and drive for 8 miles (13km) to Boa Island (pronounced Bo).*

BACK TO NATURE

If you are extremely fortunate, you may hear the distinctive call of the corncrake or land rail. Fermanagh is one of the last refuges of this bird, whose population has diminished rapidly in Britain and the rest of Europe, as it has become increasingly disturbed by mechanical methods of hay-making. Some experts feel that the complete extinction of this attractive bird is inevitable, but it can still be found here. You are, however, more likely to hear its grating 'crex-crex' call than see this secretive bird.

☑ **Boa Island,** Co Fermanagh

Two bridges connect Boa Island to the mainland. Just before the bridge at the west end is a track on the left to Caldragh cemetery, where there are two pagan idols in stone. One is called a Janus figure because it is double-faced; the other, a small, hunched figure, was moved here from Lusty Beg Island. Boa Island, with its echoes of pre-Christian Ireland, is said to be named after Badhbh, the Irish goddess of war.

▶ *Continue on the **A47** for 5 miles (8km) to Castle Caldwell.*

☒ **Castle Caldwell,** Co Fermanagh

The Fiddler's Stone at the entrance to Castle Caldwell, is a memorial to fiddler Dennis McCabe, who fell out of Sir James Caldwell's family barge on 13 August, 1770, and was drowned. The obituary ends:
On firm land only exercise your skill
That you may play and safely drink your fill.
The castle, now in ruins, had the reputation of enjoying one of the most beautiful situations of all Irish houses. The fine views are still the same, across water rich in wildlife, with bird hides that allow visitors to catch sight of many ducks, geese and grebes.

The carved stone Janus figure on Boa Island is a mysterious relic of pre-Christian times

FOR CHILDREN

Older children can enjoy a wide variety of water sports. Windsurfing, canoeing, swimming, sailing and water-skiing are all available at the Lough Melvin Holiday Centre at Garrison, south of Belleek.

▶ *Continue on the **A47** to Belleek.*

☒ **Belleek,** Co Fermanagh
This border village is famed for its fine parian china, best known

for its delicate basketwork, shamrock decoration and lustre-finish. The range of goods produced by the Belleek Pottery has expanded to include designer items alongside the classic patterns, and visitors can tour the 1857 factory, see the best examples of the china and watch exquisite craftsmanship – the result of skills handed down from generation to generation. To this, Belleek adds the lure of a restaurant where the food is served on Belleek tableware.

Visitors can witness the art of the craftspeople at Belleek

route for 2 miles (3km). Rejoin the **A46** and after 6 miles (10km) turn right, and follow signs to Monea.

6 Monea, Co Fermanagh
Monea (pronounced Mon-ay) is the ruin of a Plantation castle, remote among marshy ground on a rocky outcrop. Built by 'under-takers', or Planters, arriving from the lowlands of Scotland in the early 17th century, it has a Scottish look about it, particularly in the corbelling. The castle was captured by the Irish in 1641 and finally abandoned in 1750. There are still remnants of the bawn wall that surrounded the castle, and an ancient crannóg, or artificial island dwelling, can be picked out in the marsh in front of Monea. In the parish church is a 15th-century window, removed from Devenish.

▶ Turn left leaving Monea, then left for Enniskillen. Turn right, following signs to Boho for 5 miles (8km), then right again for Belcoo.

7 Belcoo, Co Fermanagh
Belcoo sits neatly between the two Lough Macneans, surrounded by mountains and adjacent to its neighbouring County Leitrim village, Blacklion. The two loughs are large and very beautiful.
    To the south of Lower Lough Macnean is the limestone cliff of Hanging Rock, and by the road is the Salt Man, a great lump of limestone, which, it is said, fell off the cliff and killed a man pulling a load of salt.
    Just north of Belcoo is the Holywell, traditionally visited by pilgrims in search of the curative powers of St Patrick's Well.

▶ From Belcoo, cross the border into the Republic and Blacklion for a very short distance, then cross back into Northern Ireland, taking the road along the south shore of Lower Lough Macnean. Turn right along Marlbank Scenic Loop and drive for 3 miles (5km) to Marble Arch.

▶ Take the **A46** for Enniskillen. After 13 miles (21km) turn right on the Slavin scenic

FOR HISTORY BUFFS

The narrow strip of land occupied by Belcoo was part of Black Pig's Dyke, a great prehistoric earthwork that formed part of the early boundary of Ulster. The section at the top of Lough Macnean was known as 'The Pig's Race'. The Black Pig's Dyke ran with 'The Dane's Cast' and 'The Worm Ditch', from the Atlantic to the Irish Sea. The Black Pig is a familiar emblem in Ulster folklore. There are many 'races' and paths over which the pig is reputed to have rampaged.

8 **Marble Arch,** Co Fermanagh

One of the highlights of a visit to Fermanagh, the mysterious beauty of the Marble Arch Caves, is enhanced by a ride on a quiet, flat-bottomed boat through still, dark waters. Over 300 million years of history is here among a strange landscape of chasms and valleys, amid stalactites and stalagmites. The deep gorge of Marble Arch is dramatically beautiful, and it is worth taking time to walk further into the Cladagh Glen. Common wild flowers are seen in glorious abundance and variety, as well as some Irish rarities.

▶ *Turn left, then right and drive for 4 miles (6km) to Florence Court.*

9 **Florence Court,** Co Fermanagh

Florence Court was the home of the Enniskillen family, who moved from a castle in the county town to this wild and beautiful setting in the 18th century. The house was named after a new English wife.

The present building, which dates from the middle of

RECOMMENDED WALKS

For clearly marked trails of varying lengths, difficulty and interest, try the walks in Florence Court Forest Park, through parkland, woods and open moorland.

the 18th century, is very Irish in character with exuberant rococo plasterwork of the highest order, fine Irish furniture, pleasant grounds and interesting estate buildings. In the gardens is the original Florence Court yew, the originator of all Irish yews.

▶ *From Florence Court, turn right. After a mile (1.5km) turn left on to the A32, then after 2 miles (3km) turn right for Bellanaleck.*

10 **Bellanaleck,** Co Fermanagh

A base for cruising, with a popular marina, Bellanaleck gives a glimpse of the winding, mazy ways of Upper Lough Erne, as its waters thread through 57 islands between Enniskillen and Galloon Bridge to the southeast. Here are hidden remote treasures such as Castle Balfour and the estate at Crom, rich in history and rare in wildlife.

▶ *Return to Enniskillen via the A509.*

Expansive parkland surrounds lovely Florence Court

The Heart
of Ulster

2 DAYS • 123 MILES • 198KM

The ecclesiastical capital of Ireland, Armagh is a gracious and historic city richly endowed with the culture and architecture of centuries of Christianity. Two cathedrals dedicated to Saint Patrick rise above winding streets which follow the contours of ancient earth mounds. Just outside the city is the ancient site of Emain Macha.

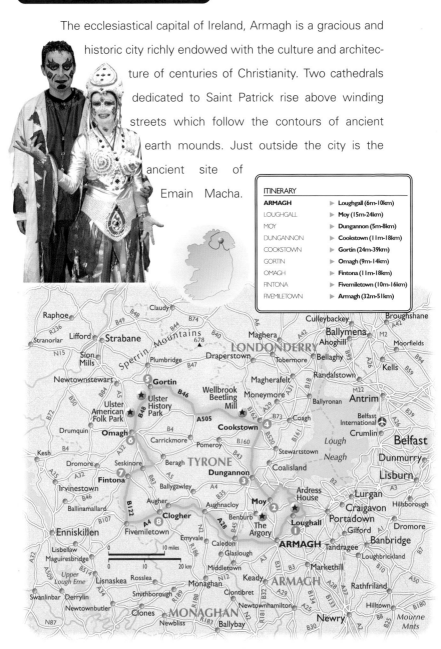

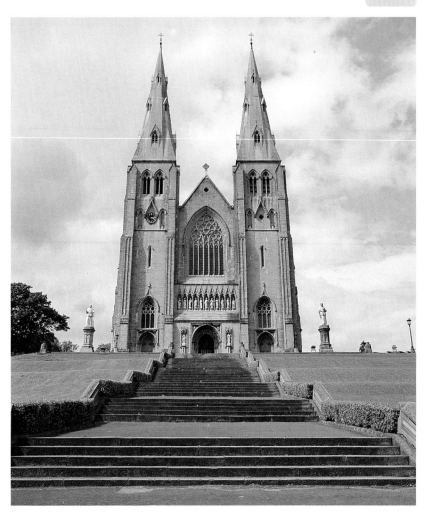

The impressive Roman Catholic Cathedral of St Patrick in Armagh was completed in 1873

ℹ️ 40, English Street, Armagh

FOR CHILDREN

Not far from Loughgall is Benburb, a hidden valley with adventurous walks, a castle on a clifftop and a restored linen mill. The Heritage Centre has a model and talks about the Battle of Benburb in 1646, when Irish forces under Owen Roe O'Neill defeated General Monroe's Scottish and English armies.

▶ Take the **B77** to Loughgall.

❶ Loughgall, Co Armagh
This is one of the pretty flower-filled villages, surrounded by orchards, in the heart of Armagh, which is known as the Orchard County. The Orange Order was founded near here after a battle in 1795.

Close by is 17th-century Ardress House, which was given an elegant new look in the 18th century with exquisite plaster-work by stuccodore Michael Stapleton, and some remarkably fine Irish furniture. Ardress still has the feel of a gentleman farmer's residence, and the restored farmyard is full of fowl, animals and traditional farming equipment. A woodland play-ground is popular with the children and there is a pretty garden and a woodland walk.

▶ Follow the **B77** for 3 miles (5km), then turn left on to the **B131**. After 2 miles (3km) turn left on to the **B28**, following the signs for Moy. After a mile (1.5km) pass Ardress House, and immediately after, branch right on to an unclassified road. Turn right again and follow signs for the **M1** for

147

3 miles (5km). At the round-about, take the B131, which becomes the B34, towards Dungannon for 3 miles (5km), then turn left on to the B106 for a further 3 miles (5km) to Moy.

2 Moy, Co Tyrone
More commonly called 'the Moy', this is on the Tyrone side of the Blackwater River.

Charlemont lies opposite on the banks of the river in County Armagh. Once one of the most important strongholds of the English, only the impressive wrought-iron gates of Roxborough House and earthworks that were artillery bastions remain. The Moy had one of the most famous horse fairs in Ireland in the 19th century, held in a fine square, where a plaque recalls a son of the village, John King, Australian soldier and explorer.

The Argory close by, situated above the river in lovely grounds, is a pleasant 19th-century house, still lit by gas and full of fascinating objects.

RECOMMENDED WALKS

An attractive stretch of the Ulster Way takes the walker along the banks of the Blackwater from Caledon in County Tyrone through Amagh to Lough Neagh.

▶ *Take the A29 to Dungannon.*

3 Dungannon, Co Tyrone
A flourishing town, this was once the chief seat of the O'Neills, kings of Ulster for 500

The wide main street of Moy, on the Tyrone-Armagh boundary

years. Now it is more famous for fine cut glass, and the Tyrone Crystal factory is a popular attraction. At Park Lane, a fishery offers trout for sale, an equestrian centre and walks.

Off the main Dungannon-Ballygawley road, at Dergenagh, is the ancestral home of Ulysses S Grant, President of the US from 1869 to 1877, restored to its appearance of 1880, and set on a farmstead worked by traditional methods of the time.

i *190 Ballygawley Road*

▶ *Continue on the A29 for 11 miles (18km) to Cookstown.*

4 Cookstown, Co Tyrone
The broad main street runs through a typical mid-Ulster farming town, but the area around Cookstown has plenty to interest the visitor.

Drum Manor Forest Park to the west is small but very attractive, with a butterfly garden, a shrub garden, a forest garden containing small plots of many tree species, and an arboretum. There is a heronry, and waterfowl inhabit the fish ponds.

In the same area is Wellbrook Beetling Mill, a

water-powered mill used for beetling or polishing, the final process in the manufacture of linen, dating from 1765. Not so long ago there would have been many such mills operating on the Ballinderry River.

The Beaghmore stone circles to the northwest of Cookstown are mysterious in their origin and purpose. Perhaps they were formed in the Stone Age or early Bronze Age for ceremonial purposes, with lines pointing to the midsummer sunrise.

[i] *The Burnavon, Burn Road*

▶ *Take the **A505** for Omagh. After 13 miles (21km) turn right on to the **B46** to Gortin for 11 miles (18km).*

FOR HISTORY BUFFS

Northeast of Cookstown is Springhill, a lovely 17th-century house with 18th- and 19th-century additions, built at a time when strength and fortification were giving way to comfort and convenience. The Lenox-Conynghams, who built Springhall and lived there for nearly 300 years, were a family of soldiers; their story, and the house, provides a fascinating view of the history of Ireland and of events further afield. The charming house has a fine oak staircase, a good library, lovely old gardens and an interesting costume museum.

SCENIC ROUTES

Linking the Cookstown-Gortin road with the Gortin-Omagh road is Gortin Lake scenic route. The blend of loughs, evergreen and deciduous forests, heather-topped moors and the village below create a fine panorama. Features with evocative names like Curraghchosaly (Moor with the Rocky Face), the meandering Owenkillew (River of the Curlew) and Mullaghbolig (Humped Top) add richness to the picture.

A splendid way to travel, and to enjoy the sights and smells of the lovely Gortin Lake scenery

5 Gortin, Co Tyrone

This beautiful, sparsely populated area is a gateway to the Sperrin Mountains. Those who want to venture further and even pan for the gold occasionally found in these hills should go north and call at the Sperrin Heritage Centre. Gortin has a fine forest park with a herd of Japanese sika deer, and the area is rich in good walks. On the Gortin side of the entrance to the forest park look out for a stone seat beside a cool stream, which has the inscription 'Rest and be thankful'.

The Ulster History Park is here, too, tracing the story of settlements in Ireland from the Stone Age to the Normans. Full-scale models of houses and monuments vividly re-create life in a mesolithic or neolithic home, and other exhibits include a round tower, monastic dwellings, a crannóg, or artifical island built as a defended lake dwelling, and a motte-and-bailey Norman structure.

Four miles (6km) from Gortin on the B48 look out for the place known locally as the Magnetic Hill, which gives the illusion that your car is travelling uphill, when it is really going downhill.

> **RECOMMENDED WALKS**
>
> From Gortin a number of walks radiate over ideal walking country, with panoramic views. Children enjoy the Burn Walk, which follows a stream all the way to the heart of Gortin village.

The Ulster American Museum has brought the New World back to the Old Country

▶ Take the **B48** to Omagh.

6 Omagh, Co Tyrone

Omagh sits high on a hill, spires and the outline of the court house giving the town a distinctive profile.

The outstanding attraction of the area is the Ulster-American Folk Park, on the A5 to Newtownstewart. It is designed very much in the American style, with costumed interpreters baking bread or spinning by a turf fire. In the Dockside Gallery you are invited to sail away to the New World. The park illustrates the two cultures in Ulster's tradition of emigration, from the reconstructed street of shops and the thatched cottages, representing the Old World (Ulster), to the American street and the log cabins, representing the New World. One of the most telling exhibits is the re-creation of the brig *Union*, an emigrant ship. Here, visitors can experience the dreadful conditions, smells and sounds of a transatlantic passage. There is an extensive programme of special events throughout the year.

i *I Market Street*

▶ *Take the **A5** signed for Belfast. After 7 miles (11km) turn right on to the **B46** for Seskinore and Fintona.*

7 Fintona, Co Tyrone
Fintona is a very quiet little village, once celebrated for its horse-drawn tram. The Forest of Seskinore is extremely productive, growing high-quality crops of hard and soft woods. It harbours a rich variety of wildlife and game. Pheasant, grouse, partridges, wild ducks and geese are reared here, as well as ornamental species such as golden pheasant and peacocks. Seskinore was once

dependent on using horse power to extract timber. Today's Forest Service has brought back Irish draught horses and trained them to this work once again.

▶ *Take the **B122** to Fivemiletown and the Clogher Valley.*

8 The Clogher Valley, Co Tyrone
Augher, Clogher and Fivemile-town are the villages of the Clogher Valley, and the names roll off the local tongue, being the stations of the old Clogher Valley railway, much loved by Ulster people.

Visitors to the tiny village of Clogher will be surprised to learn that it has a cathedral, its importance dating from the 5th century, when St Patrick made McCartan first Bishop of Clogher. The folly on a hill to the south of Clogher was a mausoleum erected by a newly rich landlord, Brackenridge, so that 'he could look down on the neighbours who had looked down on him'.

Fivemiletown has a carriage museum and recreational facilities around the lake. The

valley has three forests with different attractions – Fardross, Knockmany and Favour Royal.

▶ *Take the **A4** for Augher for 8 miles (13km), then the **A28**, passing through Aughnacloy and Caledon to Armagh.*

The lanes of rural Ireland are dotted with wayside shrines and curiosities

Mourne
Country

A town of great historic importance in the Gap of the North between Slieve Gullion and the Carlingford Mountains, Newry is close to the Mourne Mountains and Carlingford Lough. Its town hall, which actually spans the Clanrye River, has been converted into an arts centre.

2 DAYS • 95 MILES • 153KM

ITINERARY		
NEWRY	▶	**Rathfriland** (10m–16km)
RATHFRILAND	▶	**Banbridge** (10m–16km)
BANBRIDGE	▶	**Hillsborough**
		(11m–18km)
HILLSBOROUGH	▶	**Castlewellan**
		(11m–18km)
CASTLEWELLAN	▶	**Dundrum** (6m–10km)
DUNDRUM	▶	**Newcastle** (4m–6km)
NEWCASTLE	▶	**Annalong** (8m–13km)
ANNALONG	▶	**Silent Valley** (6m–10km)
SILENT VALLEY	▶	**Spelga Dam** (7m–11km)
SPELGA DAM	▶	**Rostrevor** (11m–18km)
ROSTREVOR	▶	**Warrenpoint** (4m–6km)
WARRENPOINT	▶	**Newry** (7m–11km)

ⓘ *Town Hall, Bank Parade, Newry*

▶ *Take the **A25** following signposts for Rathfriland.*

❶ Rathfriland, Co Down
A quiet village atop a steep hill, Rathfriland commands views over a tranquil valley, where shady roads wind among small farms. This is the country of Patrick Brontë, father of the famous writers Charlotte, Emily and Anne, and it is said that his stories of County Down were a memorable part of their childhood. Little Drumballyroney school, where he taught, marks the beginning of the 10-mile (16km) signposted Brontë Homeland route. In 1835, Catherine O'Hare was born in Rathfriland. She became the first woman to cross the Rocky Mountains.

▶ *Take the **B25** northwards from Rathfriland, turning left on to the **B10** for Banbridge.*

❷ Banbridge, Co Down
The steep hill in the centre of Banbridge was cut through in 1834 to spare the horses on the busy Belfast–Dublin road, and now the wide thoroughfare is divided into three with an elegant underpass. At the foot of the hill, close to the River Bann, is an elaborate monument guarded by polar bears. It commemorates Captain Crozier (1796–1848), who was second-in-command of the expedition that discovered the North-West Passage.

ⓘ *Gateway Centre, Newry Road*

▶ *Take the **A1** for Belfast. After 11 miles (18km) turn right for Hillsborough.*

❸ Hillsborough, Co Down
Take time to explore this pretty and elegant Georgian village, full of interesting shops, pubs and historic buildings. Hillsborough Castle is the residence for members of the royal family when they visit Northern Ireland, and the permanent residence of the Secretary of State. It stands in a square, not typical of an Ulster village, lined with graceful Georgian terraces. In the centre is the 18th-century market house, aligned with a fine gateway and tree-lined avenue to a fort. There was a defended settlement here in early Christian times, but the present building was rebuilt as a picturesque toy-like fort in the 18th century by the Hill family, who carefully planned the village through successive generations. The Georgian parish church adds to the harmony of Hillsborough, and the forest park has a lake with pleasant walks.

▶ *Take the road for Newry, but before joining the **A1** turn left for Dromara. After 1 mile (1.5km) turn left again and drive for 8 miles (13km) to Dromara. In Dromara, turn left following signposts for Dundrum. After 8 miles (13km) turn right and follow the **B175** for 5 miles (8km) to the junction with the **A25**. Turn right for Castlewellan.*

Castlewellan Lake, overlooked by a Victorian castle, is at the heart of the superb forest park

4 Castlewellan, Co Down
Another County Down village of steep hills, broad views and quiet tree-lined squares of pleasant terraces, Castlewellan's centre is marked by a solid market house, now a library, and its boundaries enhanced by two handsome churches.

Close to the village, the forest park covers 1,500 acres (600 hectares) of hilly ground, including a small mountain, Slievenaslat, and surrounds a beautiful lake. At its heart stands a 19th-century castle, in Scottish baronial style. It is now a conference centre. The arboretum is particularly fine, and a popular cypress, Castlewellan Gold, which was developed here, has spread the name of the forest throughout the world. Fishing, pony trekking and camping can be enjoyed here, and a Craft Centre has been set up in the handsome Grange.

FOR HISTORY BUFFS

At Drumena, 2 miles (3km) from Castlewellan, there is a good example of an elaborate stone construction, a cashel from the early Christian period with very thick walls. This cashel, overlooking Lough Island Reavy, also has a souter-rain or underground passage, used for storage or as refuge in time of danger.

▶ Take the **A50** for Newcastle. After 2 miles (3km) turn left on to the **B180**, and after 3 miles (5km) turn left again for Dundrum.

FOR CHILDREN

At Seaforde, a pretty village 3 miles (5km) north of Dundrum, is a butterfly house. It is an extraordinary experience to find that these beautiful creatures are attracted to visitors and will settle on arms and shoulders.

5 Dundrum, Co Down
You can just see the top of the keep of the Norman castle among the trees above Dundrum. John de Courcy chose a superb rocky site commanding strategic views over sea and countryside to build his castle in the 13th century, although the name 'the Fort of the Ridge' goes back to an early Christian defence. The sand dunes below

Left: a mixture of pastureland and wild moorland in the lovely Mountains of Mourne

Above: a delightful rocky cascade in the ever-popular Tollymore Forest Park near Newcastle

BACK TO NATURE

Murlough National Nature Reserve at Dundrum is as beautiful as it is interesting. The dune system here has been carefully managed and it merges into heathland, the whole area bounded by estuary and sea. The range of habitats nurture a wide variety of plants, insects and birds, and wardens lead guided walks through restricted areas. From the magnificent beach, sea birds and seals can be seen, while the inner bay estuary has a good variety of birds such as redshank, greenshank, Brent geese and godwits in the winter. Migrant birds often shelter among the marram grass and sea buckthorn in the dunes.

---

have yielded evidence of Stone-Age and Bronze-Age settlements, while at Sliddery, just south of the village, an 8-foot (2.5m) dolmen was erected, probably 4,000 years ago.

▶ Take the **A2** to Newcastle.

FOR CHILDREN

Experience warm seawater in the open air at the Tropicana in Newcastle, where water fun is provided with games and slides.

---

6 Newcastle, Co Down
When Percy French wrote of the place where 'The Mountains of Mourne sweep down to the sea', he must have had this part of County Down's

coast in mind. Newcastle itself is in the shelter of the highest of the peaks, Slieve Donard, but to the south of the town there is barely room for the road to scrape through between the mountains and the sea.

The town is a traditional seaside resort, with a promenade, parks, swimming pools and holiday recreation facilities. A magnificent beach sweeps from Dundrum to the harbour, and borders the championship golf course, Royal County Down. The staff of the Mourne Heritage Trust, who provide general information about the mountains, also organise a series of walks for the inexperienced visitor.

Two miles (3km) to the west is Tollymore, a magnificently situated and very popular forest park on the slopes of

Slievenabrock and Luke's Mountain, in the valley of the Shimna River. There are attractive walks enlivened by the picturesque cascades, bridges and numerous follies built by the Roden family.

i Central Promenade

RECOMMENDED WALKS

There are many excellent walks in the Mournes. Generally they will not be signposted, but walks leaflets are available locally. From Bloody Bridge, a short distance south of Newcastle on the A2, a path climbs the mountain along the Bloody River, so called because of the massacre in the 1641 rebellion. This is part of the Brandy Pad, a track that winds its way through the mountains by Hare's Gap to Hilltown, and which was used by smugglers distributing wines, spirits, tobacco, silks and spice, a thriving 18th-century trade.

The shoreline at Newcastle, a coastal resort and centre for the Mourne Mountains

▶ Take the **A2** following signs for Kilkeel to Annalong.

7 **Annalong,** Co Down
Two rocky clefts shelter the small fishing fleet that uses Annalong harbour, with lobster pots and fishing nets lining the stone pier. A fine corn mill right on the edge of the harbour can produce flour and oatmeal, and the Marine Park is a pleasant focal point on the shore with a play area, boat park and herb garden. A fish smokery and granite-cutting yards add activity to the narrow, winding streets and low cottages.

▶ Return to the **A2** towards Newcastle, then turn left following signs for Silent Valley for 6 miles (10km).

8 **The Silent Valley,** Co Down
Impressive gates admit the visitor to the vast area of the Silent Valley, which contains two reservoirs and dams that provide water for the Greater Belfast area. The Water Commissioners of the early part of this century planned the landscaping of the reservoirs, and the area has a peculiarly municipal feel with flowering shrubs and formal flowerbeds. The splendid mountain panoramas predominate, and today's guardians, the Department of the Environment, have provided walks, a visitors' centre and a shuttle bus (you cannot take a car up to the Silent Valley).

SPECIAL TO...

The drystone walls, or more properly, stone ditches, of the Mournes are an especially attractive feature, enclosing tiny fields and creating intruging patterns below the high peaks. Some are single width, seemingly higglegy-piggledy and gaping with holes – no mortar here – others are comapct, thick and splendidly flat on top. The Mourne Wall is quite different. Solid and massive, it provided employment between 1904 and 1922. The Wall starts and ends at the Silent Valley. Travelling 22 miles (35km), it spans the summits of 15 mountains, and encloses the entire Mourne water catchment area.

▶ Turn right and right again for Spelga Dam. After 1½ miles

*(2km) turn right on to the **B27** for Hilltown. After 5 miles (8km) turn left, still following the **B27**.*

9 Spelga Dam, Co Down
Just above Spelga is the highest point a road reaches in Northern Ireland. To the east is a good place for access into the inner Mournes, the ring of mountains – Doan, Meelbeg, Bearnagh, Donard, Lamagan and Binnian – that shields the beautiful, deep blue Lough Shannagh, and the source of the River Bann. To the north is the pretty Fofanny dam, and the Trassey river, where a path gives an approach to the north Mournes.

SCENIC ROUTES

On the road from Silent Valley, past Spelga to Rostrevor, look for the red metal gates with round knobs on the posts, which mark the water pipelines. Each mountain has its own characteristics, scattered with firs and pines and rocky outcrops, or smothered with naturalised rhododendrons. As the road dips into dark forest, there is a perfect picnic site at the Yellow River, with imaginative tables in wood and stone in an idyllic setting beside a fast-running stream.

▶ *Continue west on the **B27** and after 3 miles (5km) turn left and continue for 8 miles (13km) to Rostrevor.*

10 Rostrevor, Co Down
Rostrevor is a picturesque place with a flourishing arts festival every year, and the exotic plants and lush vegetation you will see all around you prove its claim to be the most sheltered spot in Northern Ireland, tucked as it is between Slieve Martin and the temperate waters of Carlingford Lough.

As the Mournes descend to Rostrevor the forest pines and conifers give way to an area of native oak woodland, which forms a National Nature Reserve. Climb to Cloughmore, the 'Big Stone' reputedly thrown by Finn MacCool from Slieve Foye across the lough.

A real Irish giant is buried in Kilbroney churchyard. He was the tallest man in his day at over 8 feet (2.5m) tall, and died in Marseilles in 1861. Two ancient crosses stand in this churchyard, but a Celtic bronze hand-bell, which was found in a ruined church wall, is preserved in St Mary's Church.

A granite obelisk commemorates Major General Robert Ross, who captured Washington DC in 1814, and ate the dinner prepared for the fleeing President Madison. He died three weeks later in Baltimore.

Rostrevor Forest Park and Kibroney Park have various recreational facilities, including toilets, a playground, picnic sites and a forest drive.

▶ *Take the **A2** for 4 miles (6km) to Warrenpoint.*

The restored 19th-century corn mill at Annalong overlooks the pretty little harbour

11 Warrenpoint, Co Down
Warrenpoint is a resort with a growing port where Carlingford Lough narrows to become an enclosed fiord-like waterway. The Vikings gave Carlingford its name, and this steep-sided inlet must have seemed familiar to them. Carlingford gave them excellent access for their plundering of the rich pickings of Armagh. They may have been the 'foreigners of Narrow Water' who were recorded in AD841.

The English garrison built a stronghold at Narrow Water in 1560, at a cost of £361, and the three-storey tower house with battlements, murder hole and bawn wall is a stone's throw from County Louth in Leinster.

Warrenpoint is a traditional seaside resort, with park and bandstand, marina, beach, sports and boat trips to Omeath.

▶ *Take the **A2** for a distance of 7 miles (11km) back to Newry.*

MOTORING IN IRELAND

ACCIDENTS

In the event of an accident, the vehicle should be moved off the carriageway wherever possible. (See also **Warning Triangle/ Hazard Warning Lights** page 159.)

You must also stop immediately and exchange details with the other people involved in the accident. If this is not possible you must report the accident to a member of the Garda Siochana (in the Republic) or the Police (in Northern Ireland).

If damage or injury is caused to any other person or vehicle you must stop, give your own and the vehicle owner's name and address and the registration number of the vehicle to anyone having reasonable grounds for requiring the information.

If for some reason you do not give your name and address at the time of the accident, you must report the accident to the police as soon as reasonably practicable, at least within 24 hours.

BREAKDOWNS

If the car is rented, contact the rental company who will probably have an arrangement with a motoring organisation or other breakdown service. If it is your own car, and you are a member of the Automobile Association or one of the AIT (*Alliance International de Tourisme*) driving clubs you can call on the AA rescue service run by the Automobile Association of Ireland in the Republic and the Automobile Association in Northern Ireland. The RAC (Royal Automobile Club) operates a similar service for its members, but only in Northern Ireland.

In the event of a breakdown, the vehicle should be moved off the carriageway wherever possible. (See also **Warning Triangle /Hazard Warning Lights** page 159.)

CAR HIRE

It is always best to rent a car in advance, from home if possible. Renting a car in the Republic is expensive compared with Northern Ireland. Though rates vary, smaller local firms often offer cheaper deals than the larger international companies, but always check what you are getting for your money, such as insurance and unlimited mileage. However, larger companies will often allow you to pick up your car in one town and return it in another.

Drivers must hold, and have held for one year, a valid national licence or an International Driving Permit. The minimum age for hiring a car ranges from 18 to 25, depending on the model of car. There is a maximum age limit of 70 with some companies.

Make sure you have personal insurance as well as Collision Damage Waiver (CDW).

Most cars use unleaded fuel; make sure you know what your car takes before filling the tank.

The Car Rental Council of Ireland's website (www.carrentalcouncil.ie) has information on car hire, although you can't actually reserve a car on this site.

CHILDREN

The following restrictions apply to children travelling in private motor vehicles:

Children under 3 years: front seat – appropriate child restraint must be worn, rear seats – appropriate child restraint must be worn if available.

Child aged 3 to 11 and under 1.5 metres tall: front seat – appropriate child restraint must be worn if available, if not adult seat belt must be worn. Rear seat – appropriate child restraint must be worn if available, if not adult seat belt must be worn if available.

Child aged 12 or 13 or younger child 1.5 metres or more

in height: front and rear – adult seat belt must be worn if available.

Note: under no circumstances should a rear-facing restraint be used in a seat with an airbag.

CRASH (SAFETY) HELMETS

Visiting motorcyclists and their passengers must wear crash or safety helmets.

DOCUMENTS

You must have a valid driver's licence (with an English translation if you wish to rent a car).

If you are bringing a vehicle you need its registration book with a letter of authorisation from the owner if they are not accompanying the vehicle.

DRINKING AND DRIVING

The laws regarding drinking and driving are strict and the penalties severe. The best advice is if you drink don't drive.

DRIVING CONDITIONS

Traffic drives on the left (it goes clockwise at roundabouts/traffic circles). Most signposts in the Republic give distances in kilometres: in the North, they give distances in miles. (See also **Warning Triangle /Hazard Warning Lights** page 159.)

FUEL

Fuel stations in villages in the Republic usually stay open till around 8pm and open after mass on Sundays. In Northern Ireland, where fuel is more expensive, 24 hour stations are fairly common and many stations are open on Sundays.

INSURANCE

Fully comprehensive insurance, which covers you for some of the expenses incurred after a breakdown or an accident, is advisable. Ensure that you are covered for both the Republic and Northern Ireland if you intend to cross the border.

LIGHTS

You must ensure your front and rear side lights and rear registration plate lights are lit at night. You must use headlights when visibility is seriously reduced and at night on all unlit roads and those where the street lights are more than 600 feet (185m) apart.

MOBILE PHONES

The use of a mobile phone while driving is restricted to hands-free units only in both the Republic and Northern Ireland.

ROADS
Republic of Ireland

There are some stretches of motorway in the Dublin area. The M50 encircles the east side of the city, and from it the M1 extends north as far as Dundalk, with a toll section in the Drogheda area. The M4 (via the N4) heads west, and will extend almost to Mullingar by 2006; the M7 (via the N7) goes southwest to Portlaoise.

There are a few stretches of dual carriageway on certain major arterial routes, but elsewhere the roads vary considerably, and the classification gives no reliable indication of the width or surface quality – some primary roads are little better than country lanes.

Potential hazards include the relaxed attitude of Dublin drivers to red traffic lights, while in country areas there may be loose chippings, livestock and occasionally a game of road bowls to contend with.

Northern Ireland

Motorways in the north are the M1, which heads south then west from Belfast to skirt the southern shore of Lough Neagh and end just short of Dungannon.

The M2 goes northwest from Belfast. All other major roads are fast, well-maintained and seldom congested.

ROAD SIGNS

In Gaeltacht areas of Ireland, where the Irish language is still spoken as a community language, road signs may be shown only in Irish, and this can be confusing unless you have planned your route in advance. There are Gaeltacht areas in counties Waterford, Cork, Kerry, Galway, Meath, Mayo and Donegal. If you need to ask for directions, bear in mind that some older people may speak Irish only.

Distances shown on signposts will be in kilometres in the Republic of Ireland and in miles in Northern Ireland.

ROUTE DIRECTIONS

Throughout the book the following abbreviations are used for roads:

M – Motorways
Republic of Ireland only
N – National primary/seconday roads
R – Regional roads
Northern Ireland only
A – Main roads
B – local roads

SEAT BELTS

The wearing of seat belts is compulsory for drivers and their front seat passenger. Passengers travelling in the rear seats of the vehicle must wear a seat belt if one is fitted.

SHORT CUTS

There are a couple of vehicle ferry routes that serve as useful short-cuts:

Ballyhack–Passage East crosses Waterford Harbour, and is a boon for travellers heading west from Rosslare harbour to Waterford.

Tarbert–Killimer is a 20-minute ride across the Shannon estuary, saving the need to loop around Limerick in order to get from west Kerry to west Clare.

Portaferry–Strangford at the top of the Ards Peninsula in Northern Ireland is a short hop

that saves a 50-mile (65km) drive by road.

SPEED LIMITS
Republic of Ireland

Speed limits are 48kph (30mph) in built-up areas and 100kph (60mph) elsewhere, unless otherwise indicated, and 113kph (70mph) on motorways; for non-articulated vehicles with one trailer, the maximum is 64kph (40mph).

Northern Ireland

Speed limits are 30mph (48kph) in built-up areas, 60mph (100kph) in country areas and 70mph (113kph) on dual carriageways and motorways, unless otherwise indicated; for trailers the maximum is usually 40mph (64kph).

WARNING TRIANGLE/ HAZARD WARNING LIGHTS

Hazard warning lights should be used in the event of a break-down or an accident.

If available, a red triangle should be placed on the road at least 165 feet (50m) before the obstruction and on the same side of the road.

WORDS AND PHRASES

Her are a few basic words you may find useful:

fáilte	welcome
tá/sea	yes
níl/ní hea	no
le do thoil	please
go raibh maith aguth	
	thank you
dia dhuit	hello
slán	goodbye
oscailte	open
dúnta	closed
gardaí	police
leithreas	toilet
fir	men
mná	women
an lár	middle of town
óstán	hotel
bialann	restaurant
tábhairne	pub/bar
caife	café
oifig an phoist	
	post office
oifig malairte	
	exchange office

ACCOMMODATION AND RESTAURANTS

Wherever possible the following hotels and restaurants are on the tour route and have been selected to offer a variety of hotel styles.

The AA Hotel Booking Service is a free, fast and easy way to find a place for a short break or holiday; tel: 0870 5 05 05 05. Full listings of the Irish hotels and B&Bs available through the service can be found and booked on the AA's website: www.theAA.com/getaway

Hotel prices

The hotels listed are grouped into three price categories based on a nightly rate for a double room including breakfast:
Expensive €€€/£££ – over €150/£100
Moderate €€/££ – between €75/£60 and €150/£100
Budget €/£ – under €75/£60

Restaurant prices

The restaurants listed below are grouped into three price categories based on a two-course meal for one person, without drinks:
Expensive €€€/£££ – over €40/£30
Moderate €€/££ – between €20/£15 and €40/£30
Budget €/£ – under €20/£15

TOUR 1

ENNIS, Co Clare

Cill Eoin House €–€€
Killadysert Cross, Clare Road (tel: 065 684 1668, fax: 065 684 1669).
Closed 22 Dec–9 Jan.
14 rooms.

The Cloister €–€€
Club Bridge, Abbey Street (tel: 065 682 9262).
Lovely old pub built into the cloister ruins, with a menu that features such dishes as wild venison with juniper and Armagnac sauce and poached monkfish with red-pepper sauce. Pub lunches available in the bar. Restaurant open daily 12.30–3pm, 6–9.30pm.

Cruise's Pub Restaurant €
Abbey Street (tel: 065 684 1800).
Ancient building with a good choice of favourite pub food, including Irish stew, grills and seafood. Daily 12.30–10pm.

Fountain Court €–€€
Lahinch Road (tel: 065 682 9845, fax: 065 684 5030).
Closed 21 Dec–7 Mar.
18 rooms.

Magowna €
Inch, Kilmaley (tel: 065 683 9008, fax: 065 683 9258).
Closed 24–26 Dec.
10 rooms.

Temple Gate €€–€€€
The Square (tel: 065 682 3300, fax 065 682 3322).
70 rooms.
Mainly traditional dishes with some international influences. Daily 12.45–3, 7–10.15. Closed 25 Dec.

MILLTOWN MALBAY, Co Clare

Burkes Armada €€
Spanish Point (2 miles/3km west) (tel: 065 708 4110, fax: 065 708 4632).
61 rooms.

LEHINCH, Co Clare

Grovemount House €€
Lehinch Road, Ennistymon (4 miles/6km east on N85) (tel: 065 707 1431 or 065 707 1038, fax: 065 707 1823).
Closed Nov–Apr.
8 rooms.

Moy House €€€
2 miles (3.2km) from Lahinch on Milltown Malbay road (tel: 065 708 2800, fax: 065 708 2500).
9 rooms.

BALLVAGHAN, Co Clare

Cappabhaile House €€
Newtown (0.5 mile/1km from town on Aillwee Caves road) (tel: 065 707 7260, fax: 065 707 7300).
Closed Nov–Feb.
8 rooms.

Drumcreehy €–€€
1 mile (1.5km) north on N67 (tel: 065 707 7377, fax: 065 707 7379).
10 rooms.

Gregans Castle €€
3 miles (5km) south on N67 (tel: 065 707 7005, fax: 065 707 7111).
Closed 23 Dec–14 Feb.
22 rooms.
Fine modern cuisine based on local produce and fresh fish; the lamb is specially recommended. Daily 7–8.30pm. Closed Nov–Feb.

Rusheen Lodge €€
0.5 mile (1km) north on N67 (tel: 065 707 7092, fax: 065 707 7152).
Closed mid-Nov to mid-Feb.
9 rooms.

LISDOONVARNA, Co Clare

Aran View House €
Coast Road, Doolin (4 miles/6km west) (tel: 065 707 4061 or 065 707 4420, fax: 065 707 4540).
Closed Nov–1 Apr.
13 rooms.

Cullinan's €–€€
Village centre, Doolin (4 miles/6km west) (tel: 065 707 4183, fax: 065 707 4239).
8 rooms.

Kincora Country House €€
Just outside town on Doolin road (tel: 065 707 4300, fax: 065 707 4490).
Closed Nov–Feb.
14 rooms.

BUNRATTY, Co Clare

Clover Hill Lodge €
Low Road (tel: 061 369039, fax: 061 360520).
Closed Nov–Mar.
3 rooms.

Fitzpatrick Bunratty €€€
Village centre (tel: 061 361177, fax: 061 471252).
Closed 24–26 Dec.
115 rooms.

Park House €€
Low Road (tel: 061 369902, fax: 061 369903).
Closed mid-Dec to Jan.
6 rooms.

TOUR 2
LIMERICK, Co Limerick
(See also Tour 3)
🏨 ¶�‖ **Castletroy Park** €€–€€€
Dublin Road (tel: 061 335566,
fax: 061 331117).
107 rooms.
*Fixed and à la carte menus offer
such dishes as sea bass with seared
pak choi and ginger.
Daily 12.30–2.30pm, Tue–Sat
6–9.30pm. Closed 25 and 31 Dec.*

🏨 **Clarion Hotel Limerick**
€€–€€€
Steamboat Quay (tel: 061
444100, fax: 061 444101).
Closed 24–25 Dec.
123 rooms.

¶❖ **Green Onion Caffé** €–€€
Old Town Hall Building,
Rutland Street (tel: 061 400710).
*Spearheading a culinary revival in
Limerick, the talented chef here
produces down-to-earth dishes that
are bursting with natural flavours.
Tue–Sat noon–10pm.*

🏨 **Jurys** €€
Ennis Road (tel: 061 327777,
fax: 061 326400).
Closed 24–27 Dec.
95 rooms.

🏨 **Hotel Greenhills** €€
Caherdavin (2 miles/3km) from
city centre on N18) (tel: 061
453033, fax: 061 453307).
18 rooms.

¶❖ **Patrick Puinch's** €
O'Connell Avenue (N20),
Punch's Cross (tel: 061 229588).
*Popular pub-restaurant on the
southern edge of the city, serving a
varied menu that might include beef
Wellington and vegetable lasagne.
Daily 10.30am–11.30pm.*

🏨 ¶❖ **Radisson SAS** €€
Ennis Road (tel: 061 326666,
fax: 061 327418).
154 rooms.
*Relaxing open-plan restaurant
offering seasonally interesting dishes,
such as tian of crab with roquette, or
roast rack of Limerick lamb.
Mon–Sat 6.30–10pm, Sun
12.30–2.30pm.*

🏨 **Sunville Country House** €€
Pallasgreen (tel: 061 384822,
fax: 061 384823).
6 rooms.

🏨 **White House** €
Raheen (tel/fax: 061 301709).
5 rooms.

BALLYBUNNION, Co Kerry
🏨 **Cashen Course House** €€
Golf Links Road (tel: 068 7351,
fax: 068 28934).
Closed Nov–Feb.
9 rooms.

🏨 **The Tides Guest House**
€€–€€€
On R551, near golf course (tel:
068 27980, fax: 068 27923).
5 rooms.

ADARE, Co Limerick
🏨 **Adare Lodge** €–€€
Kildimo Road (tel: 061 396629,
fax: 061 395060).
6 rooms.

🏨 **Avona House** €
Kildimo Road (tel: 061 396323,
fax: 061 396323).
Closed Nov–Mar.
4 rooms.

🏨 **Berkeley Lodge** €
Station Road (tel: 061 396857,
fax: 061 396857).
6 rooms.

🏨 **Carrigane House** €
Rienroe (tel: 061 396778).
Closed 15 Dec–10 Jan.
6 rooms.

🏨 ¶❖ **Dunraven Arms** €€
Edge of village (tel: 061 396633,
fax: 061 396541).
75 rooms.
*Modern European cuisine, with
such options as roast rib of beef with
red wine jus, and pork and apricot
terrine.
Daily 7–9.30pm, also
12.30–2.30pm Sun.*

TOUR 3
LIMERICK, Co Limerick
(See also Tour 2)
🏨 **Castle Oaks House** €€€
Castleconnel (6 miles/10km east
off N7 Dublin road) (tel: 061
377606, fax: 061 377717).
62 rooms.

🏨 **Clifton House** €–€€
Ennis Road (tel: 061 451166, fax:
061 451224).
Closed 21 Dec–2 Jan.
16 rooms.

¶❖ **Copper and Spice** €
2 Cornmarket Row (tel: 061
313620).
*Hailed by some as the best Indian
restaurant in Ireland, where authentic dishes are cooked to perfection.
Daily 5–10.30pm, Wed–Fri
12.30–2pm.*

🏨 **Jurys Inn Limerick** €€€
Lower Mallow Street (tel: 061
207000, fax: 061 400966).
Closed 24–26 Dec.
151 rooms.

¶❖ **Piccola Italia** €–€€
55 O'Connell Street (tel: 061
315844)
*In the style of a traditional trattoria,
serving pasta dishes, steaks and
seafood with Mediterranean flair.
Mon–Sat 6–11pm.*

TIPPERARY, Co Tipperary
🏨 **Ach-na-Sheen** €
Clonmel Road (tel: 062 51298,
fax: 062 80467).
Closed 11 Dec–8 Jan.
8 rooms.

CASHEL, Co Tipperary
🏨 ¶❖ **Cashel Palace** €€€
In the centre of town (tel: 062
62707, fax: 062 61521).
Closed 2 weeks Christmas–Jan.
13 rooms.
*Modern Irish cooking in historic
surroundings. Local salmon is the
signature dish.
Daily 6–7.30pm, also Mon–Thu
and Sun 12.30–3pm.*

🏨 **Dualla House** €€
Dually, northeast of Cashel off
R691 (tel: 062 61487, fax: 062
61487).
Closed Oct–Mar.
4 rooms.

🏨 **Legends Townhouse &
Restaurant** €€
R660 Holycross road (tel: 062
61292).
*Closed 23–26 Dec, 14 Feb–10 Mar,
6–20 Nov.*
7 rooms.

THURLES, Co Tipperary
🏨 **Abbeyvale House** €
Cashel Road, Holy Cross (tel:
0504 45032, fax: 0504 43032).
4 rooms.

🏨 **The Castle** €–€€
Two Mile Borris (tel: 0504
44324, fax: 0504 44352).
4 rooms.

ROSCREA, Co Tipperary
🏨 **Rackethall Country Golf &
Conference Hotel** €€
Dublin Road (tel: 0505 21748,
fax: 0505 23701).
40 rooms.

NENAGH, Co Tipperary
🏨 **Ashley Park House** €
On N52, 4 miles (6km) north
(tel: 067 38223, fax: 067 38013).
Closed 25 Dec.
5 rooms.
🏨 **Williamsferry House** €
Fintan Laylor Street (tel: 067
31118, fax: 067 31256).
Closed Christmas and New Year.
6 rooms.

PORTUMNA, Co Galway
🏨 **Shannon Oaks Hotel &
Country Club** €€€
St Joseph Road (tel: 090 974
1777, fax: 090 974 1357).
63 rooms.

MOUNTSHANNON Co
Galway
🏨 **Clareville House** €
Tuamgraney (6 miles/10km
southwest on R352) (tel: 061
922925).
Closed 20–27 Dec.
4 rooms.
🏨 **Lantern House** €
Ogonnelloe (10 miles/16km
south via R352 and R463) (tel:
061 923034, fax: 061 923139).
Closed Nov–Mar.
6 rooms.

TOUR 4
TRALEE, Co Kerry
🏨 **Abbey Gate** €€
Maine Street (tel: 066 729888,
fax: 066 712 9821).
Closed 24–26 Dec.
100 rooms.
🏨 **Ballygarry House** €€–€€€
Killarney Road (tel: 066 712
3322, fax: 066 712 7630).
Closed 20–26 Dec, 4–20 Jan.
46 rooms.
🏨 **Brianville** €
Clogherbrien, Fenit Road (tel:
066 712 6645, fax: 066 712 6645).
5 rooms.
🏨 **Meadowlands Hotel** €€€
Oakpark (tel: 066 718 0444,
fax: 066 718 0964).
Closed 24–26 Dec.
58 rooms.
🍴 **Restaurant David Norris** €€
Ivy House, Ivy Terrace (tel: 066
718 5654).
*Pretty upstairs restaurant serving
modern Irish food and European
dishes.*
Tue–Fri 5–9.30pm, Sat 7–9.30pm.

🏨 **Tralee Townhouse** €
1–2 High Street (tel: 066 718
1111, fax: 066 718 1112).
Closed 24–28 Dec.
19 rooms.

CAMP, Co Kerry
🏨 **Suan Na Mara** €
Lisnagree, Castlegregory Road
(tel: 066 713 9258, fax: 066 713
9258).
Closed mid-Nov to mid-Mar.
7 rooms.

CASTLEGREGORY, Co Kerry
🏨 **Beenoskee B&B** €
Cappateige, Conor Pass Road
(tel: 066 713 9263, fax: 066 713
9263).
5 rooms.
🏨 **Griffin's Palm Beach
Country House** €
Goulane, Conor Pass Road (tel:
066 713 9147, fax: 066 713 9073).
Closed Dec–Feb.
8 rooms.
🏨 **Sea-Mount House** €
Cappatigue, Conor Pass Road
(066 713 9229, fax: 066 713 9229).
Closed Dec–Feb.
3 rooms.
🏨 **Shores Country House**
€–€€
Cappatigue, Conor Pass Road
(tel: 066 713 9396 or 713 9195,
fax: 066 713 9196).
Closed mid-Nov to mid-Feb.
6 rooms.
🏨 **Strand View House** €
Kilcummin, Conor Pass Road
(tel: 066 713 8131, fax: 066 713
8386).
Closed 15 Dec–15 Jan.
5 rooms.

DINGLE, County Kerry
🏨 **Alpine** €–€€
Mail Road (tel: 066 915 1250,
fax: 066 915 1966).
10 rooms.
🍴 **An Vafé Liteartha** €
Dykegate Street (tel: 066 915
2204).
*Soups, sandwiches, salads, seafood
and freshly baked cakes.*
*Mon–Sat 9am–6pm (later in
summer).*
🏨 **Banbury's** €–€€
Mail Road (tel: 066 915 1244,
fax: 066 915 1786).
12 rooms.

🏨 **Cleevaun** €€
Lady's Cross, Milltown (tel: 066
915 1108, fax: 066 915 2228).
Closed mid-Dec to mid-Jan.
9 rooms.
🏨 🍴 **Doyle's Town House and
Seafood Bar** €
4 John Street (tel: 066 915 1174,
fax: 066 915 1816).
Closed mid-Nov to mid-Mar.
8 rooms.
*Seafood restaurant serving the
produce of Kerry's offshore waters
and on-shore farms (€€€).*
*Mon–Sat 6–9.30pm. Closed mid-
Dec to mid-Feb.*
🏨 **Emlagh House** €€–€€€
Edge of town (tel: 066 915 2345
or 915 2353, fax: 066 915 2369).
Closed 5 Nov–10 Mar.
10 rooms.
🏨 **Fitzgerald's Dingle Heights**
€
Ballinaboola (tel: 066 915 1543).
4 rooms.
🏨 **Gormans Clifftop House &
Restaurant** €€–€€€
Glaise Bheag, Ballydavid (tel:
066 915 5162, fax: 066 915 5003).
Closed 24–26 Dec.
9 rooms.
🏨 **Heatons** €–€€
The Wood (tel: 066 915 2288,
fax: 066 915 2324).
Closed 5 Jan–1 Feb.
16 rooms.
🏨 **Hurley's** €
An Dooneen, Kilcooley (6 miles/
10km west on R559) (tel: 066
915 5112).
Closed Nov–Mar.
4 rooms.
🍴 **Lord Bakers** €€
Main Street (tel: 066 915 1277).
*Historic pub serving good seafood
and steaks, including sole stuffed
with smoked salmon and spinach in
cheese sauce.*
Fri–Wed 12.30–2pm, 6–9.30pm.
🏨 **Milltown House** €
Milltown (tel: 066 915 1372,
fax: 066 915 1095).
Closed mid-Nov to mid-Mar.
10 rooms.

VENTRY, Co Kerry
🏨 **Mount Eagle Lodge** €–€€
On coast road (tel: 066 915 9754,
fax: 066 915 9754).
Closed Nov–Feb.
4 rooms.

TOUR 5
KILLARNEY, Co Kerry

Aghadoe Heights €€€
3 miles (5km) north off N22
Tralee road (tel: 064 31766,
fax: 064 31345).
75 rooms.
*Frederick's restaurant has long been
considered one of Ireland's finest
restaurants, blending classical
French cuisine with a strong Irish
flavour (€€€).*
*Daily 6.30–9.30pm, also
12.30–2pm Sun. Closed Jan–Mar,
residents only 25 Dec.*

Applecroft House €
Woodlawn Road (tel: 064 32782).
Closed Dec–Feb.
5 rooms.

Arbutus €€
College Street (tel: 064 31037,
fax: 064 34033).
Closed 12 Dec–30 Jan.
35 rooms.
*Traditional Irish dishes with a few
international elements (€€).*
*Daily 6.30–9pm. Closed Sun–Mon
in winter.*

Ashville €–€€
Rock Road (tel: 064 36405,
fax: 064 36778).
Closed 18–30 Dec.
10 rooms.

The Brehan €€€
Muckross Road (tel: 064 30700,
fax: 064 30701).
125 rooms.

Bricin €€
26 High Street (tel: 064 34902).
*Great for boxty (potato pancakes
with various fillings), plus seafood,
pasta dishes and Irish stew. Above a
craft shop in one of the town's oldest
buildings.*
*Tue–Sat 10am–4.30pm, also
6–9.30pm Easter–Oct.*

**Cahernane House
€€–€€€**
Muckross Road (tel: 064 31895,
fax: 064 34340).
Closed 21 Dec–31 Jan.
12 rooms.
*Classic menu might include beef
fillet with champ mash and parme-
san tulle, or monkfish with sweet
potato uree and black grape jus
(€€€).*
*Daily noon–2.30, 7–9.30pm.
Closed for lunch Dec–Jan.*

Castlerosse €€–€€€
1 mile (1.5km) from town on
R562 Kilorglin road (tel: 064

31144, fax: 064 31031).
Closed Dec–Feb.
121 rooms.

Coffey's Loch Lein €€–€€€
Golf Course Road, Fossa (tel:
064 31260, fax 064 36151).
Closed 27 Oct–1 Apr.
16 rooms.

Crystal Springs €€–€€€
Ballycasheen (tel: 064 33272 or
35518, fax: 064 35518).
6 rooms.

Darby O'Gills €€
Lissivigeen, Mallow Road
(tel: 064 34168 or 34919, fax: 064
36794).
25 rooms.

Earls Court House €€
Woodlawn Junction, Muckross
Road (tel: 064 34009, fax: 064
34366).
Closed 13 Nov–11 Feb.
20 rooms.

Fairview €€–€€€
College Street (tel: 064 34164,
fax: 064 71777).
18 rooms.

Foleys Town House €€
22–23 High Street (tel: 064
31217, fax: 064 34683).
Closed 6 Nov–16 Mar.
28 rooms.

**Gaby's Seafood Restaurant
€€€**
High Street (tel: 064 32519).
*Succulent lobster and other seafood
is cooked in a variety of ways, all
delicious.*
*Mon–Sat 6–10pm. Closed
Christmas week, late Feb to
mid-Mar.*

Glena House €€
Muckross Road (tel: 064 32705
or 34284, fax: 064 35611).
26 rooms.

Gleneagle €€€
1 mile (1.6km) south on N71
(tel: 064 36000, fax: 064 32646).
250 rooms.

Green Acres €
Fossa (tel: 064 31454).
Closed Dec–9 Jan.
8 rooms.

International €€
East Avenue Road (tel: 064
31816, fax: 064 31837).
Closed 23–27 Dec.
80 rooms.

**Kathleen's Country House
€€**
Tralee Road (tel: 064 32810,
fax: 064 32340).

Closed mid-Oct to mid-Mar.
17 rooms.

Killarney Park €€€
Kenmare Place (tel: 064 35555,
fax: 064 35266).
Closed 24–26 Dec.
72 rooms.
*A creative approach to traditional
favourites provides an interesting
choice of dishes (€€€).*
Daily 7–9.30pm.

Killarney Royal €€
College Street (tel: 064 31853,
fax: 064 34001).
29 rooms.

Killarney Villa €–€€
Waterford Road (tel/fax: 064
31878).
Closed Nov–Easter.
6 rooms.

Kingfisher Lodge €
Lewis Road (tel: 064 37131,
fax: 064 39871).
Closed 15 Dec–31 Jan.
10 rooms.

Lake €€
Muckross Road (tel: 064 31035,
fax: 064 31902).
Closed 18 Dec–10 Feb.
69 rooms.

Lime Court €
Muckross Road (tel: 064 34547,
fax: 064 34121).
Closed 24–25 Dec.
17 rooms.

Muckross Park Hotel €€€
Muckross Village (tel: 064 31938,
fax: 064 31965).
Closed Dec–Feb.
27 rooms.

**O'Donovans Farm and
Muckross Riding Stables €**
Mangerton Road, Muckross
(tel: 064 32238).
Closed 11 Nov–Feb.
6 rooms.

Old Weir Lodge €€
Muckross Road (tel: 064 35593,
fax: 064 35583).
Closed 23–26 Dec.
30 rooms.

**Quality Hotel Kilkarney
(Killarney Ryan) €€**
Cork Road (tel: 064 31555,
fax: 064 32438).
Closed Dec–Jan.
168 rooms.

Randles Court €€–€€€
Muckross Road (tel: 064 35333,
fax: 064 35206).
Closed 23–27 Dec.
52 rooms.

Scotts Garden Hotel €€
College Street tel: 064 31060,
fax: 064 36656).
Closed 24–25 Dec.
52 rooms.

Straheen House €
Ballycaxsheen, off N22 Cork
road (tel: 064 31286, fax: 064
37959).
Closed Christmas and New Year.
6 rooms.

White Gates €€
Muckross Road (tel: 064 31164,
fax: 064 34850).
Closed 21–29 Dec.

KILLORGLIN, Co Kerry

**Carrig House Country
House and Restaurant €€**
Caragh Lake (tel: 066 976 9100,
fax: 066 9766 9166).
Closed Oct–Feb.
16 rooms.

Dromin Farmhouse €€
Milltown Post Office, 2 miles
(3km) from Killorglin off N70
(tel: 066 976 1867).
Closed Nov–16 Mar.
4 rooms.

Grove Lodge €€
Killarney Road (tel: 066 976
1157, fax: 066 976 2330).
Closed 22–30 Dec.
10 rooms.

**O'Regan's Country
Home €**
Bansha, 1 mile (1.5km) from
Kilorglin off N70 (tel: 066 976
1200, fax: 066 9766 1200).
Closed 11–31 Dec.
4 rooms.

GLENBEIGH, Co Kerry

Ocean Wave €–€€
Just outside village on Killorglin
road (tel: 066 976 8249, fax: 066
976 8412).
Closed Nov–Feb.
6 rooms.

WATERVILLE, Co Kerry

Brookhaven House €
New Line Road (tel: 066 947
4431, fax: 066 947 4724).
Closed 21 Dec–Feb.
5 rooms.

Butler Arms €€€
In the centre of the village
(tel: 066 947 4144, fax: 066 947
4520).
Closed Nov–Apr.

Derrynane Bay House €
Caherdaniel, south of Waterville
on N70 (tel: 066 947 5404,
fax: 077 947 5436).
Closed Nov–23 Dec.
6 rooms.

SNEEM, Co Kerry

Great Southern €€€
Parknasilla (southeast, on N70)
(tel: 064 45122, fax: 064 45323).
24 rooms.
*Traditional dishes, including good
local seafood, have an occasional
modern twist (€€€).*
Daily 7–9pm.

Tahilla Cove €€
Tahilla, 5 miles (8km) east of
Sneem just off N70 (tel: 064
45204, fax: 064 45104).
Closed Nov–Easter.
3 rooms.

KENMARE, Co Kerry
(See also Tour 6)

d'Arcy's €€
*One of the best restaurants in town,
serving such classics as peppered
fillet of beef plus more unusual
combinations such as John Dory
with salsa, and mussels in coconut
and lime broth.*
*Daily 6.30–10pm. Closed Jan to
mid-Mar.*

Ashberry Lodge €
Ring of Kerry Road (N70)
(tel: 064 42720).
Closed 24–25 Dec.
8 rooms.

Davitts €€
Henry Street (tel: 064 42741,
fax: 064 42757).
Closed 1–14 Nov, 24–26 Dec.
11 rooms.

Mulcahy's €€
*16 Henry Street (tel: 064 42383).
Excellent modern fusion cuisine,
blending classical European cooking
with Asian influences.*
*Jun–Sep daily 6–10pm, also
noon–3 Sun; Oct–May Thu–Mon
6.15–10pm. Closed 2 weeks Nov.*

Sheen Falls Lodge €€€
Off N71 Glengarriff road, first
left after suspension bridge
(tel: 064 41600, fax: 064 41386).
Closed 2 Jan–1 Feb.
66 rooms.
*Leaning towards classical French
cuisine, the menu changes monthly
and might include Skeaghanore
duck with pistachios or pan-fried*

Valentia scallop (€€–€€€).
*Daily 7.15–9.30pm. Closed 3 weeks
before Christmas, 2 Jan–1 Feb.*

Virginia House €–€€
36 Henry Street (tel: 064 41021,
fax: 064 42415).
8 rooms.

TOUR 6
KENMARE, Co Kerry
(See also Tour 5)

Harbour Views €–€€
Castletownbere Road, Dauros
(about 5 miles/8km southwest of
Kenmare via N71 and R571)
(tel: 064 41755, fax: 064 42611).
Closed Nov–Feb.
4 rooms.

Park Hotel €€€
On R569 at top of town (tel: 064
41200, fax: 064 41402).
Closed 1–23 Dec, 2 Jan–14 Feb.
49 rooms.
*Classical dishes have a strong streak
of creativity, such as baked hake
wrapped in bacon on potato colcannon with mussel and clam chive
cream sauce (€€€).*
*Daily 11–6, 7–9. Closed Nov–Apr,
except Christmas and New Year.*

Purple Heather €
Henry Street (tel: 064 41016).
*Classic tearoom fare, plus some
excellent light meals such as wild
smoked salmon salad, vegetarian
omelette, homemade soups and Irish
cheese platters.*
Mon–Sat 11am–7pm.

Sallyport House €€–€€€
Glangarriff Road (tel: 064 42066,
fax: 064 42067).
Closed Nov–Mar.
5 rooms.

**SeaShore Farm Guest
House €€**
Tubrid (off N70 Sneem road)
(tel: 064 41270 or 41675, fax: 064
41270).
Closed 15 Nov–Feb.
6 rooms.

The Vestry €€
Templenoe (4 miles/6.5km west
on N71).
*A converted church building houses
this fine restaurant serving modern
Irish food, including local seafood,
and exotic meats, including ostrich
and kangaroo.*
*Jun–Aug daily 12.30–9pm; mid-
Mar–May and Sep–mid-Oct daily
6–9pm. Closed mid-Oct–mid-Mar.*

TOUR 7
CORK, Co Cork
(See also Tour 8)
🏨 **Ashley** €–€€
Coburg Street (tel: 021 450 1518, fax: 021 450 1178).
Closed 22 Dec–5 Jan.
27 rooms.
🍴🍴 **Café Paradiso** €
16 Lancaster Quay, Western Road (tel: 021 427 7939).
Lively vegetarian restaurant featuring seasonal produce.
🍴🍴 **Crawford Gallery Café** €–€€
Emmet Place (tel: 021 427 4415).
Within the city's art gallery, this is a popular place serving traditional Irish food. It's run by the Allen family, of the famous Ballymaloe House cookery school.
Mon–Fri 10am–5pm, Sat 10am–4.30pm.
🏨 **Fairylawn** €€
Western Road (tel: 021 454 3444, fax: 021 454 4337).
Closed 23–30 Dec.
14 rooms.
🍴🍴 **Fenn's Quay Restaurant** €€
3 Fenn's Quay (tel: 021 427 9527).
Interesting combinations of food are expertly cooked here, such as spicy Toulouse sausages with sauerkraut, mashed potato and herb jus.
Mon–Sat 10am–10pm.
🏨 **Gamish House** €–€€
1 Aldergrove, Western Road (tel: 021 427 5111, fax: 021 427 3872).
13 rooms.
🏨 🍴🍴 **Hayfield Manor** €€€
Perrott Avenue, College Road (tel: 021 484 5900, fax: 021 431 6839).
88 rooms.
The chef here is a member of the Slow Food movement and uses organic ingredients wherever possible to produce his elaborate classical French dishes (€€€).
Daily 7–10pm, Sun–Fri 12.30–2pm.
🍴🍴 **Ivory Tower** €€–€€€
American-born celebrity TV chef, Seamus O'Connell presents diners here with perhaps the most unusual combinations of flavours they've ever encountered (swordfish with banana ketchup with mango salsa, for instance).
Wed–Sat 6.30–11pm.

🍴🍴 **Jacobs** €
30a South Mall (tel: 021 425 1530).
Top quality ingredients are prepared with skill and creativity in an easygoing setting.
Mon–Sat 12.30–2.30pm, 6.30–10pm
🍴🍴 **Jacques** €€
9 Phoenix Street (tel: 021 427 7387).
A Cork favourite for more than 20 years, serving an interesting range of dishes with Mediterranean and Asian influences.
Mon–Fri noon–3pm, 6–10.30pm, Sat 6–10.30pm, Sun 4.30–9pm.
🏨 **Killarney** €€
Western Road (tel: 021 427 0290, fax: 021 427 1010).
Closed 24–25 Dec.
19 rooms.
🏨 **The Kingsley Hotel** €€€
Victoria Cross (tel: 021 480 0500, fax: 021 480 0527).
69 rooms.
🏨 **Jurys Inn** €€
Anderson's Quay (tel: 021 427 6444, fax: 021 427 6144).
Closed 24–26 Dec.
133 rooms.
🏨 **Lancaster Lodge** €€
Lancaster Quay, Western Road (tel: 021 425 1125, fax: 021 425 1126).
Closed 22–26 Dec.
39 rooms.
🏨 **Maryborough House** €€€
Maryborough Hill (tel: 021 436 5555, fax: 021 436 56623).
79 rooms.
🍴🍴 **Quay Co-op** €
24 Sullivan's Quay (tel: 021 431 7026).
Interesting vegetarian food, served in an upstairs restaurant above a wholefood shop.
Mon–Fri 9am–9pm, Sat–Sun 9am–6pm.
🏨 **Rochestown Park Hotel** €€
Rochestown Road, Douglas (tel: 021 489 0800, fax: 021 489 2178).
Closed 25–26 Dec.
160 rooms.

BLARNEY, Co Cork
🏨 **Ashlee Lodge** €€–€€€
Tower (2.5 miles/4km from Blarney on R617) (tel: 021 438 5346, fax: 021 438 5726).
10 rooms.

🏨 **Blarney Castle** €€
Village Green (tel: 021 438 5116, fax: 021 438 5542).
Closed 25 Dec.
13 rooms.
🏨 **Blarney Vale House** €
Cork Road (tel: 021 4381511).
Closed Dec–Jan.
🏨 **Killarney House** €
Station Road (tel: 021 438 1841, fax: 021 438 1841).
6 rooms.
🏨 **White House** €
Shean Lower (tel: 021 438 5338).
6 rooms.

KANTURK Co Cork
🏨 **Assolas Country House** €€
3 miles (5km) northeast, off N72 (tel: 029 50015, fax: 029 50795).
6 rooms.

MALLOW, Co Cork
🏨 **Greenfield House** €
Navigation Road (tel: 022 50231).
6 rooms.
🏨 **Longueville House** €€€
3 miles (5km) west via N72 (tel: 022 47156, fax: 022 47459).
Closed 20–27 Dec.
20 rooms.
🏨 **Oaklands House** €
Springwood, off Killarney road (N72) (tel: 022 21127, fax: 022 21127).
Closed Nov–Mar.
🏨 **Springfort Hall Country House Hotel** €€€
Off N20 Limerick road (tel: 022 21278, fax: 022 21557).
Closed 23 Dec–2 Jan.
49 rooms.

CAHER, Co Tipperary
🏨 **Caher House** €€
The Square (tel: 052 43000, fax: 052 42728).
Closed 25 Dec.
42 rooms.

LISMORE, Co Waterford
🏨 🍴🍴 **Ballyrafter House** €€
Opposite Lismore Castle (tel: 058 54002, fax: 058 53050).
Closed Nov–Feb.
10 rooms.
Modern Irish food with a strong bias towards seafood (€€–€€€).
Daily 1–2.30, 7.30–9.30. Closed Tue (except residents), 31 Oct–17 Mar.

YOUGHAL, Co Cork

Aherne's €€–€€€
163 North Main Street
(tel: 024 92424, fax: 024 93633).
Closed 24–29 Dec.
13 rooms.
French-influenced treatment of the finest local seafood draws discerning diners (€€).

Bay Views €€€
Ballycotton (southwest on coast; off N25, via R632 and R629) (tel: 021 464 6746).
Seafood – landed within sight of the restaurant – is the speciality, but doesn't dominate the menu, which might also include braised pig cheeks with swede puree. Daily 1–2.30, 7–9.30. Closed lunch Mon–Sat, Nov–Mar.

Devonshire Arms €€
Pearse Square (tel: 024 92827, fax: 024 92900).
Closed 24–31 Dec.
10 rooms.

Garryvoe Hotyel €€€
Ballycotton Bay, Castlemartyr (west of Youghal, off N25) (tel: 021 464 6718).
*Irish country cooking here features lots of locally caught fish and notable meat dishes.
Daily 1–2.30, 6.45–8.45. Closed for dinner 24 Dec, 25 Dec.*

TOUR 8
CORK, Co Cork
(See also Tour 7)

Abbeypoint House €–€€
Western Road (tel: 021 427 5526 or 427 4091, fax: 021 425 1955).
Closed 23 Dec–2 Jan.
8 rooms.

Antoine House €
Western Road (tel: 021 427 3494, fax: 021 427 3092).
7 rooms.

Café Paradiso €€
16 Lancaster Quay, Western Road (tel: 021 427 7939).
*Vegetarians are certainly in paradise here, with gourmet treatment of the finest local produce (and you can buy the chefs' cookbook).
Tue–Sat 12.30–3pm, 6.30–10.30pm. Closed Christmas week.*

Gresham Metropole €€–€€€
MacCurtain Street (tel: 021 450 8122, fax: 021 450 6450)
113 rooms.

Imperial Hotel €€–€€€
South Mall (tel: 021 427 4040, fax: 021 427 5375).
Closed 24–27 Dec.
90 rooms.

Isaacs €–€€
48 MacCurtain Street (tel: 021 450 3805).
*Modern, understated cuisine incudes satisfying stews, pastas, grills and interesting salads.
Mon–Sat 10am–10.30pm, Sun 6.30–9pm.*

Lotamore House €€–€€€
Tivoli (tel: 021 482 2344, fax: 021 482 2219).
Closed 21 Dec–6 Jan.
18 rooms.

Rose Lodge €€
Mardyke Walk, off Western Road (tel: 021 427 2958, fax: 021 427 4087).
16 rooms.

Silver Springs Moran €€–€€€
Tivoli (tel: 021 450 7533, fax: 021 450 7641).
Closed 24–26 Dec.
109 rooms.

KINSALE, Co Cork

Actons €€€
Pier Road (tel: 021 477 2135, fax: 021 477 2231).
Closed 24–27 Dec.
76 rooms.
Elegant cuisine might include canon of lamb wrapped in a black pudding mousseline and herb pancake. Daily 7–9.45pm, also 12.30–3pm Sun. Closed Jan.

Ashgrove €€
Bandon Road (tel: 021 477 4127, fax: 021 477 4127).
Closed Dec–Jan.
5 rooms.

Blue Haven Hotel and Restaurant €€–€€€
3 Pearse Street (tel: 021 477 2209, fax: 021 477 4268).
17 rooms.
*Excellent seafood is available in the atmospheric bar or lovely restaurant, with wine from French vineyards that were started by Irish exiles.
Daily, bar: 12.15–3, 6.30–10; restaurant: 7–10pm.*

Chart House Luxury Accommodation €€–€€€
6 Denis Quay (tel: 021 477 4568, fax: 021 477 7907).
Closed Christmas.
3 rooms.

Fishy Fishy Café €€
Guardwell tel: 021 477 4453).
*Seafood café serving the freshest of fish in very interesting ways, such as John Dory with tomato and coriander salsa or tiger prawns with chick peas and bacon.
Daily noon–3.45pm.*

Friar's Lodge €€
5 Friars Street (tel: 086 289 5075).
18 rooms.

The Greyhound €
Market Square (tel: 021 477 2889).
Hearty pub food, including Irish stew, seafood pancakes and home-made soups.

Harbour Lodge €€–€€€
Scilly (tel: 021 477 2376, fax: 021 477 6275).
10 rooms.

Little Skillet €€
Main Street (tel: 021 477 4202).
*Lovely atmosphere and tasty Irish food, including stews and champ.
Daily 12.30–2.30pm, 6–10.30pm.*

Long Quay House €€
Long Quay (tel: 021 477 4563 or 477 3201, fax: 021 477 4563).
Closed 15 Nov–26 Dec.
7 rooms.

Old Bank House €€€
11 Pearse Street (tel: 021 477 4075, fax: 021 477 4296).
Closed 22–27 Dec.
17 rooms.

Old Presbytery €€
43 Cork Street (tel: 021 477 2027, fax: 021 477 2166).
Closed Dec–14 Feb.
6 rooms.

Rivermount House €€
Knocknabinny, Barrells Cross (tel: 021 477 8033, fax: 021 477 8225).
Closed Dec–Jan.
6 rooms.

Trident €€–€€€
Worlds End, on the waterfront, just beyond the pier (tel: 021 477 2301, fax: 021 477 4173).
Closed 24–26 Dec.
58 rooms.
Dishes with a modern edge are

created using the finest local ingredients (€€€).
Daily 7–9.30pm, also 1–2.30pm Sun.

Waterlands €
Cork Road (tel: 021 477 2318 or 087 276 7917, fax: 021 477 4873).
Closed Dec–Feb.
4 rooms.

The White House €€
Pearse Street, The Glen (tel: 021 477 2125, fax: 021 477 2045).
Closed 24–25 Dec.
10 rooms.

CLONAKILTY, Co Cork
An Garran Coir €
Rathbarry, Rosscarbery Coast Route (tel: 023 48236, fax: 023 48236).
5 rooms.

Desert House €
Coast Road (tel: 023 33331, fax: 023 33048).
5 rooms.

Duvane €–€€
Ballyduvane (1.2 miles/2km southwest on N71) (tel: 023 33129, fax: 023 33129).
Closed Nov–Mar.
4 rooms.

Kilkern House €–€€
Rathbarry (tel: 023 40643, fax: 023 40643)
5 rooms.

The Lodge and Spa at Inchdoney Island €€
Edge of village (tel: 023 33143, fax: 023 35229).
Closed 25–26 Dec.
67 rooms.

Springfield House €
Kilkern, Rathbarry, Castlefreke (off N71 Skibbereen road) (tel: 023 40622, fax: 023 40622).
Closed Dec.
4 rooms.

ROSS CARBERY, Co Cork
Celtic Ross €€
On N71, at the edge of the village (tel: 023 48722, fax: 023 48723).
Closed mid-Jan to mid-Apr.
66 rooms.

GOUGANE BARRA, Co Cork
Gougane Barra €€
Off N22 (tel: 026 47069, fax: 026 47226).
Closed mid-Oct to mid-Apr.
25 rooms.

MACROOM, Co Cork
Castle Hotel €€
Main Street, on N22 (tel: 026 41074, fax: 026 41505)
Closed 24–28 Dec.
60 rooms.
An occasional international influence creeps in here, on a menu that might include lamb with spring onion champ and roasted root vegetables, or a starter of duck leg confit with chilli dressing.
Daily noon–3, 6–9.30.

TOUR 9
BANTRY, Co Cork
Sea View House €€€
Ballylickey, 5 miles (8km) north on N71 (tel: 027 50073, fax: 027 51555).
Closed mid-Nov to mid-Mar.
25 rooms.
Traditional Irish cuisine might include warm scallop mousse and grilled sea bass. Freshly baked bread (try the courgette and walnut) is a highlight (€€).
Daily from 7pm, also Sunday lunch.

Westlodge €€€
On the outskirts of town overlooking the bay (tel: 027 50360, fax: 027 50438).
Closed 23–27 Dec.
90 rooms.

SKIBBEREEN, Co Cork
Baltimore Harbour €€€
Baltimore (tel: 028 20361, fax: 028 20466).
Closed Jan.
64 rooms.
The Clipper restaurant serves accomplished cuisine using the very best west Cork produce.
Daily 6.30–9.30pm (brasserie menu available during the day in the bar).

Casey's of Baltimore €€
Village centre (tel: 028 20197, fax: 028 20509).
Closed 20–27 Dec.
14 rooms.
Excellent seafood, served simply, comes direct from Baltimore's fishing fleet; the seafood chowder is legendary (€€€).
Daily 12.30–2.30, 6.30–9.

Eldon €€
Bridge Street (tel: 028 22000, fax: 028 22191).
Closed 24–27 Dec.
19 rooms.

Ilenroy House €
10 North Street (tel: 028 22751 or 22193, fax: 028 23228).
5 rooms.

SKULL, Co Cork
Adele's €–€€
Main Street (tel: 028 28459).
Lovely tearoom fare, plus a daily changing menu of first-rate seafood and pasta dishes.
Easter–Jun, Sep–Nov Wed–Sun 9.30am–6pm; Jul–Aug daily 9.30am–6pm. Closed Nov–Easter.

Rock Cottage €€
Barnatonicane (tel: 028 35538, fax: 028 35538).
3 rooms.

MIZEN HEAD, Co Cork
Carraig-Mor House €
Toormore Bay, Goleen (tel: 028 28410, fax: 028 28410).
Closed 24–26 Dec.
5 rooms.

Good Things Café €
Ahakista Road, Durrus (tel: 027 61426).
Unpretentious little bistro offering the best of local produce, including artisan cheeses, in creative dishes.
Wed–Mon 10.30am–5pm, 6.30–8.30pm.

Heron's Cove €
The Harbour, Goleen (tel: 028 35225, fax: 028 35422).
Closed Christmas and New Year.
5 rooms.
Casual restaurant specialising in seafood such as Dunmanus Bay scallops and an exceptional fisherman's broth (€€).
May–Oct daily noon–10pm.

TOUR 10
WATERFORD, Co Waterford
(See also Tour 15)
Arlington Lodge €€€
John's Hill (tel: 051 878584, fax: 051 878127).
Closed 24–27 Dec.
20 rooms.

Athenaeum House €€–€€€
Christendon, Ferrybank (tel: 051 833999, fax: 051 833977).
29 rooms.

Belmont House €
Belmont Road, Rosslare Road, Ferrybank (tel: 051 832174).
Closed Nov–Apr.
6 rooms.

¶¶ Bodega! €–€€
54 John Street (tel: 051 844177).
*Lively haunt of Waterfords 20-
somethings, with loud music and
excellent continental cuisine.
Mon–Fri noon–2.30pm, Mon–Sat
6–10pm (10.30 Sat).*

Bridge Hotel €€€
1 The Quay (tel: 051 877222,
fax: 051 877229).
*Closed Christmas and first 2 weeks
Jan.*
133 rooms.

Faithlegg House €€€
Faithlegg (tel: 051 382000,
fax: 051 382010).
82 rooms.

Granville €€€
The Quay (tel: 051 305555,
fax: 051 305566).
Closed 25–26 Dec.
100 rooms.

**Sion Hill House and
Gardens** €€–€€€
Sion Hill, Ferrybank (tel: 051
851558, fax: 051 851678).
Closed mid-Dec to early Jan.
4 rooms.

Tower €€–€€€
The Mall (tel: 051 875801,
fax: 051 870129).
Closed 24–28 Dec.
139 rooms.

¶¶ Waterford Castle €€€
The Island (tel: 051 878203,
fax: 051 879316).
19 rooms.
*Modern Irish cuisine, with a classi-
cal influence and strong emphasis on
seafood (€€€).
Daily 7–8.30pm, also
12.30–1.45pm Sat–Sun. Closed
Christmas, early Jan.*

¶¶ Wine Vault €–€€
High Street (tel: 051 853444).
*In a city famed throughout history
for its wine merchants, this restaurant matches wonderful bistro food
with great vintages.
Mon–Sat 12.30–2.30pm,
5.30–10.30pm.*

DUNMORE EAST, Co
Waterford
The Beach Guest House €€
Lower Village (tel: 051 383316,
fax: 051 383319).
Closed Nov–Feb.
7 rooms.

**¶¶ The Strand Seafood
Restaurant** €€
*Overlooking Waterford Harbour.
Intimate restaurant serving such
outstanding dishes as wild salmon
with green gooseberry sauce and
lemon sole stuffed with seafood
mousse.
Mar–Oct daily 6.30–10pm;
Nov–Dec and Feb Wed–Sun
6.30–10pm. Closed Jan.*

TRAMORE, Co Waterford
Cliff House €–€€
Cliff Road (tel: 051 381497 or
391296, fax: 051 381497).
Closed 20 Dec–Jan.
6 rooms.

¶¶ Coast €€
Upper Branch Road (tel: 051
393646).
*Trendy gourmet restaurant serving
modern international cuisine such as
chargrilled Asian chicken and pan-
fried Barbary duck with honey and
sherry sauce.
Tue–Sun 6.30–10.30pm, Sun
1–2.30pm, also Sun evenings
Jul–Aug. Closed 24 Dec–1 Jan.*

Glenorney €€
Newtown (tel: 051 381056,
fax: 051 381103).
Closed Christmas.
6 rooms.

Majestic €€
(tel: 051 381761, fax: 051
381766).
60 rooms.

DUNGARVAN, Co Waterford
An Bohreen €
Killineed West (tel: 051 291010,
fax: 051 291011).
Closed Nov–mid-Mar.
4 rooms.

Castle Country House €€
Millstreet, Cappagh (tel: 058
68049, fax: 058 58099).
Closed Dec–Feb.
5 rooms.

Gortnadiha House €–€€
Ring (tel: 058 46142, fax: 058
46444).
Closed Christmas and New Year.
3 rooms.

Lawlors €€–€€€
Town centre (tel: 058 41122 or
41056, fax: 058 41000).
Closed 25 Dec.
89 rooms.

Powersfield House €€
Ballinamuck West (tel: 058
45594, fax: 058 45550).
6 rooms.

Sliabh gCua Farmhouse €€
Touraneena, Ballinamult
(tel: 058 47120).
Closed Nov–Mar.
3 rooms.

¶¶ The Tannery €€
Quay Street (tel: 058 545420).
*Innovative chef Paul Flynn adds his
own special flair to traditional Irish
and European dishes.
Tue–Sun 12.30–2.30pm,
6.30–9.30pm. Closed Sat lunch,
Mon.*

CAPPOQUIN, Co Waterford
Richmond House €€–€€€
On Dungarvan road (tel: 058
54278, fax: 058 54988).
Closed 23 Dec–20 Jan.
9 rooms.

LISMORE, Co Waterford
(See also Tour 7).

CASHEL, Co Tipperary
(See also Tours 3 and 10))
Baileys of Cashel €€
Main Street (tel: 062 61937,
fax: 062 63957).
Closed 24–28 Dec.
9 rooms.

¶¶ Chez Hans €€
Moor Lane (tel: 062 61177).
*This restaurant in a former
Wesleyan chapel, is getting great
reviews for its menu of familiar
favourites, cooked to perfection.
Open Tue–Sat 6–10pm.*

Thornbrook House €
Dualla Road (tel: 062 62388,
fax: 062 61480).
Closed Nov–Mar.
5 rooms.

CLONMEL, Co Tipperary
**¶¶ Angela's Wholefood
Restaurant** €
14 Abbey Street (tel: 052 26899).
*Satisfying lunch menu, including
soups, salads, sandwiches and such
dishes as spicy Moroccan lamb stew;
great for breakfast too.
Mon–Fri 9am–5.30pm, Sat
noon–5pm.*

¶¶ Mr Bumbles €€
Richmond House, Kickham
Street (tel: 052 29188).
Bright, split-level bistro with a menu

of international dishes, including superb fish and Tipperary beef. Mon–Fri 5–9.30, Sat 6–10pm, also noon–2.30pm Thu, Fri and Sun.

🏨 ♟️ **Minella** €€€
South of river (tel: 052 22388, fax: 052 24381).
Closed 24–28 Dec.
70 rooms.
Traditional hotel-style menu using local produce (€€)
Daily 12.30–2.30, 6.30–9.30.

TOUR 11

ATHLONE, Co Westmeath

🏨 **Glasson Golf Hotel and Country Club** €€€
Glasson (tel: 090 648 5120, fax: 090 648 5444).
29 rooms.

🏨 ♟️ **Hodson Bay** €–€€€
Hodson Bay (tel: 090 644 2000, fax: 090 644 2020).
133 rooms.
Daily-changing menu might include turf-smoked chicken breast or Ballinstelligs Bay lobster (€€€).
Daily 12.30–2.30, 7–9.45.

♟️ **Left Bank Bistro** €–€€
Fry Place (tel: 090 649 4446).
The cuisines of Italy, France and Asia combine on a menu that ranges from Thai spiced chicken to classic beef fillet.
Tue–Sat 10am–9.30pm.

🏨 **Riverview House** €
Galway Road, Summerhill (tel: 090 649 4532, fax: 090 649 4532).
Closed 18 Dec–1 Mar.
4 rooms.

🏨 **Shelmalier House** €
Cartontroy, Retreat Road (tel: 090 647 2245, fax: 090 647 3190).
Closed 20 Dec–31 Jan.
7 rooms.

🏨 ♟️ **Wineport Lodge** €€€
Glasson (tel: 090 643 9010, fax: 090 648 5471).
Closed 24–26 Dec.
10 rooms.
Wholesome local produce, such as Lissadel oysters or carved rack of lamb, are served in generous portions and there's an excellent wine list (€€–€€€).
Daily 6–10pm.

MULLINGAR, Co Westmeath

🏨 **Bloomfield House** €€€
Belvedere (tel: 044 40894, fax: 044 43767).
111 rooms.

🏨 **Crookedwood House** €€
Crookedwood (tel: 044 72165, fax: 044 72166).
Closed Christmas.
8 rooms.

🏨 **Hilltop House** €
Delvin Road, Rathconnell (tel: 044 48958, fax: 044 48013).
Closed Nov–Feb.
5 rooms.

🏨 **Mullingar Park** €€€
Dublin Road (tel: 044 44446, fax: 044 35937).
Closed 24–25 Dec.
95 rooms.

BIRR, Co Offaly

🏨 **Country Arms** €€–€€€
Near the church (tel: 0509 20791, fax: 0509 21234).
24 rooms.

TOUR 12

DROGHEDA, Co Louth

🏨 **Boyne Valley Hotel & Country Club** €€
Stameen, Dublin road. (tel: 041 983 7737, fax: 041 983 9188).
73 rooms.

MONASTERBOICE, Co Louth

🏨 **Tullyesker Country House** €
Tullyesker (tel: 041 983 0430).
Closed Dec–Jan.
5 rooms.

SLANE, Co Meath

🏨 **Conyngham Arms** €€
Village Centre (tel: 041 988 4444, fax: 041 982 4205).
16 rooms.

NAVAN, Co Meath

🏨 **Ardboyne** €€
Dublin Road (tel: 046 902 3119, fax: 046 902 2355).
Closed 24–26 Dec.
5 rooms.

♟️ **Hudson's Bistro** €€
Railway Street (tel: 046 29231).
Bright and cheerful bistro with an international menu, including Greek kebabs and Thai curry.
Mon–Sat 6–11pm, Sun 6–9pm.

🏨 **Killyon** €
Dublin Road (tel: 046 907 1224, fax: 046 907 2766).
Closed 24–26 Dec.
6 rooms.

🏨 **Newgrange** €€
Bridge Street (tel: 046 907 4100, fax: 046 907 3977).
Closed 25 Dec.
62 rooms.

TOUR 13

DUBLIN, Co Dublin

🏨 **Abberley Court** €
Belgard Road, Tallaght (south of city at junction of N81 Tallaght by-pass and Belgard Road) (tel: 01 459 6000, fax: 01 462 1000).
Closed 25 Dec.
40 rooms.

🏨 **Aberdeen Lodge** €€
53 Park Avenue, Ballsbridge, Dublin 4 (tel: 01 283 8155, fax: 01 283 7877)
16 rooms.

🏨 **Abrae Court** €€
9 Zion Road, Rathgar (tel: 01 492 2242, fax: 01 492 3944).
Closed Christmas.
14 rooms.

🏨 **Berkley Court** €€€
Lansdowne Road, Dublin 4 (tel: 01 665 3200, fax: 01 661 7238).
186 rooms.

🏨 **Bewleys Hotel Ballsbridge** €€
Merrion Road, Ballsbridge, Dublin 4 (tel: 01 668 1111, fax: 01 668 1999).
Closed 24–26 Dec.
220 rooms.

🏨 **Bewleys Hotel Leopardstown** €€
Central Park, Leopardstown, Dublin 18 (tel: 01 293 5000, fax: 021 293 5099).
306 rooms.

🏨 **Bewleys Hotel Newlands** €€
Newlands Cross, Naas Road On N7, off M50 junction 9 (tel: 01 464 0140, fax: 01 464 0900).
Closed 24–26 Dec.
258 rooms.

🏨 **Browne's Townhouse and Brasserie** €€€
22 St Stephen's Green, Dublin 2 (tel: 01 638 3939, fax: 01 638 3900).
Closed 24 Dec–3 Jan.
11 rooms.

🏨 **Burlington** €€€
Upper Leeson Street, Dublin 4 (tel: 01 660 5222, fax: 01 660 8496).
500 rooms.

Buswells €–€€
23–25 Molesworth Street,
Dublin 2 (tel: 01 614 6500,
fax: 01 676 2090).
Closed 25–26 Dec.
69 rooms.

Camden Court €€
Lower Camden Street, Dublin 2
(tel: 01 475 9666, fax: 01 475
9677).
Closed Christmas/New Year.
246 rooms.

Carnegie Court €€
North Street, Swords, off N1
north of Dublin Airport (tel: 01
840 4384, fax: 01 840 4505),
Closed 25–26 Dec.
36 rooms.

Cassidys €€–€€€
Cavendish Row, O'Connell
Street Upper, Dublin 1 (tel: 01
878 0555, fax: 01 878 0687).
Closed 24–26 Dec.
88 rooms.

Charleville Lodge Guest House €€
268–272 North Circular Road,
Phibsborough, Dublin 7 (tel: 01
838 6633, fax: 01 838 5854).
Closed 21–26 Dec.
30 rooms.

The Clarence €€€
6–8 Wellington Quay, Dublin 2
(tel: 01 407 0800, fax: 01 407
0820).
Closed 24–27 Dec.
50 rooms.
*Modern European cooking, using
mostly organic ingredients.*
(€€–€€€).
*Daily 6.30–10.30pm, Sun–Fri
12.30–2.30pm.*

Clarion Hotel Dublin IFSC €€€
North Wall Quay, Dublin 1
(tel: 01 433 8800).
*Modern Irish theme with interesting
flavour combinations.*
*Daily 6–midnight, Mon–Fri
noon–2.30pm.*

Dobbins Wine Bistro €–€€
15 Stephen's Lane, off Upper
Mount Street, Dublin 2 (tel: 01
676 4679).
*Foodies' favourite serving innova-
tive Continental cuisine.*
*Mon–Fri 12.30–2.30pm, Tue–Sat
7.30–10.30pm.*

Eliza Lodge €€€
23–24 Wellington Quay, Dublin
2 (tel: 01 671 8044, fax: 01 671
8362).

Closed 23 Dec–2 Jan.
18 rooms.

Finnstown Country House €€€
Newcastle Road, Lucan (west of
the city off the N4) (tel: 01 601
0700).
*Victorian dining room with fixed
price and à la carte menus of international food.*
Mon–Sat 12.30–2.30, 7.30–9.30.

Fitzwilliam Hotel €€€
St Stephen's Green, Dublin 2
(tel: 01 478 7000, fax: 01 676
7488).
12 rooms.
*Thornton's, the hotel's restaurant,
overlooks the green and produces
contemporary dishes with intense
flavours (€€€).*
Tue–Sat 12.30–1.45pm, 7–10pm.

Glenorga €€
64 Merrion Road, Ballsbridge,
Dublin 4 (tel: 01 668 3661,
fax: 01 668 3698).
Closed 21 Dec–12 Jan.
13 rooms.

Govinda's €
4 Aungier Street, Dublin 2
(tel: 01 475 0309).
*Vegetarian restaurant serving gener-
ous and satisfying dishes with
European and Asian influences.*
Mon–Sun 9pm.

Gresham €€€
O'Connell Street, Dublin 1 (tel:
01 874 6881, fax: 01 878 7175).
289 rooms.

Herbert Park Hotel €€€
Ballsbridge, Dublin 4 (next to
the RDS) (tel: 01 667 2200,
fax: 01 667 2595).
153 rooms.

Irish Film Centre Café Bar €
Temple Bar, Dublin 2
*Trendy place for an inexpensive
meal, with Irish and international
cuisine on the menu. Live music or
comedy at weekends.*
*Daily 12.30–3, 6–9 (lunch from
1pm Sat–Sun).*

Jacob's Ladder €€
4 Nassau Street, Dublin 2
(tel: 01 670 3865).
*Punchy modern treatment of tradi-
tional Irish dishes with an emphasis
on healthy eating. Possibly the best
colcannon in Ireland.*
*Tue–Sat 12.30–2.30pm, Tue–Fri
6–10pm, Sat 7–10pm. Closed 24
Dec–4 Jan.*

Jurys Green Isle €€
Naas Road (6 miles/10km southwest) (tel: 01 459 3406, fax: 01
459 2178).
90 rooms.

Jurys Hotel and Towers €€
Pembroke Road, Ballsbridge,
Dublin 4 (tel: 01 660 5000,
fax: 01 667 5276).
303 rooms.

Jurys Montrose €€
Stillorgan Road, Dublin 4 (tel:
01 269 3311, fax: 01 269 1164).
178 rooms.

Jurys Tara Hotel €€
Merrion Road, Dublin 4 (tel: 01
269 4666, fax: 01 269 1027).
113 rooms.

Longfield's €
Fitzwilliam Street Lower,
Dublin 2 (tel: 01 676 1367,
fax: 01 676 1542).
26 rooms.

Lord Edward €€
23 Christ Church Place, Dublin
8 (tel: 01 454 2420).
*A lengthy menu of fresh fish and
shellfish dishes.*
*Mon–Fri noon–2.30pm, Mon–Sat
6–10.30pm. Closed 24 Dec–3 Jan.*

Lyndon €€
26 Gardiner Place, Dublin 1 (tel:
01 878 6950, fax: 01 878 7420).
9 rooms.

McEniff Grand Canal Hotel €€–€€€
Grand Canal Street, Dublin 4
(tel: 01 646 1000, fax: 01 645
1001).
142 rooms.

McEniff Skylon €€
Upper Drumcondra Road,
Dublin 9 (on M1 between
airport and city) (tel: 01 837
9121, fax: 01 837 2778).
88 rooms.

Marine €€€
Sutton Cross, Dublin 13 (tel: 01
839 0000, fax: 01 839 0442).
Closed 25–27 Dec.
48 rooms.

Mercer €€€
Lower Mercer Street, Dublin 2
(tel: 01 478 2179, fax: 01 478
0328).
Closed 24–26 Dec.
41 rooms.

Merrion Hotel €€€
Upper Merrion Street, Dublin 2
(tel: 01 603 0600, fax: 01 603
0700).
145 rooms.

🏨 The Morrison €€€
Lower Ormond Quay, Dublin 1
(tel: 01 887 2400, fax: 01 878 3185).
Closed Christmas.
94 rooms.

🏨 Mount Herbert €€€
Herbert Road, Lansdowne Road, Dublin 4 (tel: 01 668 4321, fax: 01 660 7077).
Closed 21–27 Dec.
185 rooms.

🏨 Ormond Quay €€–€€€
7–11 Upper Ormond Quay, Dublin 1 (tel: 01 872 1811, fax: 01 872 1362).
Closed 24–25 Dec.
62 rooms.

🏨 Plaza Hotel €€
Belgard Road, Tallaght, Dublin 24 (6 miles/10km south, at end of M50) (tel: 01 462 4200, fax: 01 462 4600).
Closed 24–30 Dec.
122 rooms.

🏨 Red Cow Morans €€–€€€
Red Cow Complex, Naas Road, Dublin 22 (tel: 01 459 3650, fax: 01 459 1588).
Closed 24–26 Dec.
123 rooms.

🍽️ Restaurant Patrick Gilbaud €€€
21 Upper Merrion Street, Dublin 2 (tel: 01 676 4192).
Ireland's finest restaurant. Expect plenty of flair and innovation in the French cuisine here.
Open Tue–Sat 12.30–2.45, 7–10.45.

🍽️ Restaurant 23 at The Gresham Hotel €€€
O'Connell Street, Dublin 1 (tel: 01 817 6116 or 874 6881.
Traditional fare with a modern touch.
Mon–Sat 5.30–10.30. Closed Sun, Bank Hols, 2 weeks at Christmas.

🏨 Royal Dublin €€–€€€
O'Connell Street, Dublin 1 (tel: 01 873 3666, fax: 01 873 3120).
Closed 24–25 Dec.
117 rooms.

🏨 The Shelbourne €€€
27 St Stephen's Green, Dublin 2 (tel: 01 663 4500, fax: 01 661 6006).
190 rooms.

🏨 Stillorgan Park €€–€€€
Stillorgan Road, Dublin 4 (tel: 01 288 1621, fax: 01 283 1610).
125 rooms.

🏨 Temple Bar €€–€€€
Fleet Street, Temple Bar, Dublin 2 (tel: 01 677 3333, fax: 01 677 3088).
Closed 23–25 Dec.
129 rooms.

🍽️ Yamamori Noodles €–€€
71–72 South Great George's Street, Dublin 2 (tel: 01 475 5001).
Lively Japanese restaurant with a good choice of excellent and authentic dishes.
Sun–Wed 12.30–11pm, Thu–Sat 12.30–11.30pm.

KILLINEY, Co Dublin
🏨 Fitzpatrick Castle €€€
On Killiney Hill (tel: 01 230 5400, fax: 01 230 5430).
113 rooms.

BRAY, Co Wicklow
🏨 Royal €€€
Main Street (tel: 01 286 2935, fax: 01 286 7373).
91 rooms.

🍽️ Tree of Idleness €€
Seafront (tel: 01 286 3498)
Greek Cypriot restaurant with all the favourites on the menu, including moussaka, taramasalata and roast sucking pig.
Tue–Sun 7.30–11pm.

🏨 🍽️ Woodville €
Ballywaltrim Lane (tel: 01 286 3103, fax: 01 286 3103).
Closed 15 Dec– 7 Jan.
4 rooms.

ROUNDWOOD, Co Wicklow
🍽️ Roundwood Inn €€
Main Street (R755) (tel: 01 281 8107)
Lovely old coaching inn serving superb food, including Irish stew and fresh local lobster and salmon.
Wed–Fri 7–9.30pm, Sat–Sun 1–2.30pm.

🏨 Wicklow Way Lodge €€
Old Bridge (tel: 01 281 8489, fax: 01 281 8189).
Closed Dec–Jan.
5 rooms.

GLENDALOUGH, Co Wicklow
🏨 Glendalough €€
Edge of village (tel: 0404 45135, fax: 0404 45142).
Closed Dec–Jan.
44 rooms.

BLESSINGTON, Co Wicklow
🏨 Downshire House Hotel €€
On N81 (tel: 045 865199, fax: 045 865335).
Closed 22 Dec–6 Jan.
14 rooms.

TOUR 14
KILKENNY, Co Kilkenny
🏨 Alcantra €–€€
Maidenhill, Kells Road (tel: 056 776 1058, fax: 056 776 1058).
Closed 21–31 Dec.
4 rooms.

🏨 Butler House €€–€€€
Patrick Street (tel: 056 776 5707, fax: 056 776 5626).
Closed 24–29 Dec.
13 rooms.

🍽️ Café Sol €–€€
6 William Street (tel: 056 776 4987.
Brightly decorated café with basic breakfast and lunch menus, and more interesting Southern American and Mediterranean dishes at dinner.
Mon–Fri 10–9, Sat 10–5.

🍽️ Kilkenny Design Restaurant €
The Parade (tel: 056 772 2118).
Classy cafeteria with a good range of salads, soups, platters and pastries.
Mon–Sat 9–5, also Sun 10–5 May–Dec.

🏨 🍽️ Kilkenny River Court Hotel €€–€€€
The Bridge, John Street (tel: 056 772 3388, fax: 056 772 3389).
Closed 24–26 Dec.
40 rooms.
A Mediterranean twist is given to the modern cooking here, producing such dishes as wild mallard with a red wine reduction.

🏨 Lacken House €€–€€€
Dublin Road (tel: 056 776 1085, fax: 056 776 2435).
Closed 24–26 Dec.
11 rooms.

🏨 Langtons €€–€€€
69 John Street (tel: 056 776 5133, fax: 056 776 3693).
Closed Good Fri, 25 Dec.
14 rooms.

🏨 Newpark €€
(tel: 056 776 0500, fax: 056 776 0555).
111 rooms.

🏨 Shillogher House €–€€
Callan Road (tel: 056 776 3249 or 776 4865, fax: 056 776 4865).
6 rooms.

¶¶ Zuni €€
26 Patrick Street (tel: 056 772 3999).
This restaurant offers international specialities, such as tempura king prawns with sesame toast and Moroccan lamb.
Daily 6–9.30pm (closes at 9pm Sun).

THOMASTOWN, Co Kilkenny
⌂ Abbey House €–€€
Jerpoint Abbey (tel: 056 772 4166, fax: 056 772 4192).
Closed 31–30 Dec.
6 rooms.
⌂ Carrickmourne House €–€€
New Ross Road (tel: 056 772 4124, fax: 056 772 4124).
5 rooms.
⌂ ¶¶ Mount Juliet Conrad €€€
On N9 (tel: 056 777 3000, fax: 056 777 3019).
32 rooms.
Fresh vegetables and herbs from the kitchen garden add to the imaginative European dishes.
Daily 7–9.45pm.
¶¶ Water Garden €
On the Kilkenny road (tel: 056 772 4690).
Nice little community/charity tearoom serving home baked goodies, plus meals made with local organic produce and cheese.
Tue–Fri 10am–5pm, Sun 12.30–5pm. Closed Sun Christmas–Easter.

NEW ROSS, Co Wexford
⌂ Greenpark €
Creakan Lower (tel: 051 421028, fax: 051 421028).
Closed Dec–Feb.
3 rooms.
⌂ Oakwood House €
Ring Road, Mountgarrett (tel: 051 425494, fax: 051 425494).
Closed Nov–Mar.
4 rooms.

CARLOW, Co Carlow
⌂ Dolmen €€€
Kilkenny Road (tel: 059 914 2002, fax: 059 914 2375).
490 rooms.
⌂ Seven Oaks €€
Athy Road (tel: 059 913 1308, fax: 059 913 2155),
Closed 25–26 Dec.
59 rooms.

PORTLAOISE, Co Laois
⌂ The Heritage Hotel €€€
(tel: 0502 78588, fax: 0502 78577).
110 rooms.
⌂ Ivyleigh House €€
Bank Place, Church Street (tel: 0502 22081, fax: 0502 63343).
Closed 20 Dec–4 Jan.
6 rooms.
⌂ O'Sullivan €€
8 Kelly Ville Park (tel: 0502 22774).
6 rooms.

ABBEYLEIX, Co Laois
⌂ Abbeyleix Manor Hotel €€
South on N8 (tel: 0502 30111, fax: 0502 30220).
Closed 25–26 Dec.
23 rooms.

THURLES, Co Tipperary
⌂ Inch House Country House €€
2.5 miles (4km) from Thurles on the Nenagh road (tel: 0504 51348 or 51251, fax: 0504 51754).
5 rooms.

CASHEL, Co Tipperary
(See also Tours 3 and 10)
⌂ Aulber House €€
Deerpark ROI (tel: 062 63713, fax: 062 63715).
Closed 23–27 Dec.
12 rooms.
⌂ Ashmore House €–€€
John Street (tel: 062 61286, fax: 062 62789).
5 rooms.

TOUR 15
WEXFORD, Co Wexford
¶¶ Bohemian Girl €
2 Selskar Street (tel: 053 24419).
Great pub lunches include fresh oysters, homemade soups, sandwiches and pates.
Daily 12.30–3pm.
⌂ Clonard House €–€€
Clonard Great (tel: 053 43141, fax: 053 43141).
Closed Nov–Feb.
9 rooms.
⌂ Darral House €€
Spawell Road (tel: 053 24264, faxc: 053 24284).
Closed 20 Dec–1 Jan.
4 rooms.
⌂ ¶¶ Ferrycarrig €€–€€€
Ferrycarrig Bridge (tel: 053

20999, fax: 053 20982).
102 rooms.
Classically inspired cuisine, with eight choices per course (€€€).
Daily 7–10.15pm. Closed some days; call for information.
¶¶ Forde's Restaurant €€
The Crescent (tel: 053 23832).
Elegant waterfront bistro with a long menu of excellent, imaginative dishes.
Daily 6–10.30pm.
⌂ Killiane Castle €€
Drinagh (tel: 053 58885, fax: 053 58885).
Closed Dec–Feb.
8 rooms.
¶¶ Mange2 €€
100 South Main Street (tel: 053 24419).
Essentially French cuisine, but with other influences here and there.
Daily 6–10.30pm, also 012.30–2.30pm Tue–Fri and Sun.
⌂ Maple Lodge €–€€
Castlebridge (tel: 053 59195, fax: 053 59195).
Closed mid-Nov to mid-Mar.
4 rooms.
⌂ Mount Auburn €–€€
1 Auburn Terrace, Redmond Road (tel: 053 24609, fax: 053 24609).
Closed 20–28 Dec.
6 rooms.
⌂ O'Briens Auburn House €–€€
2 Auburn Terrace, Redmond Road (tel: 053 23605, fax: 053 42725).
Closed 18 Dec–2 Jan.
5 rooms.
⌂ Rathaspeck Manor €
Rathaspeck (tel: 053 42661).
Closed 8 Nov–Jun.
6 rooms.
⌂ River Bank House Hotel €€–€€€
By Wexford Bridge on R741 (tel: 053 23611, fax: 053 23342).
Closed 24–25 Dec.
23 rooms.
⌂ Slaney Manor €€
Ferrycarrig (tel: 053 20051 or 20144, fax: 053 20510).
Closed Christmas week.
8 rooms.
⌂ Talbot €€–€€€
Trinity Street (tel: 053 22566, fax: 053 23377).
Closed 24–25 Dec.
98 rooms.

White's €
Georges Street (tel: 053 22311,
fax: 053 45000).
76 rooms. (Reopening 2006 after
redevelopment.)

**¶¶¶ Whitford House Hotel
Health and Leisure Club €€€**
New Line Road (tel: 053 43444,
fax: 053 46399).
36 rooms.
*French and other European dishes
are produced with excellent Wexford
produce (€€€).*
*Daily 7–9pm, also 12.30–3pm Sun.
Closed 23 Dec–2 Jan.*

COURTOWN HARBOUR,
Co Wexford
Bay View €€
Town centre (tel: 055 25307,
fax: 055 25576).
Closed 30 Nov–14 Mar.
17 rooms.

Courtown €€
(tel: 055 25210, fax: 055 25304)
Closed mid-Nov to early March.
21 rooms.

GOREY, Co Wexford
¶¶¶ Ashdown Park €€
The Coach Road (tel: 055 80500,
fax: 055 80777).
Closed 24–25 Dec.
60 rooms.
*Modern British cuisine, with
Mediterranean accents, featuring
local fish and game in season (€€).*
*Daily 6.30–9.30pm, also
12.30–2.30pm Sun.*

Hillside House €–€€
Tubberduff (tel: 055 21726 or
22036, fax: 055 22567).
Closed 20–28 Dec.
6 rooms.

Marlfield House Hotel €€€
(tel: 055 21124).
*Elegant dining in Regency mansion,
with daily changing menu of classical Mediterranean cuisine.*
Daily 7–9pm, also 12.30–1.45 Sun.

**Woodlands Country House
€€**
Killinierin (tel: 0402 37125 or
37133, fax: 0402 37133).
Closed Sep–May.
60 rooms.

ENNISCORTHY, Co Wexford
Ballinkeele House €€–€€€
Ballymurn (tel: 053 38105,
fax: 053 38468).
5 rooms.

Lemongrove House €–€€
Blackstoops (tel: 054 36115,
fax: 054 36115).
Closed 20–31 Dec.
9 rooms.

Riverside Park €€
The Promenade (tel: 054 37800,
fax: 054 37900).
60 rooms.

Treacys €€€
Templeshannon (tel: 054 37789,
fax: 054 37733).
Closed 23–25 Dec.
59 rooms.

NEW ROSS, Co Wexford
(See also Tour 14)
Cedar Lodge Hotel €€–€€€
Carrigbyrne, Newbawn (tel: 051
428386, fax: 051 428222).
Closed 21 Dec–1 Jan.
28 rooms.

WATERFORD, Co Waterford
(See also Tour 10)
Brown's Town House €€
29 South Parade (tel: 051
870594, fax: 051 871923).
Closed 20 Dec–29 Jan.
6 rooms.

**Diamond Hill Country
House €–€€**
Diamond Hill, Slieverue (tel:
051 832855, fax: 051 832254).
Closed 22–27 Dec.
17 rooms.

¶¶¶ Dooley's €€–€€€
30 The Quay (tel: 051 873531,
fax: 051 870262).
Closed 25–27 Dec.
113 rooms.
*Broadly international menu might
include cod fillet wrapped in
cabbage leaves, with carrot and
cardamom purée (€€€).*
*Daily 6–9.30pm, also 12.30–3pm
Sun.*

**Foxmount Country House
€€**
Passage East Road, Dunmore
Road (tel: 051 874308, fax: 051
854906).
Closed early Nov–early Mar.
5 rooms.

Ivory's Hotel €€–€€€
Tramore Road (tel: 051 358888,
fax: 051 358899).
Closed 24–28 Dec.
40 rooms.

McEniff Ard Ri Hotel €€
Ferrybank (tel: 051 832111, fax:
051 832863). *Closed 24–27 Dec.*
98 rooms.

Waterford Manor €€
Killotteran, Butlerstown (tel: 051
377814, fax: 051 354545).
21 rooms.

BALLYHACK, Co Wexford
Marsh Mere Lodge €
Near Ballyhack ferry (tel: 051
389186).
4 rooms.

KILMORE QUAY, Co Wexford
Quay House €€
On main street (tel: 053 29988,
fax: 053 29808).
8 rooms.

ROSSLARE, Co Wexford
Churchtown House €€
On Rosslare–Rosslare Harbour
link road (tel: 053 32555, fax: 053
32577).
Closed Nov–Feb.
12 rooms.

Crosbie Cedars €€
Rosslare village (tel: 053 32124,
fax: 053 32243).
Closed 24–25 Dec.
34 rooms.

Euro Lodge €
(tel: 053 35118 or 33994, fax: 053
35120).
Closed Nov–Mar.
38 rooms.

¶¶¶ Kelly's Resort €
On Wexford road (tel: 053 32114,
fax: 053 32222).
Closed mid-Dec to late Feb.
99 rooms.
*Smart, intimate restaurant with
daily changing menu of steaks,
seafood and more challenging
conceptions. Local produce is
handled with panache (€€€).*
Daily 1–1.30, 7.30–9.30.

Kilrane House €
Kilrane village (tel: 053 33135,
fax 053 33739).
Closed 25–28 Dec.
5 rooms.

The Light House €
Main Road (tgel: 053 33214,
fax: 053 33214).
Closed Oct–Feb.
4 rooms.

**Mount Pleasant Country
House €€**
Mount Pleasant (tel: 053 35631,
fax: 053 35631).
4 rooms.

Oldcourt House €
Off N11 at St Patrick's Church
(tel: 053 33895 or 086 374 2568).
Closed Dec–Feb.
6 rooms.

TOUR 16
SLIGO, Co Sligo
Aisling €
Cairns Hill (tel/fax: 071 916
0704).
Closed 24–26 Dec.
5 rooms.

Austie's/The Elsinore €–€€
Rosses Point Road, Rosses Point
(4 miles/6.5km northwest)
(tel: 071 917 7111).
*Nautical-style pub restaurant over-
looking Sligo Bay, with substantial
pub food featuring local seafood,
steaks and curry.*
*Daily 5.30–9.30pm, also
12.30–3.30pm Sun.*

Chestnut Lawn €
Cummeen, Strandhill Road
(tel: 071 916 2781, fax: 071 916
2781).
Closed 21 Dec–21 Jan.
3 rooms.

Crazy Jane's €
Rockwood Parade (tel: 071 914
1976).
*All-day breakfasts, pasta dishes,
quiches, chicken supreme, snacks in a
waterfront location.*
*Mon–Sat 9am–6pm (to 9pm
Jun–Aug).*

Sligo Park Hotel €€
Pearse Road (tel: 071 916 0291,
fax: 071 916 9556).
138 rooms.

Tower €€
Quay Street (tel: 071 914 4000,
fax: 071 914 6888).
Closed 24–28 Dec.
58 rooms.

The Wunding Stair €
Hyde Bridge House (tel: 071 914
1244).
*Simple, healthy self-service food –
organic salads, additive free sandwiches, homemade soups – in a
second-hand/antiquarian bookshop.*
Mon–Sat 10am–6pm.

LISSADELL, Co Sligo
Rowanville Lodge €
1 mile (1.5km) north of Grange
on N15 (tel: 071 916 3958).
Closed Nov–Apr.
3 rooms.

BUNDORAN, Co Sligo
Dùn Na Si €
Bundoran Road, Ballyshannon
(7 miles/11km northeast on
N15) (tel: 071 985 2322).
7 rooms.

TOUR 17
CARRICK-ON-SHANNON,
Co Leitrim
Caldra House €€
Caldragh (1.5 miles/2.5km north
off R280) (tel: 071 962 3040,
fax: 071 962 3040).
3 rooms.

The Landmark Hotel €€€
(tel: 071 962 2222, fax: 071 962
2233).
Closed 24–25 Dec.
50 rooms.

LONGFORD, Co Longford
**Longford Country House-
Cuminskeys €–€€**
Ennybegs (tel: 043 23320,
fax: 043 23516).
6 rooms.

ROSSCOMMON, Co
Roscommon
Gleesons Townhouse €
Market Square (tel: 090 662
6954, fax: 090 662 7425).
19 rooms.

TOUR 18
WESTPORT, Co Mayo
Atlantic Coast Hotel €€
The Quay (tel: 098 29000,
fax: 089 29111).
Closed 23–27 Dec.
85 rooms.
*Modern international cuisine imight
include pan-roasted five-spice duck
or black pudding stuffed guinea fowl
supreme (€€€).*
Daily 6.30–9.15pm.

Bella Vita €
High Street (tel: 098 29771).
*Cosy, friendly Italian wine
bar/restaurant with great antipasti.*
Tue–Sun 6–10pm.

Bertra House €
Thornhill, Murrisk (southwest
on R335 Louisburgh road)
(tel: 098 64833, fax: 098 64969).
5 rooms.

Carrabaun House €
Carrabaun, Leenane Road
(tel: 098 26196, fax: 098 28466).
Closed 16–31 Dec.
6 rooms.

**Hotel Westport
Conference and Leisure
Centre €€€**
Newport Road (tel: 098 25122,
fax: 098 26739).
129 rooms.

Knockranny Lodge €€€
Knockranny (tel: 098 28595,
fax: 098 28805).
Closed Dec–Jan.
16 rooms.

Lemon Peel €–€€
The Octagon (tel: 098 26929).
*Smart bistro serving tasty modern
Irish cuisine with some international
elements (Cajun crusted salmon;
pork in black bean sauce on Chinese
noodles).*
Tue–Sun 5–11pm.

Linden Hall €
Altamount Street (tel: 098
27005).
Closed 21 Dec–9 Jan.
4 rooms.

**The Olde Railway
€€–€€€**
The Mall (tel: 098 25166 or
25606, fax: 098 25090).
24 rooms.
*Simple but excellent food, showing
classic and traditional Irish roots.
Fresh local lobster is a speciality
(€€€).*
Daily 6.30–9.30pm.

Quay Cottage €€
The Quay (tel: 098 26412).
*Fresh, succulent fish, including wild
local salmon, plus steaks and other
daily specials. Daily 6–10pm.*
Closed Sun & Mon Nov–Apr.

Seabreeze €
Kilsallagh (southwest on R335
Louisburgh road) (tel: 098
66548).
3 rooms.

The Wyatt €€
The Octagon (tel: 098 25027).
Closed 25–26 Dec.
53 rooms.

ACHILL ISLAND, Co Mayo
Achill Cliff House €–€€
Keel (tel: 098 43400, fax: 098
43007).
Closed 23–26 Dec.
10 rooms.

Fincorry House €
Breanascill Bay, Atlantic Drive
(tel: 098 45755 or 086 304 8039,
fax: 098 45755).
Closed Nov–Feb.
6 rooms.

🏠 **Gray's** €€
Dugort (tel: 98 43244 or 43315).
Closed 25 Dec–1 Jan.
5 rooms.

🏠 **Lavelles Seaside House** €
Dooega (tel: 098 45116 or 01 282 8142).
Closed 2 Nov to mid-Mar.
14 rooms.

BALLINA Co Mayo
🏠 🍴 **Teach Iorrais** €€
Creesala (tel: 097 86888, fax: 097 86855).
31 rooms.
Modern European dishes, including pan-fried breast of duck with vanilla mash. Try the wonderful parsnip ice cream (€€€).
Daily 7–10pm.

KNOCK, Co Mayo
🏠 **Belmont** €€
On N17 Galway road (tel: 094 938 8122, fax: 094 938 8532).
Closed 25–26 Dec.
63 rooms.

🏠 **Knock House Hotel** €€
Ballyhaunis Road (tel: 094 938 8088, fax: 094 938 8044).
68 rooms.

TOUR 19
GALWAY, Co Galway
🏠 **Almara House** €–€€
2 Merlin Gate, Merlin Park, Dublin Road (tel: 091 755345 or 086 245 1220, fax: 091 771585).
Closed 20–30 Dec.
4 rooms.

🏠 **Ardawn House** €–€€
31 College Road (tel: 091 568833 or 564551, fax: 091 563454).
Closed 21–26 Dec.
8 rooms.

🏠 **Ardilaun Conference and Leisure Centre** €€€
Taylor's Hill (tel: 091 521433, fax: 091 521546).
Closed 22–27 Dec.
89 rooms.

🏠 **Atlantic Heights** €–€€
2 Cashelmara, Knocknacarra Cross, Salthill (tel: 091 529466 or 528830, fax: 091 529466).
Closed Nov–Mar.
6 rooms.

🏠 **Brennans Yard** €€–€€€
Lower Merchants Road (tel: 091 568166, fax: 091 568262).
Closed 21–28 Dec.
45 rooms.

🍴 **The Cobblestone** €
Kirwan's Lane (tel: 091 567227).
Excellent vegetarian dishes, such as 'beanie shepherd's pie' or vegetable-and-walnut bake, plus some meat and fish dishes, and great baked goods.
Daily 9am–7pm.

🏠 **Corrib Haven Guest House** €
107 Upper Newcastle (tel: 091 524171, fax: 091 582414).
Closed mid-Dec to mid-Jan.
9 rooms.

🏠 **Corrib Haven Guest House** €
107 Upper Newcastle (tel: 091 524171, fax: 091 582414).
Closed mid-Dec to mid-Jan.
9 rooms.

🏠 **The Four Seasons** €
23 College Road (tel: 091 564078, fax: 091 569765).
5 rooms.

🏠 🍴 **Galway Bay Hotel Conference and Leisure Centre** €€€
The Promenade, Salthill (tel: 091 520520, fax: 091 520530).
153 rooms.
Fresh fish majors on the modern French menu, and lobster is the signature dish (€€€).
Daily 6.30–9.30pm, also 12.30–2.30pm Sun.

🏠 **Glenlo Abbey Hotel** €€€
Bushypark (tel: 091 526666, fax: 091 527800).
46 rooms.

🏠 **The Harbour** €€–€€€
The Harbour (tel: 091 569466, fax: 091 569455).
Closed 23–27 Dec.
96 rooms.

🏠 **Jurys Galway Inn** €€
Quay Street (tel: 091 566444, fax: 091 568415).
Closed 24–26 Dec.
128 rooms.

🏠 **Killeen House** €€–€€€
Killeen, Bushypark (on N59 towards Moycullen) (tel: 091 524179, fax: 091 528065).
Closed 23–28 Dec.
6 rooms.

🍴 **Kirwan's Lane** €€
Kirwan's Lane (tel: 091 568266).
One of Galway's best restaurants, offering a continental menu, including a superb mille-feuille of fresh crab and such meat dishes as stuffed guinea fowl.

Daily 12.30–2.30, 6–10.30. Closed Sun Sep–Jun.

🏠 **Lochlurgain** €€–€€€
22 Monksfield, Upper Salthill (tel: 091 529595, fax: 091 522399).
Closed 26 Oct–13 Mar.
13 rooms.

🏠 **Marian Lodge** €–€€
Knocknacarra Road, Salthill Upper (tel: 091 521678, fax: 091 528103).
Closed 23–28 Dec.
6 rooms.

🏠 **Menlo Park Hotel** €€€
Terryland (tel: 091 761122, fax: 091 761222).
Closed 24–25 Dec.
64 rooms.

🍴 **Nimmo's** €–€€
Long Walk, Spanish Arch (tel: 091 561114).
Trendy wine bar with seasonally changing menu, strong on seafood in summer and game in winter.
Tue–Sun 12.30–3pm, 7–10pm.

🏠 **Oranmore Lodge** €€–€€€
Oranmore (tel: 091 794400, fax: 091 790227).
Closed 22–27 Dec.
56 rooms.

🏠 🍴 **Park House Hotel and Park Room Restaurant** €€–€€€
Forster Street, Eyre Square (tel: 091 564924, fax: 091 569219).
Closed 24–26 Dec.
57 rooms.
Wide choice of dishes that are traditional, but not old-fashioned. Plenty of seafood (€€€).
Daily 6–10, Sun–Fri 12.30–2.30.

🏠 🍴 **Radisson SAS Hotel** €€€
Lough Atalia Road (tel: 091 538300, fax: 091 538380).
217 rooms.
Modern European menu features a different chef de partie each month (€€€).
Daily 6–10.30pm, also 12.30–3pm Sun.

🍴 **River God Café** €–€€
Quay Street (tel: 091 565811).
Satisfying comfort food, such as Connemara casserole of cod and potatoes.
Daily 5–10.30pm.

🏠 **Victoria** €€
Victoria Place, Eyre Square (tel: 091 567433, fax: 091 565880).
Closed 25 Dec.
57 rooms.

Westwood House Hotel €€€
Dangan, Upper Newcastle (on the N6) (tel: 091521442, fax: 091 521400).
Closed 24–25 Dec.
58 rooms.

CARNA, Co Galway
Carna Bay Hotel €€–€€€
On R340 (tel: 095 32255, fax: 095 32530).
Closed 23–26 Dec.
26 rooms.

Cashel House €€€
Cashel (8 miles/13km beyond Carna on R342) (tel: 095 31001, fax: 095 31077).
Closed 4 Jan–4 Feb.
32 rooms.

Hillside House B&B €
Kylesalia, Kilkieran (5 miles/8km east of Carna on R340) (tel: 095 33420, fax: 095 33624).
Closed Oct–Mar.
4 rooms.

Zetland Country House €€€
Cashel Bay (8 miles/13km beyond Carna on R342) (tel: 095 31111, fax: 095 31117).
Closed Nov–9 Apr.
19 rooms.

ROUNDSTONE, Co Galway
Eldons €€
On the main street (tel: 095 35933 or 35942, fax: 095 35871).
Closed 4 Nov–16 Mar.
13 rooms.
Fish predominates on the menu, with chicken and steak dishes as an alternative – all accurately cooked with clear flavours.
Daily 6.30–9.30pm.

Ivy Rock House €
Letterdyfe (tel: 095 35872, fax: 095 35959).
Closed Oct–Mar.
6 rooms.

O'Dowd's Seafood Restaurant €–€€
Roundstone Harbour (tel: 095 35809).
Traditional restaurant serving wonderful seafood, including chowder, crab claws in garlic butter, whole lobster, and fishermen's platters.
Easter–mid-Oct daily noon–10pm.

CLIFDEN, Co Galway
Abbeyglen Castle €€
Sky Road (tel: 095 21201, fax: 095 21797).
Closed 5 Jan–1Feb.
44 rooms.

Alcock and Brown Hotel €€
Town centre (tel: 095 21206 or 21086, fax: 095 21842).
Closed 23–25 Dec.
19 rooms.
Plenty of fish from the local harbour on a menu of Irish cuisine with strong international influences (€€€).
Daily, lunch from 12.30, dinner from 6pm.

Ardagh Hotel and Restaurant €€€
Ballyconneely Road (tel: 095 21384, fax: 095 21314). Closed Nov–Mar.
19 rooms.
Modern cuisine features some inspired combinations: pot-roast venison with sweet red cabbage, honey-roast monkfish on baby spinach, Thai-style mussels (€€€).
Daily 7.15–9.30pm.

Ardmore House €
Sky Road (tel: 095 21221, fax: 095 21100).
Closed Oct–Mar.
6 rooms.

Ben View House €
Bridge Street (tel: 095 21256, fax: 095 21226).
10 rooms.

Buttermilk Lodge €€
Westport Road (tel: 095 21951, fax: 095 21953).
Closed 3 Jan–10 Feb.
11 rooms.

Byrne's Mal Dua House €€
Galway Road (tel: 095 21171 or 0800 904 7532, fax: 095 21739).
14 rooms.

Dan O'Hara's Farmhouse €
Lettershea (5 miles/8km east on N59) (tel: 095 21246 or 21808, fax: 095 22098).
Closed Nov–Mar.
4 rooms.

Dun Ri €–€€
Hulk Street (tel: 095 21625, fax: 095 21635).
Closed 3 Nov–Feb.
10 rooms.

Faul House €
On the Ballyconneely road (tel: 095 21239, fax: 095 21998).
6 rooms.

Kinstown House €
Bridge Street (tel: 095 21470, fax: 095 21530).
8 rooms.

Mallmore House €
Ballyconneely Road (tel: 095 21460).
Closed Oct to mid-Mar.
6 rooms.

O'Grady's €€
Market Street (tel: 095 21450.
Superb fresh seafood, including Clifden lobster and fillet of Cleggan brill. Also beef, lamb and pork.
Apr–Oct Mon–Sat 12.30–2.30pm, 6.30–10pm.

Rock Glen Country House Hotel €€€
1.5 miles (2km) from town (tel: 095 21035 or 21393, fax: 095 21737).
Closed mid-Nov to mid-Feb, but open New Year.
26 rooms.
Lavishly furnished scenic restaurant serving intricate, creative Irish dishes with strong hints of Pacific Rim and French cuisine (€€).
Daily 7–9pm.

The Signal €€
Rear of Station House Hotel, on the N59 (tel: 095 22946).
Modern continental cuisine with plenty of originality and rich flavours, as in blackened turbot with smoked oysters.
May–Sep Wed–Sun 6.30–9.30pm.

Two Dog Café €
Church Street (tel: 095 22186).
Internet café serving wholesome soups, salads, baguettes, and pastries with Italian coffee.

KYLEMORE ABBEY, Co Galway
Kylemore House €
On shore of Lake Kylemore (tel: 095 41143, fax: 095 41143).
Closed Nov–Feb.
6 rooms.

Renvyle House Hotel €€–€€€
Renvyle (west off N59) (tel: 095 43511, fax: 095 43515).
Closed 6 Jan–14 Feb.
68 rooms.
Unusual combinations with clear flavours distinguish the menu here,

including perfectly roasted monkfish
(€€).
Daily 7–9pm.

LEENAUN, Co Galway
🏨 **Killary Lodge** €
3 miles (5km) west on Clifden
road (tel: 095 42276 or 42245,
fax: 095 42314).
12 rooms.

OUGHTERARD, Co Galway
🏨 **The Boat Inn** €€
Village centre (tel: 091 552196,
fax: 091 552694).
Closed 25 Dec.
11 rooms.
🏨 **Waterfall Lodge** €€
On N59 (tel: 091 552168).
6 rooms.
🏨 **Lakeland Country House** €
Portcarron Bay (off N59) (tel:
091 552121 or 552146, fax: 091
552146).
Closed 10 Dec–16 Jan.
9 rooms.

TOUR 20
LONDONDERRY, Co
Londonderry
🍴 **Badger's** £
16–18 Orchard Street (tel: 028
7136 0763).
Cosy pub serving hot sandwiches
('damper melts') and such dishes
as steak and Guinness casserole.
Mon noon–3pm, Tue–Thu
noon–7pm, Fri–Sat noon–9.30pm.
🏨 **Beech Hill Country House**
£££
32 Ardmore Road (tel: 028 7134
9279 fax: 028 7134 5366).
Closed 24–25 Dec.
17 rooms.
🍴 **Brown's Bar & Brasserie** ££
1–2 Bond's Hill, Waterside (tel:
028 7134 5180).
Classy and peaceful place serving
some of the best food in the city.
Modern Irish cuisine blends with
Italian and Thai.
Tue–Fri noon–2.30pm,
5.30–10pm, Sat 5.30–10.30.
🏨 **City Hotel** ££
Queen's Quay (tel: 028 7136
5800, fax: 028 7136 5801).
Closed 24–27 Dec.
145 rooms.
🏨 **Clarence House** £–££
15 Northland Road (tel: 028
7126 5342, fax: 028 7126 5377).
10 rooms.

🏨 **Quality Hotel Davincis** ££
15 Culmore Road (tel: 028 7127
9111, fax: 028 7127 9222).
Closed 25 Dec.
67 rooms.
🏨🍴 **Tower Hotel Derry** ££
Off the Diamond (tel: 028 7137
1000, fax: 028 7137 1234).
Closed 24–27 Dec.
93 rooms.
Modern menu inspired by
Mediterranean and Pacific Rim
cuisine (£).
Daily 12.30–2.30pm, dinner from
6pm. Closed Christmas.
🏨 **White Horse** £–££
68 Clooney Road, Campsie
(tel: 028 7186 0606, fax: 028 7186
0371).
57 rooms.

LETTERKENNY, Co Donegal
🏨 **Castle Grove Country**
House ££–£££
Castlegrove, Ballymaleel (tel:
074 915 1118, fax: 074 915 1384).
15 rooms.
🏨 **Mount Errigal** ££
Derry Road, Ballyraine (tel: 074
912 2700, fax: 074 912 5085).
82 rooms.
🏨 **Pennsylvania House** ££
Curraghleas, Mountain Top
(tel: 074 912 6808, fax: 074 912
8905). *Closed 20–26 Dec.*
5 rooms.

DUNFANAGHY, Co Donegal
🏨 **Arnolds** €€
(tel: 074 913 6208, fax: 074 913
6352).
Closed Nov to mid-Mar.
30 rooms.

TOUR 21
LARNE, Co Antrim
🏨 **Derrin** £
2 Prince's Gardens (tel: 028 2827
3269 or 2827 3762, fax: 028 2827
3269).
Closed 25–26 Dec.
6 rooms.
🏨 **Manor** £
23 Oler Fleet Road, Harbour
Highway (tel: 028 2827 3305,
fax: 028 2826 0505).
Closed 25–26 Dec.
8 rooms.

CARNLOUGH, Co Antrim
🏨 **Londonderry Arms** ££
20 Harbour Road (tel: 028 2888
5255, fax: 028 2888 5263).
Closed Christmas.
35 rooms.

GLENGARIFF, Co Antrim
🏨 **Sanda** £
29 Kilmore Road (tel: 028 2177
1785).
2 rooms.

CUSHENDALL, Co Antrim
🏨 **The Meadows** £
81 Coast Road (tel: 028 2177
2020).
6 rooms.

CUSHENDUN, Co Antrim
🏨 **Drumkeerin** £
201A Torr Road (tel: 028 2176
1554, fax: 028 2176 1556).
3 rooms.
🏨 **The Villa Farm House** £
185 Torr Road (tel: 028 2176
1252, fax: 028 2176 1252).
3 rooms.

BALLYCASTLE, Co Antrim
🏨 **Marine** ££
1 North Street (tel: 028 2076
2222, fax: 028 7076 9507).
32 rooms.

GIANT'S CAUSEWAY Co
Antrim
🍴 **Smuggler's Inn** £
306 Whitepark Road, opposite
entrance to Giant's Causeway
(tel: 028 2073 1577).
Local ingredients, such as salmon,
duck and game, are matched with
creative sauces.
Daily noon–2.30pm, 4–9pm.

BUSHMILLS, Co Antrim
🏨 **Bayview** £–££
2 Bayhead Road, Portballintrae
(north off A2) (tel: 028 2073
4100, fax: 028 2073 4330).
25 rooms.
🏨 **Bushmills Inn** ££
9 Dunluce Road (tel: 028 2073
2339, fax: 028 2073 2048).
32 rooms.
🏨 **Whitepark House** £
Ballintoy (tel: 028 2073 1482).
3 rooms.

PORTRUSH, Co Antrim
🏠 **Beulah Guest House £**
16 Causeway Street (tel: 028
7082 2413, fax: 028 7082 5900).
Closed 25–26 Dec.
11 rooms.
🍴 **Café in the Centre £**
Dunluce Avenue (tel: 028 7082
4444)
*Sandwiches, salads, omelettes and
steaks are on the menu here, alongside the famous Ulster Fry.
Jul–Aug daily 10–8, Easter–Jun
and Sep daily noon–5, Oct Sat–Sun
noon–5. Closed Nov–Easter.*
🏠 **Harbour Heights £**
17 Kerr Street (tel: 028 7082
2765, fax: 028 7082 2558).
10 rooms.
🏠 **Magherabuoy House ££**
41 Magheraboy Road (tel: 028
7082 3507, fax: 028 7082 4687).
40 rooms.
🏠 **Ramore £££**
The Harbour (tel: 028 7082
4313).
*Pacific rim dishes encapsulate fresh,
vibrant flavours.
Daily 12.15–2.15, 5–10. Closed
25 Dec.*
🏠 **Royal Court Hotel ££**
233 Ballybogey Road (tel: 028
7082 2236, fax: 028 7082 3176).
Closed 26 Dec.
18 rooms.

LIMAVADY, Co Londonderry
🏠 **Gorteen House £–££**
Deerpark, Roemill Road
(tel: 028 7772 2333, fax: 028 7772
2333).
26 rooms.
🍴 **The Lime Tree ££**
60 Catherine Street (tel: 028
7776 4300).
*Down-to-earth neighbourhood
restaurant serving generous
portions of excellent traditional
Irish dishes.
Tue–Sat 6–9pm.*
🏠 **Radisson Roe Park Hotel
& Golf Resort £££**
1 mile (1.5km) outside the town
(tel: 028 7772 2222, fax: 028 7772
2313).
118 rooms.

BALLYMENA, Co Antrim
🏠 **Galgorm Manor £££**
1 mile (1.5km) outside
Ballymena on A42, between
Galgorm and Cullybacky

(tel: 028 2588 1001, fax: 028 2588
0080).
24 rooms.

TOUR 22
BELFAST
🍴 **Aldens £**
229 Upper Newtownards Road
(tel: 028 9065 0079).
*Modern European cuisine in a chic
modern restaurant.
Mon–Fri noon–2.30pm, Mon–Sat
6–10pm. Closed Sun.*
🏠 **Ashberry Cottage £**
19 Rosepark Central (tel: 028
9028 6300).
3 rooms.
🏠 **Ash Rowan £–££**
12 Windsor Avenue, between
Lisburn and Malone roads
(tel: 028 9066 1758, fax: 028 9066
3227).
5 rooms.
🍴 **Beatrice Kennedy £££**
44 University Road (tel: 028
9020 2290).
*Eclectic menu in Parisian brasserie-
style surroundings.
Tue–Sun 5–10.30pm (also
12.30–3pm Sun). Closed Mon,
24–26 Dec, 1 Jan, Easter.*
🍴 **Bourbon £££**
60 Great Victoria Street (tel: 028
9033 2121).
*Modern European food, with such
interesting dishes as cinnamon
braised pork belly and duck and
ham hock crubeens.
Mon–Fri noon–3pm, daily
5–11pm.*
🍴 **Cayenne £££**
7 Ascot House, Shaftesbury
Square (tel: 028 9033 1532).
*Brash, lively restaurant of celebrity
chef, Paul Rankin, serving a mix
of Pacific, Oriental, Indian and
Mediterranean food.
Mon–Fri noon–2.15pm, daily
6–11.15pm. Closed 25–26 Dec,
12 Jul.*
🏠 **Crescent Townhouse ££**
13 Lower Crescent (tel: 028
9032 3349, fax: 028 9032 0646).
Closed 25–27 Dec, part of Jul.
11 rooms.
🍴 **Flour Crepe Room 46 £**
46 Upper Queen Street (tel: 028
9033 9966).
*Crêpes, sweet and savoury, are
made to order.
Mon–Sat noon–8pm.*

🏠 **Jurys Belfast Inn ££**
Fisherwick Place, Great Victoria
Street (tel: 028 9053 3500,
fax: 028 9053 3511).
Closed 24–26 Dec.
190 rooms.
🏠 **Malmaison Belfast £££**
34–38 Victoria Street (tel: 020
7479 9512).
62 rooms.
🍴 **Metro BrasserieEuropean
£–££**
13 Lower Crescent (tel: 028
9032 3349)
*Modern brasserie with casual
atmosphere and contemporary
cooking.*
🍴 **Nick's Warehouse ££**
35–39 Hill Street (tel: 028 9043
9690).
*Trendy converted warehouse offering
hearty food with world-wide origins,
from Scandinavia to the
Mediterranean.
Mon–Fri noon–2.30pm,
6–9.30pm, Sat 6–9.30pm.*
🏠 **Ramada Belfast £–££**
117 Milltown Road, Shaws
Bridge (tel: 028 9092 3500,
fax: 028 9092 3600).
120 rooms.
🍴 **Restaurant Michael Deane
££–£££**
38–40 Howard Street (tel: 028
9033 1134).
*Celebrity chef Deane maintains a
hands-on presence here, providing
accomplished renditions of modern
British and Irish dishes. Fine dining
upstairs; more relaxed brasserie
downstairs.
Wed–Sat 7–9pm, also 12.15–2pm
Fri. Closed Sun–Tue, Christmas,
New Year, Easter, 2 weeks Jul.*
🍴 **Shu £££**
253 Lisburn Road (tel: 028 9038
1655).
*Trendy eatery for discerning
gourmets, offering a globetrotting
menu of stylishly presented food.
Mon–Sat 12.30–2.30, 6–10. Closed
Sun, 24–26 Dec, 12–14 Jul.*
🏠 **Tara Lodge £–££**
36 Cromwell Road (tel: 028 9059
0900, fax: 028 9059 0901).
Closed 25–29 Dec, 9–14 Jul.
19 rooms.
🍴 **Ta Tu ££**
701 Lisburn Road (tel: 028 9038
0818).
*Fashionable bar-restaurant with
international dishes on the menu.*

TENsq £££
10 Donegall Square (tel: 028
9024 1001, fax: 028 9024 3210).
23 rooms.

CULTRA, Co Down
**Clandeboye Lodge
Hotel ££**
10 Estate Road, Clandeboye
(southeast via A2 and B170)
(tel: 028 9185 2500, fax: 028 9185
2772).
Closed 25–26 Dec.
43 rooms.
*In woodland surroundings, this
hotel restaurant serves seasonally
inspired modern classics (££).
Daily noon–2.30, 6.30–9.30.*
The Old Inn ££
15 Main Street, Crawfordsburn
(east off A2) (tel: 028 9185 3255).
*Modern British dishes, such as
gratin of Dublin Bay prawns, pan-
fried Ulster beef with red wine, and
Finnebrogue venison with sweet
potato.
Daily 12.30–2.30pm, Mon–Sat
7–9.30pm. Closed 25 Dec.*
Shanks £££
The Blackwood, Crawfordsburn
(east off A2) (tel: 028 9185 3313).
*Award-winning restaurant offering
essentially classical cooking with
restrained international influences;
exceptional seafood. Tue–Fri lunch
and dinner, Sat dinner only.
Closed Sun–Mon, 25–26 Dec,
Easter Tue and 2 weeks mid-Jul.*

NEWTOWNARDS, Co Down
Ballycastle House £
20 Mountstewart Road (5
miles/8km southeast on A20)
(tel: 028 4278 8357).
3 rooms.
Ballynester House £
1a Cardy Road, off Mount
Stewart Road (tel: 028 4278
8386, fax: 028 4278 8986).
3 rooms.
Edenvale House £
130 Portaferry Road (tel: 028
9181 4881, fax: 028 9182 6192).
Closed 24–26 Dec.
3 rooms.

PORTAFERRY, Co Down
The Narrows ££
8 Shore Road (tel: 028 4272
8148, fax: 028 4727 8105).
13 rooms.

Portaferry ££
10 The Strand (tel: 028 4272
8231, fax: 028 4272 8999).
Closed 24–25 Dec.
14 rooms.

**TOUR 23
ENNISKILLEN,** Co Fermanagh
Dromard House £
Tamlaght (3 miles/5km east on
A4) (tel: 028 6638 7250).
Closed 24–26 Dec.
4 rooms.
Killyhevlin ££
2 miles (3km) south off the A4
(tel: 028 6632 3481).
Closed 25 Dec.
43 rooms.
Willowbank House £
60 Bellevue Road (tel: 028 6632
8582, fax: 028 6632 8582).
Closed Christmas.
5 rooms.

FLORENCE COURT, Co
Fermanagh
**Arch House Tullyhona
Farm £**
Marble Arch Road,
Florencecourt (tel: 028 6634
8452, fax: 028 6634 8452).
4 rooms.

**TOUR 24
ARMAGH,** Co Armagh
Charlemont Arms Hotel £
57–65 English Street (tel: 028
3752 2028, fax: 028 3752 6979).
Closed 25–26 Dec.
30 rooms.

DUNGANNON, Co Tyrone
Cohannon Inn £
212 Ballynakilly Road
(tel: 028 877 24488, fax 028 8775
2217).
42 rooms.
Grange Lodge ££
7 Grange Road (tel: 028 8778
4212, fax: 028 8778 4313).
Closed 21 Dec–9 Jan.
5 rooms.
**Millbrook Bed and
Breakfast £**
46 Moy Road (tel: 028 8772
3715).
3 rooms.
**Reahs Restaurant and
Luxury Accommodation £££**
24 Killyman Road (tel: 028 8772
5575, fax: 028 8772 6676).
7 rooms.

OMAGH, Co Tyrone
Hawthorn House ££
72, Old Mountfield Road
(tel: 028 8225 2005, fax: 028 8225
2005).
*Exciting contemporary cooking and
innovative seafood dishes.
Daily, lunch from noon, dinner from
7pm.*

**TOUR 25
CASTLEWELLAN,** Co Down
Slieve Croob Inn £
Seeconnell Centre, 119
Clanvaraghan Road (1
mile/1.5km from town on A25)
(tel: 028 4377 1412, fax: 028 4377
1162).
7 rooms.

NEWCASTLE, Co Down
Briers Country House £
39 Middle Tollymore Road
(off B180) (tel: 028 4372 4347,
fax: 028 4372 6633).
8 rooms.
**Burrendale Hotel and
Country Club ££**
51 Castlewellan Road (tel: 028
4372 2599, fax: 028 4372 2328).
69 rooms.
Enniskeen House ££
98 Bryansford Road (tel: 028
4372 2392, fax: 028 4372 4084).
Closed 12 Nov–14 Mar.
12 rooms.
Grasmere £
16 Margerite Park, Bryansford
Road (tel: 028 4372 6801).
3 rooms.
Slieve Donard ££
Downs Road (tel: 028 4372 1066.
028 4372 4830).
130 rooms.

ANNALONG, Co Down
Glassdrumman Lodge £££
85 Mill Road (tel: 028 4376 8451,
fax: 028 4376 7041).
10 rooms.

WARRENPOINT, Co Down
The Duke ££
7 Duke Street (above the Duke
Bar) (tel: 028 4175 2084).
*Creative cooking here has won criti-
cal acclaim for such dishes as seared
chile beef with crunchy vegetables
and Thai rice and excellent seafood.
Tue–Sat 6–10pm, Sun 5.30–9pm.*

FESTIVALS AND EVENTS

JANUARY
Funderland
This event beats the winter weather by constructing a temporary theme park inside the Royal Dublin Society, complete with white-knuckle rides, stalls and such entertainment as a high-wire motorcycle act.
Boxing Day–mid January.
For information: tel: 061 419 988; www.funfair.ie/www.rds.ie).

Yeats Winter School
The writer's home town, Sligo, plays host to this weekend of lectures and tours of the countryside that inspired his work.
Late Jan.
For information: tel: 071 42693; www.yeats-sligo.com

FEBRUARY
All Ireland Dancing Championships
The whole world knows about Irish dancing these days, and this popular week-long event in Ennis, Co Clare, is a hotly contested competition that's a qualifier for the World Dancing Championship.
Early February.
For information: tel: 01 475 1053

Six Nations Rugby Tournament
The national teams of Ireland, England, Scotland, Wales, France and Italy compete at the Lansdowne Road rugby ground in Dublin, with a great atmosphere at the 50,000-capacity venue and in the surrounding pubs.
Certain Saturdays, early February–April.
For information: tel: 01 668 4601; www.6-nations-rugby.com

Antiques and Collectibles Fair
Newman House, on St Stephen's Green, Dublin hosts this event, with about 60 antiques dealers specialising in small pieces and collectors' items.

Four Sundays in February.
For information: tel: 01 716 7422.

Jameson Dublin International Film Festival
Showcasing around a hundred full-length and short films from more than 30 countries.
Mid-February.
For information: tel: 01 661 6216; www.dublinfilmfestival.net

MARCH
St Patrick's Day
The patron saint of Ireland is commemorated across the country on 17 March, and most major cities will have lively celebrations and perhaps a parade (see also St Patrick's Festival, below).

St Patrick's Festival
St Patrick's Day is celebrated throughout Ireland. Dublin's event stretches to a full-scale five-day festival with concerts, fireworks, street theatre and, of course, the St Patrick's Day Parade through the city.
Starts 16 March.
For information: tel: 01 676 3205; www.stpatricksfestival.ie

Limerick Spring Festival
A highlight of this lively festival is the International Marching Band Parade and Competition, with 20 or so bands from several countries taking part.
Mid- to late March.
For information: tel: 061 400255; www.limerick.ie

Galway Four Seasons Walking Festival
This is the springtime event – there are also summer, autumn and winter festivals, and all feature organised walks to explore Connemara and the Aran Islands. The festival is based at the Connemara Walking Centre in Clifden.
Late March.
For information: tel: 095 21379; www.walkingireland.com

Pan Celtic International Festival
Celebrating the music, dance and culture of the Celtic nations. Held in a different location each year.
March/April, during week after Easter.
For information: www.panceltic.com

Titanic – Made in Belfast
A week-long festival recalling the positive aspects of the Titanic era in Belfast's shipyards and factories, including living history events, exhibitions, boat trips, talks, storytelling for children, concerts and a memorial service for those who died when Titanic sank.
Late March–early April.
For information: www.titanic.com

Irish Grand National
The highlight of the Easter Festival at Fairyhouse racecourse is the Irish Grand National, the most valuable and prestigious National Hunt race in the country.
March or April, Easter weekend.
For information: tel: 01 825 6167; www.fairyhouseracecourse.ie

APRIL
Belfast Film Festival
More than 130 movies are screened at this celebration of the moving image, including international premieres, classics and short films.
Early April.
For information: tel: 028 9032 5913; www.niftc.co.uk

Wexford Book Festival
Six days of adults' and children's events, featuring the best of Irish and European authors, including a popular Sports Writers Night.
Mid-July.
For information: tel: 053 22226; www.wexfordbook.com

Cathedral Quarter Arts Festival

Cutting edge and culturally diverse events in and around Belfast's Cathedral Quarter cover performing and visual arts, with such innovative ideas as graffiti art and comic-book culture, Irish, world and rock music, plus world-class comedy, modern theatre and circus arts.
For information: tel: 028 9023 2403 (box office: 028 9024 6609); www.cqaf.com

Shannon Dol-fun

The waters of the west coast are home to a number of bottlenose dolphins and this festival, based at Kilrush, celebrates their presence with dolphin-watching trips, talks, kids' activities and a costume parade.
Late April–early May.
For information: tel: 065 905 2326; www.shannondolphins.ie

Carlsberg Kilkenny Rhythm n' Roots Festival

A big line-up of bands from Ireland and American, playing blues, bluegrass, appalachian, cajun, country-rock and traditional Irish music.
Late April–early May.
For information: tel: 056 779 0057; www.kilkennyroots.com

MAY
Wicklow Gardens Festival Co

Wicklow is known as the 'Garden of Ireland' and this festival provides the chance for visitors to tour some private gardens in addition to those that are always open to the public. A total of around 40 gardens are involved.
Beginning of May–mid-August.
For information: tel: 0404 20070; www.wicklow.ie/tourism

West Cork Walking Festival

An opportunity to enjoy superb walks of varying lengths amid spectacular west coast scenery, plus talks and entertainment.
For information: tel: 028 22812; www.westcork.ie

Heineken Green Energy International Music Festival

Big names from the world of pop music feature in concerts at Dublin Castle.
Early May.
For information: tel: 01890 925100

Belfast City Marathon

Celebrating its 25th year in 2006, this event attracts thousands of runners, and there's also a wheelchair event, a marathon walk, a relay race and a fun run.
Early May.
For information: tel: 028 9027 0345; www.belfastcity-marathon.com

Northwest 200

Motorcycle road race from Portrush to Portstewart along Co Antrim's country lanes – one of Northern Ireland's biggest sporting events, drawing an international crowd.
Mid- to late May.
For information: tel: 028 7035 5800; www.northwest200.fm.

Lord Mayor's Show

Marking the end of each Lord Mayor's term of office, there's a big parade through Belfast city centre, starting from Writer's Square.
21 May.
For information: tel: 028 9027 0222.

Galway Early Music Festival

Celebrating European music and dance of the 12th–18th centuries, this four-day festival attracts the finest exponents from Ireland and elsewhere to the medieval streets of Galway city. There are concerts, workshops and masterclasses in medieval, renaissance and baroque music.
Late May.
For information: tel: 087 930 5506; www.galwayearlymusic.com

Fleadh Nua

A week-long festival of traditional music and dancing, held in Ennis, Co Clare, including concerts, workshops, informal sessions, ceilis, exhibitions, lectures and film shows.
Late May.
For information: tel: 065 684 0406 or 086 825 0300; www.fleadhnua.com

JUNE
Dublin Writers Festival

Writers from many countries converge on Dublin for readings, discussions, lectures, music, film and children's events.
For information: tel: 01 671 3639; www.dublinwritersfestival.com

Smithwick's Cat Laughs Comedy Festival

A front-runner for the title of best comedy festival in the world, held in Kilkenny, Co Kilkenny, featuring an international line-up of big-name comedians in stand-up, skits, improv and film.
Early June.
For information: tel: 056 776 3837; www.smithwickscatlaughs.com.

Music in Great Irish Houses

A series of chamber music concerts by world-class performers, held in the stately surroundings of various Irish mansions and historic buildings.
Early–mid-June.
For information: 01 664 2822; www.musicirishhouses.com

Listowel Writers' Week

A lively literary festival drawing a number of internationally known writers to this Co Kerry town to give readings and talks, conduct workshops and launch new books. Also film and music events, competitions and children's events.
Early June.
For information: tel: 068 21074; www.writersweek.ie.

Bloomsday

Dublin celebrates its James Joyce heritage by commemorating the 24 hours in the life of Leopold Bloom that are the subject of his Ulysses. There are special ceremonies at the Joyce Museum and city restaurants

and pubs join in with their own festivities.
Mid-June.
For information: tel: 01 878 8547; www.jamesjoyce.ie

Budweiser Irish Derby
The most historic horse racing event of the year, held at Ireland's premier track, The Curragh in Co Kildare.
Late June.
For information: tel: 045 441205; www.curragh.ie

Strawberry Festival
A long-time favourite in the Co Wexford calendar, this festival features lots of entertainment (including the Carlsberg Rhythm Route), arts and crafts, funfair, demonstrations and exhibitions… but, most of all, fresh strawberries in profusion.
For information: www.strawberryfestival.ie

Killarney Summerfest
A comprehensive range of family entertainments includes big-name stadium rock concerts, classical music, busking and other street entertainment, comedy, theatre, dance, kid's events and outdoor activities.
Late June–mid July.
For information: tel: 064 61560; www.killarneysummerfest.com

JULY
Dublin Jazz Week
Concerts, workshops, master classes, film featuring established musicians and rising stars from the US and Europe.
Early July.
For information: tel: 01 877 9001; www.esb.ie

American Independence Celebrations
Ireland's strong links with the US are reflected in the existence of the Ulster American Folk Park and they celebrate the Fourth of July in style, with living history enactments, bluegrass, jazz and folk music and traditional American games.
2–4 July.
For information: tel: 028 8224 3292; www.folkpark.com

Drogheda Samba Festival
A carnival atmosphere prevails during this celebration of Brazilian dance, with dancing, international bands, street theatre and a parade.
Early July.
For information: tel: 041 983 8332 or 086 812 3310; www.solo.ie//samba/

Clonmel Junction Festival
A lively mix of theatre, art, concerts and free daytime events.
Early July.
For information: tel: 052 29339; www.junctionfestival.com

Oxegen
A mammoth two-day rock music festival at Punchestown Racecourse, with five stages and more than 80 bands, including the biggest names of the moment (Green Day, Foo Fighters, The Prodigy, New Order and others in 2005).
Early July.
For information: www.oxegen.ie Ticket hotline: 0818 719300 (Republic of Ireland) or 0870 243 4455 (Northern Ireland).

Hooves and Grooves Festival
Exactly what it sounds like, this festival features horseracing and music – a perfect combination for the Irish in particular. As well as harness racing and masses of gigs, there's street theatre, street markets and water sports.
Early July.
For information: tel: 053 52900 (Wexford Tourism); www.hoovesandgrooves.com

Battle of the Boyne
Commemoration In Belfast and other cities of Northern Ireland, the Protestant community remember the historic battle with parades and other celebrations. It's also known as Orangeman's Day.
12 July.
For information: tel: 028 9032 2801.

Galway Arts Festival
Hailed as Ireland's biggest and most exciting arts festival, this is

a two-week event covering both visual and performing arts.
Mid- to late July.
For information: tel: 091 509700; www.galwayartsfestival.com

International Rose Week
A fragrant festival in which rose breeders from across the globe submit entries for judging at Sir Thomas and Lady Dixon Park in Belfast. In addition to the flowers and garden walks, there are plant and craft stalls and entertainment.
Mid- to late July.
For information: tel: 028 9027 0467

Ballyshannon Music Festival
Ireland's oldest and biggest traditional music festival, bringing top bands and soloists to this corner of Co Donegal.
Late July.
For information: www.ballyshannonfolkfestival.com

Croagh Patrick Pilgrimage
More than 25,000 pilgrims climb Ireland's holy mountain to honour the patron saint.
Last Sunday in July.
For information: tel: 098 64114; www.croagh-patrick.com

Galway Races
The summer festival meeting is one of the great events of the social calendar, with much more going on than horse racing.
Late July.
For information: tel: 091 753870; www.galwayraces.com

Lughnasa Fair
A medieval extravaganza, based at the great waterfront castle at Carrickfergus, Co Antrim, with traditional food and entertainment, crafts, medieval games and participants in medieval costume.
Late July.
For information: tel: 028 4336 6455.

Belfast Pride
A week of parties, drama, music, dance and other evens culminates in a spectacular parade around the city centre, ending

with a party in Writer's Square. For information: www.belfastpride.com

AUGUST
Dublin Horse Show
This event at the RDS is an acknowledgement of the Irish love of horses and a great social event. In addition to the show jumping and other competitions, there are lots of exhibitors, an arts and crafts exhibition, music and children's entertainment. For information: tel: 01 240 7213; www.dublinhorseshow.com

Matchmaking Festival
Famous traditional festival (the original singles event) in the spa town of Lisdoonvarna, Co Clare, with music, dancing and perhaps romance. *Late August–early October.* For information: tel: 065 707 4005; www.matchmakerireland.com

Baltimore Regatta
Waterborne events in Roaringwater Bay, Co Cork. *First Monday in August.* For information: www.baltimore-sailing-club.com

Puck Fair
Ancient festival honouring a goat that reputedly alerted the town to impending danger. There's music, theatre, a procession and a ceremony in which a goat is crowned. *10th–12 August.* For information: www.puckfair.ie

Kilkenny Arts Festival
A comprehensive festival of all the arts, including theatre and dance, visual arts, literature and all kinds of music – world, jazz, classical, traditional Irish. *Mid-August.* For information: tel: 056 775 2175 or 056 776 3663; www.kilkennyarts.ie

Connemara Pony Show
The premier event (among several) that showcase the sturdy little breed of pony that

originated in and still come from Co Galway. *Mid-August.* For information: tel: 095 21863; www.cpbs.ie

Rose of Tralee Festival
Much more than just a beauty pageant, though entrants of Irish descent come to Tralee, Co Kerry, from across the globe to take part. Lots of other events and festivities. *Late August.* For information: tel: www.rose-oftralee.ie

Cork Art Fair
Cork's City Hall plays host to a contemporary art fair featuring original paintings and sculptures by Irish and foreign artists. *Late August.* For Information: tel: 01 499 2244 or 087 617 5418; www.corkart-fair.com

Fleadh Cheoil na hEireann
The grandaddy of all traditional music festivals in Ireland, at a different location each year. *Late Aug.* For information: tel: 074 912 5133.

Festival of World Cultures
Bringing internationally renowned performers of music, theatre, dance, circus and film together with local acts amid a real carnival atmosphere in Dun Laoghaire, Co Dublin. *Late August.* For information: tel: 01 204 7271.

Ould Lammas Fair
Held in Ballycastle, on the north Co Anrim coast, this is one of the oldest fairs in Ireland, with a huge street market, various entertainments and the chance to try the local delicacies, dulce (edible seaweed) and yellow man (confectionery). *Last Monday and Tuesday in August.* For information: tel: 028 2076 2024 (Ballycastle Tourist Information Centre).

Clarenbridge Oyster Festival
Heralding the start of the oyster season in Co Galway, this is a nine-day feast of oysters (and other seafood) and entertainment. *Late August–early September.* For information: 091 796 6766; www.clarenbridge.com

SEPTEMBER
Appalachian & Bluegrass Music Festival
The Ulster American Folk Park in Co Tyrone stages this popular event, the largest of its kind in Europe, with musicians from North America and Europe. *Early September.* For information: tel: 028 8224 3292; www.folkpark.com

Heritage Week
Ireland's contribution to European Heritage Days consists of a week of nationwide events at various historic properties, parks and gardens and other venues. Sunday events are usually free of charge. *Early–mid-September.* For information: tel: 01 888 3164 or 01 888 3146; www.environ.ie or contact local tourist offices.

All-Ireland Hurling and Gaelic Football Finals
Two of Ireland's best-loved sports reach their annual pinnacle at Croke Park in Dublin. It's comparable to the Super Bowl and if you can't get tickets, soak up the atmosphere in a pub – anywhere in Ireland. *Hurling Final, early September, Gaelic Football, mid-September.* For information: tel: 01 836 3222; www.gaa.ie

Cape Clear International Storytelling Festival
An ancient art form is kept alive at this lively event on Cape Clear island, Co Cork, proving conclusively that the Irish really do have a way with words. For information: tel: 028 39116; http://indigo.ie/~stories/

Blackstairs Blues Festival
The town of Enniscorthy, Co Wexford, is jumping during this

festival, which features a good range of blues, from acoustic guitar and harmonica duos to big bands.
Mid-September.
For information: tel: 087 622 1589;
www.blackstairsblues.com

Galway Art Fair
Brings together exhibitions from around 40 Irish and foreign artists and galleries, totalling thousands of original art works to see and buy, hosted by the Corrib Great Southern, Galway.
Late September.
For information: tel: 01 499 2244 or 087 617 5418;
www.galwayartfair.com

Galway International Oyster Festival
Parties, parades, concerts, beauty contests, the World Oyster Opening Champion-ships, and lots of oyster-eating and Guinness-drinking.
Late September.
For information: tel: 091 522066;
www.galwayoysterfest.com

Dublin Theatre Festival
Features the best of Irish and international drama, including classics and new works, staged by every major Irish company.
Late September–mid-October.
For information: tel: 01 474 0154, www.
dublintheatrefestival.com

OCTOBER
Ballinasloe Horse Fair
Originating in 1700, this is one of the oldest Horse Fairs in Europe and attracts huge crowds of up to 100,000 to a town that has an equestrian flavour all year round.
Early October.
For information: tel: 0909 643453 www.ballinasloe.com

Autumn Flavours Festival
The village of Kinsale, Co Cork, has a reputation for good eating all year round, culminating in this celebration of food and drink.
Early October.
For information: tel: 021 477 2234 (Kinsale Tourist

Information Office, open Mar-Oct) or 021 477 4026 (Kinsale Chamber of Tourism).

Cork Film Festival
Celebrating its 50th year in 2005, this excellent festival is internationally renowned for is eclectic mix of screenings and events. It includes short films, big budget blockbusters, inde-pendent and foreign-language films and documentaries.
Early to mid-October.
For information: tel: 021 427 1711; www.corkfilmfest.org

Ideal Homes Exhibition
A showcase for everything that's new and exciting in home design and lifestyle, including show homes, themed pavilions, food and drink, health and beauty, and hundreds of exhibitors. Held at the Royal Dublin Society's Simonscourt Pavilion.
Late October.
For information: tel: 01 490 0600; www.idealhome.ie

Wexford Opera Festival
Nearly 20 evening events and double that amount during the day, with performers from all over the world taking part in productions staged exclusively for the festival.
Late October–early November.
For information: tel: 053 22400;
www.wexfordopera.com

Belfast Festival at Queens
Ireland's largest arts festival with world-class concerts of all types of music, dance, comedy, litera-ture and visual arts.
Late October–early November.
For information: tel: 028 9097 2600; www.belfastfestival.com

Adidas Dublin Marathon
Dublin's Georgian streets are thronged by enthusiastic crowds cheering on the thousands of runners in this long-established event which attracts serious international athletes as well as amateurs and celebrity fundrais-ers. It's known world-wide as 'the friendly marathon'.
Late October.

For information: tel: 01 623 2250;
www.dublincitymarathon.ie

Guinness Jazz Festival
40,000 music fans gather in Cork for Europe's friendliest jazz festival, which features the biggest international names over a four-day period, plus fringe events.
Late October.
For information: tel: 021 425 5100 (Cork Kerry Tourism);
www.corkjazzfestival.com

NOVEMBER
Enterprising Limerick Crafts and Gifts Exhibition
The biggest event of its kind in the Shannon region, with more than 50 exhibitors of high qual-ity crafts gathering in the City Hall.
Late November.
For information: tel: 086 243 6347

DECEMBER
National Crafts Fair of Ireland
Perfect for Christmas shopping, this show brings together crafts-people and craft shops and galleries from all over Ireland at Dublin's RDS exhibition hall.
Early December.
For information: tel: 01 670 2186; www.rds.ie

Limerick Christmas Racing Festival
Three days of post-Christmas horse racing at Limerick Racecourse.
26–28 December.
For information: tel: 061 229377; www.limerick-racecourse.com

Leopardstown National Hunt Festival
Thoroughbred National Hunt (over jumps) racing at Leopardstown Racecourse, just south of Dublin.
26–28 December.
For information: tel: 01 289 2888; www.leopardstown.com

PRACTICAL INFORMATION

TOUR INFORMATION
The addresses, telephone numbers and opening times of the attractions mentioned in the tours, including the telephone numbers of the Tourist Information Centres are listed below tour by tour.

TOUR 1

_i_ Arthur's Row, Ennis. Tel: 065 6828366.
_i_ Cliffs of Moher. Tel: 065 7081171.

Ennis
Riches of Clare Museum
Arthur's Row, Ennis, Co Clare. Tel: 065 6823382. *Open Jun–Sep daily; Oct–May, Tue–Sat.*

Ennis Friary
Ennis, Co Clare. Tel: 065 29100. *Open May–Sep, daily 9.30–6.30; last admission 5.45pm.*

3 Cliffs of Moher
O'Brien's Tower
Liscannor, Co Clare. Tel: 061 360788. *Open May–Oct daily 10–6; last admission 5.30pm.*

5 Lisdoonvarna
Spa Wells Health Centre
The Sulphur Hill, Lisdoonvarna, Co Clare. Tel: 065 7074023. *Open Jun–Oct daily 10–6.*

6 Kilfenora
The Burren Centre
Kilfenora, Co Clare. Tel: 065 7088030. *Open mid-Mar–May, Sep–Oct, daily 10–5; Jun–Aug, daily 9.30–6; last tour an hour before closing.*

7 Kinvarra
Dunguaire Castle
Kinvarra, Co Clare.

Tel: 091 637108. *Open May–mid-Oct, daily 9.30–5.30; last admission 4.30pm.*

Thoor Ballylee
Gort, Co Galway. Tel: 091 631436. *Open May–Sep, daily 10–6.*

8 Quin
Knappogue Castle
Quin, Co Clare. Tel: 065 368103. *Open Apr–Oct, daily 9.30–5.30; last admission 4.30pm.*

Craggaunowen Project
Kilmurry, Sixmilebridge, Co Clare. Tel: 061 360788. *Open Apr–Oct, daily 10–6; last admission 5pm.*

9 Bunratty
Bunratty Castle
Bunratty, Co Clare. Tel: 061 360788. *Open Sep–May, daily 9.30–5.30; Jun–Aug, daily 9–6.30; last admission 4.30pm.*

Special to…
Bunratty Castle Banquets
Bunratty, Co Clare. Tel: 061 360788. *Open all year, at 5.30pm and 8.45pm, subject to demand.*

Cratloe Woods House
Shannon Dual Carriageway, Cratloe, Co Clare. Tel: 061 327028. *Open Jun–mid-Sep Mon–Sat by appointment only.*

Dromore Nature Reserve
Ruan, Ennis, Co Clare. Tel: 065 6837166. *Open daily 10–6; last admission 5.15pm.*

For children
Aillwee Cave
Ballyvaghan. Tel: 065 7077067. *Open daily 9.30–6.30.*

TOUR 2

_i_ Arthur's Quay, Limerick. Tel: 061 317522.
_i_ St John's Church, Listowel. Tel: 061 22590.
_i_ Heritage Centre, Adare. Tel: 061 396666.

Limerick
The Georgian House
2 Pery Square, Limerick, Co Limerick, Tel: 061 314130. *Open Mon–Fri 10–4.30 or by appointment at weekends.*

The Hunt Museum
The Custom House, Rutland Street, Limerick, Co Limerick. Tel: 061 312833. *Open Mon–Sat 10–5, Sun 2–5.*

2 Foynes
Flying Boat Museum
Foynes, Co Limerick. Tel: 069 65416. *Open Apr–Oct, daily 10–6; last admission 5pm.*

3 Glin
Glin Castle and Gardens
Glin, Co Limerick. Tel: 068 34173. *Open late Mar–Nov. Telephone for information.*

9 Rathkeale
Castle Matrix
Rathkeale, Co Limerick. Tel: 069 64284. *Open Apr–Sep, Sat–Thu, (visitors are requested to telephone before visiting).*

10 Adare
Heritage Centre
Main Street, Adare, Co Limerick. Tel: 061 396666. *Open Apr–Sep, daily 9–6.*

For history buffs
King John's Castle
Limerick, Co Limerick. Tel: 061 360788. *Open Apr–Oct daily 9.30–6,*

Nov–Mar 10.30–4.30; last admission one hour before closing.

For history buffs
Irish Palatine Heritage Centre
Rathkeale, Co Limerick. Tel: 069 63511. *Open Jun–Sep, Mon–Sat 10–5, Sun 2–6, closed 12–2.*

TOUR 3

_i_ Arthur's Quay, Limerick. Tel: 061 317522.
_i_ EXCEL, Tipperary. Tel: 062 51457.
_i_ Heritage Centre, Cashel. Tel: 062 61333.
_i_ Connolly Street, Nenagh. Tel: 067 31610.
_i_ Killaloe Heritage Centre, Killaloe. Tel: 061 376866.

2 Cashel
Rock of Cashel
Cashel, Co Tipperary. Tel: 062 61437. *Open daily, mid-Sep to mid-Mar, mid-Jun to mid-Sep 9–4.30; mid-Mar to mid-Jun 9–5.30.*

Bru Boru Heritage Centre
Cashel, Co Tipperary. Tel: 062 61122. *Open: centre Apr–Sep, 9–5. Theatre Jun–Sep, Tue–Sat 9am–midnight, Sun–Mon 9–5.*

8 Thurles
Famine Museum
St Mary's Church, Thurles, Co Tipperary. Tel: 0504 21133. *Open May–Sep, Sun–Fri.*

4 Roscrea
Roscrea Heritage Centre and Damer House
Roscrea Castle, Roscrea, Co Tipperary. Tel: 0505 21850. *Open Apr–Oct, daily, 10–6; last admission 5.15pm.*

Practical • Information

5 Nenagh
Nenagh District Heritage Centre
Nenagh, Co Tipperary.
Tel: 067 32633.
Open Mon–Fri 9.30–5.

6 Portumna
Portumna Castle
Portumna, Co Galway.
Tel: 090 9741658.
Open late Mar–mid-Apr, daily 10–5; mid-Apr–Oct, daily 10–6.

7 Mountshannon
Lough Derg Holy Island
Mountshannon, Co Clare.
Open daily. Tel: 061 921351 for boat trip.

8 Killaloe
Brian Boru Heritage Centre
Killaloe, Co Clare. Tel: 061 376866.
Open May–Sep, daily 10–6.

Special to...
Bolton Library
Cashel, Co Tipperary.
Tel: 062 61232.
Open May–Sep daily.

TOUR 4
---

[i] Ashe Memorial Hall, Denny Street, Tralee, Co Kerry. Tel: 066 7121288.
[i] The Pier, Dingle, Co Kerry. Tel: 066 9151188.

Tralee
Kerry the Kingdom
Tralee, Co Kerry. Tel: 066 7127777.
Open Mar–Oct, daily 10–6; Aug 10–7, Nov–Dec 2–5.

Siamsa Tire
Town Park, Tralee, Co Kerry. Tel: 066 7123055.
Apr–Oct 8.30pm.

For children
Tralee–Blennerville train
Tralee, Co Kerry. Tel: 066 7121288.
Telephone for information.

Blennerville Windmill
Tralee, Co Kerry. Tel: 066 7127777 or 7121064.
Telephone for information.

Aquadome
Tralee, Co Kerry. Tel: 066 7129150.
Telephone for times.

4 An Daingean (Dingle)
Dolphin Boat Trips
Dingle Boatmen's Association, Dingle Pier, Dingle, Co Kerry. Tel: 066 51967.
Sailings depart daily, weather permitting.

For children
Dingle Oceanworld
Near Dingle Harbour, Dingle, Co Kerry. Tel: 066 9152111.
Open daily 10–6.

6 Dunbeg
Dunbeg Fort
Fahan, Ventry, Co Kerry.
Tel: 066 9159070.
Open all year. Telephone for details.

7 Fahan
Famine Cottage
Fahan, Co Clare. Tel: 066 9156241.
Open May–Oct, daily 9–6.

8 Ceann Sléibhe (Slea Head)
Blasket Centre
Dún Chaoin, Dingle Peninsula, Co Kerry.
Tel: 066 9156444.
Open Easter–Sep, daily 10–6 (Jul–Aug 10–7).

For children
Freshwater Experience
Emlagh, Lispole, Co Kerry.
Tel: 066 9151045.
Open daily 9–5 (Jul–Aug 9–6).

11 Gallarus Visitor Centre
Dingle, Co Kerry. Tel: 066 9155333.
Open Apr–Sep 9–9; Oct–Mar 9–5.

TOUR 5
---

[i] Beech Road, Killarney.
Tel: 064 31633.
[i] Kenmare Heritage Centre, Kenmare. Tel: 064 41233.

2 Glenbeigh
Kerry Bog Village Museum
Glenbeigh, Co Kerry.
Tel: 066 9769184.
Open Mar–Nov daily 8.30–7; Nov–Mar on request.

3 Cahersiveen
Valentia Island Ferry
Cahersiveen, Co Kerry.
Tel: 066 9476141.
Open Apr–Sep, daily 8.30am–10.30pm.

The Barracks Heritage Centre
Bridge Street, Cahersiveen, Co Kerry. Tel: 066 9472589.
Open all year, Tue–Fri 11–5.

5 Sneem
Derrynane House
Caherdaniel, Co Kerry.
Tel: 066 9475113.
Open Nov–Mar, Sat–Sun 1–5; Apr, Oct, Tue–Sun 1–5; May–Sep, Mon–Sat 9–6, Sun 11–7; last admission 45 minutes before closing.

8 Ladies View
Killarney National Park Centre
Muckross House, Muckross, Co Kerry.
Tel: 064 31440.
Open mid-Mar–Oct, daily 9–6 (Jul–Aug 9–7).

Muckross House
Killarney, Co Kerry. Tel: 064 31440.
Open daily, Nov–mid-Mar, 9–5.30; mid-Mar–Jun, Sep–Oct, 9–6; Jul, Aug 9–7.

Recommended walks
Ross Castle
Ross Road, Killarney, Co Kerry. Tel: 064 35851.
Open daily, Apr 10–5; May, Sep 10–6; Jun–Aug 9–6.30; Oct, Tue–Sun 10–5.

Back to nature
Skellig Experience Heritage Centre
Skellig, Co Kerry. Tel: 066 9476306.
Open daily Apr, May, Sep–Nov 10–6; Jun–Aug 10–7; last admission one hour before closing.

TOUR 6
---

[i] Kenmare Heritage Centre, Kenmare. Tel: 064 41233.
[i] Town Centre, Glengarriff. Tel: 027 63084.

For history buffs
Kenmare Heritage Centre
Kenmare. Tel: 064 41233.
Open Easter–Sep.

1 Glengarriff
Garinish Island
Reached by boat from Blue Pool, Glengarriff, Co Cork.
Tel: 027 63333.
Open Mar, Oct, Mon–Sat 10–4.30, Sun 1–5; Apr–Jun, Sep, Mon–Sat 10–6.30, Sun 11–6.30; Jul, Aug, Mon–Sat 9.30–6.30, Sun 11–6.30.

Bamboo Park
N71, Glengarriff, Co Cork.
Tel: 027 63570.
Open all year, daily 9–7.

3 Castletown Bearhaven
Call of the Sea
North Road, Castletown Bearhaven, Co Cork.
Tel: 027 70835.
Open Mon–Fri 10–5, Sat–Sun 1–5.

Dursey Island Cable Car
Castletown Bearhaven, Co Cork. Tel: 027 73017.
Cable car operates all year, weather permitting, Mon–Sat 9–11, 2.30–5, 7–8, Sun 9–10.15, 12–1, 7–8.

TOUR 7
---

[i] Grand Parade, Cork City. Tel: 021 4255100.
[i] Town Centre, Blarney. Tel: 021 4381624.
[i] Heritage Centre, Lismore. Tel: 058 54975.
[i] Heritage Centre, Market Square, Youghal. Tel: 024 20170.

Cork
Cork City Gaol
Sundays Well, Cork, Co Cork. Tel: 021 4305022.

*Open Mar–Oct, daily
9.30–5; Nov–Feb 10–4.*

Crawford Art Gallery
Emmet Place, Cork, Co
Cork. Tel: 021 4273377.
*Open Mon–Sat 10–5; last
admission 4.15pm.*

See also Tour 8
❶ Blarney
Blarney Castle
Barney, Co Cork. Tel: 021
35321.
*Open all year, Mon–Sat
9–6.30, Sun 9.30–5.30.*

❷ Kanturk
Rural Farm Museum
Mealehara, Co Cork.
Tel: 029 51319.
Open all year daily.

❹ Mitchelstown
Mitchelstown Caves
Burncourt, Cahir, Co
Tipperary. Tel: 052
67246.
Open all year, daily 10–6.

❺ Caher
Caher Castle
Caher, Co Tipperary.
Tel: 052 41011.
*Open mid-Mar–mid-Oct
daily 9.30–5.30 (to 7pm
mid-Jun to mid-Sep); mid-Oct
to mid-Mar, 9.30–4.30; last
admission 45 minutes before
closing.*

❼ Lismore
Lismore Castle Gardens
Lismore, Co Waterford. Tel:
058 54424.
*Open Apr–Sep, daily
1.45–4.45 (from 11am in
high season).*

Lismore Heritage Centre
The Courthouse, Lismore,
Co Waterford. Tel 058
54975.
*Open Apr–Oct, daily
9.30–5.30, Sun 12–5.30.*

❽ Youghal
Heritage Centre
Market Square, Youghal,
Co Cork. Tel: 024 20170
or 92447.
*Open all year, ex 2 weeks
at Christmas/New Year,
Mon–Sat 10–5.30.*

For history buffs
Queenstown Story
Cobh Heritage Centre,
Cobh, Co Cork. Tel: 021
4813591.
*Open Feb–Dec, daily 10–6;
last admission 5pm.*

For children
Fota Island Wildlife Park
Carrigtwohill, Co Cork.
Tel: 021 812678.
*Open Apr–Sep, Mon–Sat
10–6, Sun 11–6; Oct,
Sat–Sun 11–6; last
admission 5pm.*

[i] Grand Parade, Cork.
Tel: 021 4255100.
[i] Pier Road, Kinsale.
Tel: 021 4772234.
[i] 25 Ashe Street,
Clonakilty. Tel: 023 33226.

Cork
Cork Public Museum
Fitzgerald Park, Cork, Co
Cork. Tel: 021 4270679.
*Open Mon–Fri, 11–1,
2.15–5, Sun 3–5.*

❶ Kinsale
Charles Fort
Summercove, Kinsale,
Co Cork. Tel: 021 772263.
*Open all year, ex mid-Mar to
mid-Apr, daily 10–6; last
admission 5.15pm.*

❷ Clonakilty
Timoleague Castle
Gardens
Clonakilty, Co Cork.
Tel: 023 46116.
*Open Jun–Aug, Mon–Sat
11–5.30, Sun 2–5.30; other
times by arrangement.*

Michael Collins Memorial
Centre
Woodfield, Co Cork.
Tel: 023 33226.
Open all year, daily.

Arigideen Heritage Park
Castleview, Clonakilty, Co
Cork. Tel: 023 46107.
*Open mid-Jun to mid-Sep,
Mon–Sat 10.30–5; other
times by appointment.*

❻ Gougane Barra
Forest Park
Coillte Teoranta,
Inchigeelagh, Macroom,
Co Cork. Tel 026 42837.
*Open all year daily, except
during tree harvesting times.*

For children
Cork Harbour Cruises
Kennedy Pier, Cobh,
Co Cork. Tel: 021 4811485.
*Cruises Jun–Sep at 12, 2, 3
and 3.50.*

[i] The Old Courthouse,
The Square, Bantry.
Tel: 027 50229.
[i] North Street,
Skibbereen. Tel: 028 21766.

Bantry
Bantry House Gardens
Bantry, Co Cork. Tel: 027
50047.
*Open 17 Mar–Oct, daily
10–6.*

❷ Skibbereen
Skibbereen Heritage
Centre
Upper Bridge Street,
Skibbereen, Co Cork.
Tel: 028 40900.
*Open mid-Mar–Oct,
Tue–Sat 10–6 (daily late
May–mid-Sep); last
admission 5.15pm.*

Sherkin Island Ferry
Baltimore. Tel: 028 20125.
*All year daily, outward
9–8.30, return 9.45–8.45.
Sightseeing and fishing tours
also available.*

Cape Clear Heritage
Centre
Cape Clear Island,
Co Cork. Tel: 028 39119.
Telephone for opening times.

❸ Skull
Skull Planetarium
Skull Community College,
Skull, Co Cork. Tel: 028
28552.
Telephone for opening times.

Cape Clear Ferry
Pier Road, Skull, Co Cork.
Tel: 028 28278.

Operates *all year daily
(weather permitting).*

❹ Mizen Head
Mizen Head Visitor
Centre
Mizen, Goleen, Co Cork.
Tel: 028 35115.
*Open mid-Mar–Oct, daily
10.30–5 (Jun–Sep 10–6);
Nov–mid-Mar, weekends
11–4.*

[i] The Quay, Waterford.
Tel: 051 875823.
[i] Town Centre, Tramore,
Co Waterford. Tel: 051
381572.
[i] The Courthouse,
Dungarvan, Co Waterford.
Tel: 058 41741.
[i] Heritage Centre,
Lismore. Tel: 058 54975.
[i] Castle Car Park, Cahir.
Tel 052 41453.
[i] Heritage Centre,
Cashel. Tel: 062 61333.
[i] Sarsfield Street,
Clonmel. Tel: 052 22960.
[i] Heritage Centre, Main
Street, Carrick-on Suir.
Tel: 051 640200.

Waterford
Waterford Crystal Visitor
Centre
Waterford, Co Waterford.
Tel: 051 332500.
*Open Jan–Feb, Nov–Dec,
daily 9–5; Mar–Oct, daily
8.30–6. Factory tours
Mar–Oct, daily 8.30–4.15;
Nov–Feb, Mon–Fri 9–3.15.*

Reginald's Tower
The Quay, Waterford,
Co Waterford. Tel: 051
858958.
*Open Easter–May, daily
10–5; Jun–Sep, daily
9.30–6.30; Oct, daily 10–5.*

❸ Tramore
Stradbally Hall, Demesne
and Steam Museum
Stradbally, Co Waterford.
Tel: 0502 25160.
*Telephone for opening times;
railway runs bank hols and in
summer on request.*

4 Dungarvan
Waterford County Museum
St Augustine Street, Dungarvan, Co Waterford. Tel: 058 45960.
Open all year, Mon–Fri, 10–1, 2–4.30 (5 in summer); also Sat in summer.

5 Cappoquin
Cappoquin House and Gardens
Cappoquin, Co Waterford. Tel: 058 54004.
Open Apr–Jul, Mon–Sat, 9–1.

6 Lismore
Lismore Castle Gardens
Lismore, Co Waterford. Tel: 058 54424.
Open Apr–Sep, 1.45–4.45 (from 11 in high season).

Lismore Heritage Centre
The Courthouse, Lismore, Co Waterford. Tel: 058 54975.
Open Apr–Oct, daily 9.30–5.30, Sun 12–5.30.

7 Caher
Caher Castle
Caher, Co Tipperary. Tel: 052 41011.
Open mid-Mar to mid-Oct daily 9.30–5.30 (7pm mid-Jun to mid-Sep); mid-Oct to mid-Mar, 9.30–4.30; last admission 45 minutes before closing.

Swiss Cottage
Kilcommon, Co Tipperary. Tel: 052 41144 or 41011.
Open mid-Mar–Apr, Tue–Sun 10–1, 2–4.30 (till 6 in Apr).

8 Cashel
Rock of Cashel, Co Tipperary. Tel: 062 61437.
Open daily, mid-Sep to mid-Mar, mid-Jun to mid-Sep 9–4.30; mid-Mar to mid-Jun 9–5.30.

9 Clonmel
Clonmel Museum of Transport
Gortnafleur Business Park, Clonmel, Co Tipperary. Tel: 052 29727. *Open all year,*

Mon–Sat 10–6; also Sun Jun–Aug 2.30–6.

South Tipperary County Museum
The Borstal, Clonmel, Co Tipperary. Tel: 052 34550.
Open all year, Tue–Sat 10–5.

10 Carrick-on-Suir
Ormond Castle
Off Castle Street, Carrick-on-Suir, Co Tipperary. Tel: 051 640787.
Open mid-Jun to mid-Sep, daily 9.30– 6.30; last admission 5.45pm.

Heritage Centre
Main Street, Carrick-on-Suir, Co Tipperary. Tel: 051 640200.
Open daily 10–4 (5 Jun–Sep; may vary weekends).

Tipperary Crystal
Ballynoran, Carrick-on-Suir, Co Tipperary. Tel: 051 641188.
Open Mon–Fri 9–5.30, Sat 9.30–5, Sun 11–5. Tours Mon–Fri 10–3.30.

TOUR 11

i Athlone Castle, Athlone. Tel: 090 6472107 (seasonal).
i Market House, Mullingar. Tel: 044 48650.
i Clonmacnoise. Tel: 090 9674134 (seasonal).

Athlone
Athlone Castle and Visitor Centre
St Peters Square, Athlone, Co Westmeath. Tel: 090 6494630.
Open May–Sep, daily 10–4.30.

1 Mullingar
Tullynally Castle and Gardens
Castlepollard, Co Westmeath. Tel: 044 61159.
Gardens May–Aug, daily 2–6; Castle mid-Jun–Jul, 2–6.

2 Tullamore
Locke's Distillery Museum
Kilbeggan, Co Offaly. Tel: 0506 32134.

Open Nov–Mar, 10–4, Apr–Oct 9–6.

Tullamore Dew Heritage Centre
Bury Quay, Tullamore, Co Offaly. Tel: 0506 25015.
Open daily, May–Sep 9–6; Oct–Apr 10–5, Sun 12–5.

4 Clonmacnoise
Shannonbridge, Co Offaly. Tel: 090 9674195.
Open mid-May–Dec, daily 9–7.

For Children
Clonmacnoise and West Offaly Railway Bog Tour
Shannonbridge, Co Offaly. Tel: 090 9674114.
Open Apr–early Oct, daily 10–5.

TOUR 12

i Mayoralty Street, Drogheda. Tel: 041 9845684.
i Ludlow Street, Navan. Tel: 046 9073426.

2 Mellifont
Old Mellifont Abbey
Tullyallen, Co Louth. Tel: 041 9826459.
Open May–Oct, daily 10–6. Last admission 5.15pm.

3 Newgrange
Brú na Boinne Visitor Centre
Newgrange and Knowth Dunore, Drogheda, Co Meath. 041 9880300.
Open daily from 9 or 9.30, closing time varies. Knowth open May–Oct only.

4 Slane
Slane Castle
Slane, Co Meath. Tel: 041 9884400.
Open May–early Aug, Mon–Thu noon–5.

5 Kells
Kells Heritage Centre
Headfort Place, Kells, Co Meath. Tel: 046 9247840.
Open Oct–Apr, Mon–Sat 10–5; May–Sep, Mon–Sat 10–5.30, Sun and bank hols 2–5.30.

7 Tara
Hill of Tara Visitor Centre
St Patrick's Church, Hill of Tara, Co Meath. Tel: 046 9025903.
Open May–Oct, daily 10–6; last admission 5.15pm.

For history buffs
Trim Castle
Trim, Co Meath. Tel: 046 9438619.
Open May–Oct, daily 10–6.

For children
Newgrange Farm
Newgrange, Slane, Co Meath. Tel: 041 9824119.
Open Easter Sat–Aug, 10–5.

TOUR 13

i Suffolk Street, Dublin. Tel: 01 605 7799.
i Glendalough Visitor Centre, Glendalough. Tel: 0404 45325 (seasonal).

1 Dun Laoghaire
National Maritime Museum of Ireland
Haigh Terrace, Laoghaire, Co Dublin. Tel: 01 2800969.
Open mid-Jun–Oct, Tue–Sun, 1–5.

James Joyce Museum
Joyce Tower, Sandycove, Co Dublin. Tel: 01 2809265.
Open Mar–Oct, Mon–Sat 10–1, 2–5, Sun & bank hols, 2–6.

3 Bray
Heritage Centre
Old Courthouse, Bray, Co Wicklow. Tel: 01 2867128.
Open Mon–Fri, 9.30–1, 2–4.30, Sat 10–3.

Kilruddery House and Gardens
Bray, Co Wicklow. Tel: 01 2862777.
Open Apr–Sep, daily 1–5.

4 Enniskerry
Powerscourt Gardens and House Exhibition
Enniskerry, Co Wicklow. Tel: 01 2046000.
Open daily 9.30–5.30.

5 Roundwood
Mount Usher Gardens
Ashford, Co Wicklow.
Tel: 0404 40116.
*Open early Mar–Oct, daily
10.30–6.*

6 Glendalough
Visitor Centre
Glendalough, Co Wicklow.
Tel: 0404 45352.
*Open mid-Mar to mid-Oct,
daily 9.30–6.*

Avondale House and
Forest Park
Rathdrum, Co Wicklow.
Tel: 0404 46111.
*Open all year, daily from
11am.*

8 Blessington
Russborough House
Blessington, Co Wicklow.
Tel: 045 865239.
*Open Apr & Oct, Sun &
bank hols 10–5; May–Sep,
daily 10–5.*

10 Killakee
Rathfarnham Castle
Rathfarnham, Dublin 14.
Tel: 01 4939462.
*Open May–Oct, daily
9.30–5.30.*

Special to...
Guinness Storehouse
St James Gate, Dublin 8.
Tel: 01 4538364.
*Open all year, daily 9.30–5;
Jul, Aug 9.30–8.*

For children
Clara Lara Funpark
Vale of Clara, Rathdrum,
Co Wicklow. Tel: 0404
46161.
*Open May–early Sep, daily
10–6.*

Recommended walks
Marlay Park
Rathfarnham, Dublin 14.
Tel: 01 4934059.
Open daily 10–8.

For history buffs
Pearse Museum
St Enda's Park, Grange
Road, Rathfarnham,
Dublin 16. Tel: 01 4934208.
*Open all year, daily 10–1,
2–4 (5 or 5.30 in summer).*

TOUR 14

i Shee Alms House,
Rose Inn Street, Kilkenny.
Tel: 056 7751500.
i The Quay, New Ross.
Tel: 051 421857.
i Tullow Street, Carlow.
Tel: 059 9131554.
i Market House, Kildare.
Tel: 045 521240.
i James Fintan Lawlor
Avenue, Portlaoise. Tel:
0502 21178.

Kilkenny
Kilkenny Castle
The Parade, Kilkenny, Co
Kilkenny. Tel: 056 21450.
*Open Apr–May, daily
10.30–5; Jun–Aug, daily
9.30–7; Sep 10–6.30;
Oct–Mar, 10.30–12.45,
2–5.*

1 Thomastown
Jerpoint Abbey
Thomastown, Co Kilkenny.
Tel: 056 24623.
*Open Mar–May, mid-
Sep–Oct, daily 10–5;
Jun–mid-Sep, daily 9.30–
6.30; Nov 10–4; last admis-
sion one hour before closing.*

4 Kildare
Irish National Stud,
Japanese Gardens and St
Fiachras Garden
Tully, Co Kildare. Tel: 045
521617 or 045 522963.
*Open mid-Feb to mid-Nov
daily 9.30–6; last admission
5pm.*

5 Portlaoise
Emo Court
Emo, Co Laois. Tel: 0502
26573.
*Gardens open all year daily
during daylight hours. House
open for guided tours mid-
Jun–mid-Sep 10.30–5; last
tour 4.30pm.*

9 Fethard
Fethard Folk and
Transport Museum
Cashel Road, Fethard. Co
Tipperary. Tel: 052 31516.
Open May–Oct, daily 10–6.

Back to nature
John F Kennedy Park and
Arboretum
New Ross, Co Wexford.
Tel: 051 388171.
*Open Oct–Mar, daily 10–5;
Apr, Sep, daily 10–6.30;
May–Aug, daily 10–8; last
admission 45 minutes before
closing.*

TOUR 15

i Crescent Quay,
Wexford. Tel: 053 23111.
i Town Centre, Gorey.
Tel: 055 21248.
i The Castle, Enniscorthy.
Tel: 054 34699.
i The Quay, New Ross.
Tel: 051 421857.
i 41, The Quay, Water-
ford. Tel: 051 875823.
i Rosslare Harbour,
Kilrane, Rosslare. Tel: 053
33232.

Wexford
Irish National Heritage
Park
Ferrycarrig, Co Wexford.
Tel: 053 20733.
*Open, daily 9.30–6.30; last
admission 5pm.*

3 Enniscorthy
Wexford County Museum
Castle Hill, Enniscorthy, Co
Wexford. Tel: 054 35926.
*Open Jun–Sep, daily 10–6;
Oct–Nov, Feb–May, daily
2–5.30; Dec–Jan Sun 2–5.*

National 1798 Rebellion
Centre
Millpark Road, Enniscorthy,
Co Wexford. Tel: 054
37596.
*Open Mon–Sat 9.30–6, Sun
11–6; last admission 5pm.*

4 New Ross
The *Dunbrody*
South Quay, New Ross,
Co Wexford. Tel: 051
425239.
*Open Apr–Sep, daily 9–6;
Oct–Mar, daily noon–5.*

Dunbrody Abbey Visitor
Centre
Campile, Co Wexford.
Tel: 051 388603.
Open May–Sep, daily 10–6.

---

5 Waterford
Waterford City Municipal
Art Collection
City Hall, The Mall,
Waterford, Co Waterford.
Tel: 051 873501.
*Open Mon–Fri 10–1, 2–5;
May–Sep, Sat–Sun 11–4.*

Garter Lane Arts
Centre
O'Connell Street,
Waterford, Co Waterford.
Tel: 051 855038.
*Open Tue–Sat 12–6. Check
before visiting as opening
times are subject to seasonal
variations.*

7 Ballyhack
Ballyhack Castle
Ballyhack, Co Wexford.
Tel: 051 389468.
*Open Jun–Sep, daily
9.30–6.30.*

8 Hook Head
Hook Lighthouse Visitor
Centre
Hook Head, Co Wexford.
Tel: 051 397055.
*Open Mar–Oct, daily
9.30–5.30; Nov–Feb 10–5.*

9 Fethard
Tintern Abbey
Fethard, Co Wexford.
Tel: 051 562650.
*Open mid-Jun–Sep,
9.30–6.30; last admission
5.45pm.*

TOUR 16

i Temple Street, Sligo.
Tel: 071 9161201.
i The Bridge, Bundoran.
Tel: 071 9841350.

2 Lissadell
Lissadell House
Drumcliffe, Co Sligo.
Tel: 071 9163150.
*Open Jun–mid-Sep, Tue–Sun
10–1, 2–5.*

7 Lough Gill
Parkes Castle
Fivemile Bourne, Co
Leitrim. Tel: 071 9164149.
*Open mid-Mar–Oct, daily
10–6; last admission
5.15pm.*

8 Dromahair
Lake Isle of Innisfree
Lough Gill, Co Sligo.
Tel: 071 9164266.
*Cruises operate Jun–Sep
12.30–5.30.*

10 Strandhill
Carrowmore Megalithic
Cemetery
Strandhill, Co Sligo. Tel: 071
9161534.
*Open Easter–Oct, daily
10–5.15.*

For history buffs
Creevykeel Court
Tomb
Dundoran Road,
Cliffoney, Co Sligo. Tel: 071
9161021.
Open at all times.

TOUR 17

i King House, Boyle.
Tel: 071 9662145.
i The Marina, Carrick-
on-Shannon. Tel: 071
9620170.
i 45 Dublin Street,
Longford. Tel: 043 46566.
i Harrison Hall,
Roscommon. Tel: 090
6626342.

Boyle
King House
Boyle, Co Roscommon.
Tel: 071 9663242.
*Open Apr–Sep, daily 10–6;
last admission 5pm.*

Back to nature
Lough Key Forest Park
Boyle, Co Roscommon.
Tel: 071 9662363.
Open daily.

2 Longford
Carrigglas Manor
Longford, Co Longford.
Tel: 043 45165.
*Telephone for details of tours
and opening times.*

3 Roscommon
Roscommon County
Museum
The Square, Roscommon,
Co Roscommon. Tel: 090
6625613. *Open Apr–Oct,
Mon–Sat 10–5.30;
Nov–Mar by appointment.*

4 Castlerea
Clonalis House
Castlerea, Co Roscommon.
Tel: 0907 20014.
*Open Jun–mid-Sep, Tue–Sun
12–5.*

TOUR 18

i James Street, Westport.
Tel: 098 25711.
i Cashel, Achill Island.
Tel: 098 47353.
i Cathedral Road, Ballina.
Tel: 096 70848.
i Town Centre, Knock.
Tel: 094 9388193.
i Mill Museum, Tuam.
Tel: 093 25486.
i Town Centre,
Castlebar. Tel: 094 9021207.

Westport
Westport Heritage
Centre
James Street, Westport,
Co Mayo.
Open all year.

Westport House
Westport, Co Mayo.
Tel: 098 25430.
Open Mar–Oct 11.30–5.

4 Knock
Knock Shrine
Knock, Co Mayo. Tel: 094
9388100.
*Open late Apr–Oct, main
ceremony Mon–Sat 2.15,
Sun 2.30, 7 Masses daily.*

Knock Folk Museum
Knock, Co Mayo. Tel: 094
9388100.
Open May–Oct, 10–6.

5 Tuam
Tuam Mill Museum
Shop Street, Tuam,
Co Mayo. Tel: 093 25486.
Open Mon–Sat 10–6.

8 Castlebar
Museum of Country Life
Turlough Park, Turlough,
Castlebar, Co Mayo.
Tel: 094 9031173.
*Open all year, Tue–Sat 10–5,
Sun 2–5.*

For history buffs
Ballintobber Abbey,
Ballintobber, Claremorris,

Co Mayo. Tel: 094
9030934. *Telephone for
opening times and tours.*

**Ceide Fields Visitor
Centre and Site**
West of Ballycastle, Co
Mayo. Tel: 096 43325.
*Open mid-Mar–Nov 10–5
(Jun–Sep 10–6).*

TOUR 19

i Forster Street, Galway.
Tel: 091 537700.
i Galway Road, Clifden.
Tel: 095 21163.
i Main Street, Oughter-
ard. Tel: 091 552808.

Galway
Nora Barnacle House
Museum
Bowling Green, Galway,
Co Galway. Tel: 091
564743. *Open mid-May to
mid-Sep, Mon–Sat 10–5.*

2 Rossaveel
Aran Island Ferries
Rossaveel, Co Galway.
Tel: 091 568903.
*Sailings daily, outward:
10.30am, 6pm (also 1pm
Jun–Sep); return 9am, 5pm
(also 12, 7.30pm Jun–Sep).*

4 Gortmore
Patrick Pearse's Cottage
Rosmuck, Co Galway.
Tel: 091 574292.
*Open mid-Jun to mid-Sep,
daily 10–6.*

6 Roundstone
Roundstone Music and
Crafts
Roundstone, Co Galway.
Tel: 095 35808.
*Open Jul–Aug, daily 9–7;
May–Oct, daily 9.30–6.*

8 Kylemore Abbey
Connemara, Co Galway.
Tel: 095 41146.
Open all year, daily 9–5.30.

10 Oughterard
Aughnanure Castle
Oughterard, Co Galway.
Tel: 091 552214.
*Open May–mid-Sep, daily
9.30–6; mid-Sep–Oct,
Sat–Sun 9.30–6.*

Back to nature
Connemara National Park
Visitor Centre
Letterfrack, Co Galway.
Tel: 095 41054.
*Open mid-Mar–Oct, daily
10–5.30.*

TOUR 20

i 44, Foyle Street,
Londonderry. Tel: 028
71267284.
i Blaney Road, Letter-
kenny. Tel: 074 9121160.

**1 The Grianán of
Aileach**
Burt, Inishowen, Co
Donegal. Tel: 077 68000.

4 Rathmullan
The Flight of the Earls
Heritage Centre
Tel: 074 58131.
*Open mid-May–Sep, Mon–
Sat 10–6, Sun 12–6.30.*

11 Glenveagh
Columcille Heritage
Centre
Gartan, Churchill. Tel: 074
9137306.
*Open Easter, & 1st Sun in
May–last Sun in Sep, Mon–
Fri 10.30–6.30, Sun 1–6.30.*

Back to nature
Glenveagh National Park
Churchill, Co Donegal.
Tel: 074 9137090.
*Open mid-Oct to mid-Mar,
daily 9.30–5; mid-Mar to
mid-Oct daily 9.30–6; last
admission 45 minutes before
closing.*

Glebe House and Gallery
Churchill. Tel: 074 37071.
*Open Easter, mid-May–Sep,
daily, except Fri 11–6.30.*

TOUR 21

i Narrow Gauge Road,
Larne. Tel: 028 28260088.
i Sheskburn House,
7 Mary Street, Ballycastle.
Tel: 028 20762024.
i Giant's Causeway,
Bushmills. Tel: 028 20731855.
i Dunluce Centre,
Sandhill Drive, Portrush.
Tel: 028 70823333.

[i] 7 Connell Street, Limavady. Tel: 028 77760307.

Larne
Carnfunnock Country Park
Coast Road, Larne, Co Antrim. Tel: 028 28270541.
Open daily.

5 Glenariff
Glenariff Forest Park
Glenariff, Co Antrim.
Tel: 028 29556000.
Open daily, 10–sunset.

7 Ballycastle
Ballycastle Museum
59 Castle Street. Tel: 028 20762942.
Open Jul, Aug daily 12–6 or by arrangement.

Rathlin Island
Ferry from The Harbour, Ballycastle, Co Antrim.
Tel: 028 20769299.
Phone for details.

8 Carrick-a-Rede
Carrick-a-Rede Rope Bridge
Larrybane, Co Antrim.
Tel: 028 20731159.
Open mid-Mar to mid-Jun, Sep–mid-Oct 10–6; mid-Jun–Aug 10–7.

9 Giant's Causeway
60 Causeway Road, Bushmills, Co Antrim.
Tel: 028 20731582.
Open all year. Shop open Mar–mid-Dec daily; mid-Dec–Feb, phone for details.

Causeway School Museum
Causeway Road, Bushmills, Co Antrim. Tel: 028 20731777.
Open Jul–Aug daily 11–5.

10 Bushmills
Bushmills Distillery
Bushmills, Co Antrim.
Tel 028 20733218.
Open Apr–Oct, Mon–Sat, 9.30–5.30, Sun 12–5.30. Last tour 4pm; Nov–Mar, Mon–Fri, 5 tours daily, 10.30–3.30; Sat–Sun 3 tours daily 1.30, 2.30, 3.30.

11 Portrush
Dunluce Castle
Bushmills, Co Antrim.
Tel: 028 20731938.
Open Apr–Sep, Mon–Sat, 10–6, Sun 2–6; Jul, Aug, Sun 12–6; Oct–Mar, Tue–Sat 10–4, Sun 2–4.

12 Downhill
Downhill and Mussenden Temple
Bishop's Gate, 42 Mussenden Road, Castlerock, Coleraine, Co Londonderry. Tel: 028 70848728.
Grounds daily, dawn to dusk; Temple Mar–Jun, Sep, 11–6; Jul–Aug, 11–7.30; Oct 11–5.

Benone Tourist Complex
53 Benone Avenue, Limavady, Co Londonderry. Tel: 028 77750555.
Open Apr–Jun 9am–dusk; Jul–Aug 9am–10pm; Sep 9am–dusk; Oct–Mar 9–5.

13 Limavady
Roe Valley Country Park
Limavady, Co Londonderry. Tel: 028 77722074.
Open daily.

14 Ballymoney
Leslie Hill Open Farm
Ballymoney, Co Antrim.
Tel: 028 27666803.
Open Jul & Aug, Mon–Sat 11–6, Sun 2–6.

For children
Portrush Countryside Centre
Portrush, Co Antrim.
Tel: 028 70823600.
Open Jul, Aug 12–8.

Dunluce Centre
10 Sandhill Drive, Portrush, Co Antrim.
Tel: 028 70824444.
Open Easter–mid-Apr, Jul, Aug, daily 10.30–6.30; mid-Apr, May, Sat–Sun 12–6.30; Jun Mon–Fri 10–5; Sep–Mar, Sat–Sun 12–5.

TOUR 22

[i] Belfast Welcome Centre, 59 North Street, Belfast. Tel: 028 90246609.

[i] 31 Regent Street, Newtownards. Tel: 028 91826846.
[i] The Stables, Castle Street, Portaferry.
Tel: 028 42729882.
[i] The St Patrick Centre, 53A, Market Street, Downpatrick. Tel: 028 44612233.

Belfast
City Hall
Donegall Square, Belfast.
Tel: 028 90270456.
Open for tours, Jun–Sep, Mon–Fri 11, 2, 3, Sat 2.30; Oct–May, Mon–Fri 11, 2.30, Sat 2.30.

Ulster Museum
Botanic Gardens, Botanic Avenue, Belfast. Tel: 028 90383000.
Open Mon–Fri 10–5, Sat 1–5, Sun 2–5.

1 Cultra
Ulster Folk and Transport Museum
Cultra, Co Down. Tel: 028 90428428.
Open at 10 Mon–Sat, 11 on Sun. Closing times vary from 4 to 6 according to season.

2 Newtownards
Scrabo Tower and Country Park
Newtownards, Co Down.
Tel: 028 91811491. *Country Park open Jul–Sep, Sat–Thu. Scrabo Tower open Jun–Sep, Sat–Thu 11–6.30.*

3 Greyabbey
Grey Abbey
Greyabbey, Co Down.
Tel: 028 90543037.
Open Apr–Sep, Tue–Sat, 10–7, Sun 2–7; Oct–Mar, Sat 10–4, Sun 2–4.

Mount Stewart
Greyabbey, Co Down.
Tel: 028 42788387.
House open: Apr, Oct, Sat–Sun 1–6; Easter, daily 1–6; May–Sep, Wed–Mon 1–6; last tour at 5. Garden: Apr–Sep, daily 11–6; Oct, Sat–Sun 10.30– 6; also Sun during Mar 2–5.

6 Portaferry
Exploris
The Rope Walk, Castle Street, Portaferry, Co Down. Tel: 028 42728062.
Open Apr–Aug, Mon–Fri 10–6, Sat 11–6, Sun 12–6; Sep–Mar, Mon–Fri 10–5, Sat 11–5, Sun 1–5.

7 Strangford
Castle Ward
Strangford, Downpatrick, Co Down. Tel: 028 44881204.
Open mid-Mar–Apr, Sep–Oct, Sat, Sun & bank hols 1–6; May, Wed–Mon 1–6; Jun–Aug 1–6.

8 Downpatrick
Down Cathedral
The Mall, English Street, Downpatrick, Co Down.
Tel: 028 44614922.
Open Mon–Sat 9.30–4.30, Sun 2–5.

Down County Museum
The Mall, English Street, Downpatrick, Co Down.
Tel: 028 44615218.
Open Mon–Fri 10–5, Sat–Sun 1–5.

Inch Abbey
Downpatrick, Co Down.
Tel: 028 90235000.

10 Nendrum Monastic Site
Mahee Island, Comber, Co Down. Tel: 028 90543037.
Open Apr–Sep, Tue–Sat 10–7, Sun 2–7; Oct–Mar, Sat 10–4, Sun 2–4.

Back to nature
Castle Espie Wildfowl and Wetlands Centre
Ballydrain Road, Comber, Co Down. Tel: 028 91874146.
Open Mar–Oct, Mon–Fri 10.30–5 (5.30 Jul, Aug), Sat–Sun 11–5.30; Nov–Feb, Mon–Fri 11–4, Sat–Sun 11–4.30.

TOUR 23

[i] Wellington Road, Enniskillen. Tel: 028 66323110.

Practical • Information

Enniskillen

Enniskillen Castle
Castle Barracks, Enniskillen,
Co Fermanagh. Tel: 028
66325000.
*Open Mon 2–5, Tue–Fri
10–5.*

Castle Coole
Enniskillen, Co Fermanagh.
Tel: 028 66322690.
*Open Apr, Sep, Sun and
bank hols 1–6; Easter, daily
1–6; May–Aug, Fri–Wed
1–6; last tour 5.15pm.*

[1] Devenish
Devenish Island
Co Fermanagh. Tel: 028
66323110.
*Ferry operates Good Friday–
mid-Sep, daily 10, 1, 3, 5.*

[2] Castle Archdale
Kesh, Co Fermanagh.
Tel: 028 68621588.
*Park open all year 9am–
dusk. Museum and Visitor
Centre open Easter Sun
12–6, May bank hol 11–6;
Jul–Aug, Tue–Sun 11–7.*

White Island Ferry
Castle Archdale, Kesh,
Co Fermanagh. Tel: 028
68621892.
Seasonal, phone for details.

[3] Belleek
Belleek Pottery Visitor
Centre
Belleek, Co Fermanagh.
Tel: 028 68658501.
*Open Apr–Jun, Sep, Mon–Fri
9–6, Sat 10–6, Sun 2–6;
Jul–Aug, Mon–Fri 9–8, Sat
10–6, Sun 11–6; Oct
Mon–Fri 9–5.30, Sat
10–5.30, Sun 2–6;
Nov–Mar, Mon–Fri 9–5.30.*

[8] Marble Arch
Marble Arch Caves
Marlbank Scenic Loop,
Florencecourt, Co
Fermanagh. Tel: 028
66348855.
*Open mid- to late Mar–Sep,
10–4.30; may close after
heavy rain.*

[9] Florence Court
Florence Court village,
Co Fermanagh. Tel: 028

66348249.
*Open mid-Mar–May, Sep,
Sat, Sun & Bank Holidays
12–6; Jun–Aug, daily 12–6.*

[10] Bellanaleck
Crom Estate
Newtownbutler, Co
Fermanagh. Tel: 028
67738118.
*Open mid-Mar–Sep,
Mon–Sat 10–6, Sun 12–6.*

TOUR 24

[i] 40 English Street,
Armagh. Tel: 028 37521800.
[i] 190 Ballygawley Road,
Dungannon. Tel: 028
87767259.
[i] The Burnavon,
Burn Road, Cookstown.
Tel: 028 86766727
[i] 1 Market Street,
Omagh. Tel: 028 82247831.

Armagh

Emain Macha, Navan Fort
81 Killylea Road, Armagh,
Co Armagh. Tel: 028 3752
1800.

[1] Loughgall
Ardress House
Ardress, Co Armagh.
Tel: 028 38851236.
*Open mid-Mar–late Sep,
Sat–Sun 2–6.*

[2] Moy
The Argory
Moy, Dungannon, Co
Tyrone. Tel: 028 87784753.
*Open mid-Mar–May, Sep,
Sat, Sun & bank hols 2–6;
Jun–Aug 2–6.*

[3] Dungannon
Tyrone Crystal
Killybrackey, Coalisland
Road, Dungannon, Co
Tyrone. Tel: 028 87725335.
*Open daily, seasonal times;
call for details.*

Grant Ancestral Home
45 Dergna Road,
Dungannon, Co Tyrone.
Tel: 028 85551733.
*Open Mar–May, Oct,
Mon–Fri 10.30–4.30;
Jun–Sep, Mon–Sat 10–6.30,
Sun 2–6; last admission one
hour before closing.*

[4] Cookstown
Drum Manor Forest Park
Cookstown, Co Tyrone.
Tel: 028 86762774.
Open daily dawn to dusk.

Wellbrook Beetling Mill
20, Wellbrook Road,
Corkhill, Cookstown, Co
Tyrone. Tel: 028 86748210.
*Open mid-Mar–Jun, Sep, Sat,
Sun & Bank Holidays 12–6;
Jul & Aug, daily 12–6.*

[5] Gortin
Gortin Glen Forest Park
Lislap, Omagh, Co Tyrone.
Tel: 028 81648217.
Open daily dawn-dusk.

Ulster History Park
Cullion, Lislap, Omagh, Co
Tyrone. Tel: 028 81648188.
*Open Apr–Sep, Mon–Sat
10.30–6.30, Sun 11.30–7;
Oct–Mar Mon–Fri 10–5;
last admission 1.5 hours
before closing.*

[6] Omagh
Ulster-American Folk Park
Mellon Road, Castletown,
Omagh, Co Tyrone. Tel: 028
82243292.
*Open Apr–Sep, Mon–Sat
10.30–4.30, Sun and bank
hols 11–5.*

[8] The Clogher Valley
Fivemiletown Coach and
Carriage Museum
Fivemiletown, Co Tyrone.
Tel: 028 89521221.
Telephone for details.

For children
Benburb Valley Heritage
Centre
Milltown Road, Benburb,
Dungannon, Co Tyrone.
Tel: 028 37549885.
Open daily 10–5.

TOUR 25

[i] 200 Newry Road,
Banbridge. Tel: 028
40623322.
[i] Newcastle Centre,
Central Promenade,
Newcastle. Tel: 028
43722222.

[4] Castlewellan
Castlewellan Forest Park
Main Street, Castlewellan,
Co Down. Tel: 028
43778664.
Open daily, 10am–dusk.

For children
Seaforde Butterfly House
Seaforde, Co Down.
Tel: 028 44811225.
*Open Apr–Sep, Mon–Sat
10–5, Sun 1–6.*

[5] Dundrum
Dundrum Castle
Dundrum, Co Down.
Tel: 028 90543037.
*Open Apr–Sep, Tue–Sat,
10–7, Sun 2–7; Oct–Mar,
Sat 10–4, Sun 2–4.*

[6] Newcastle
Mourne Heritage Trust
87, Central Promenade,
Newcastle, Co Down.
Tel: 028 43724059.
Open all year, Mon–Fri, 9–5.

Tollymore Forest Park
Tullybrannigan Road,
Newcastle, Co Down.
Tel: 028 43722428.
Open 10–sunset.

[7] Annalong
Annalong Corn Mill
The Harbour, Annalong, Co
Down. Tel: 028 3026887.
Telephone for details.

**[8] The Silent Valley
Visitor Centre**
Head Road, Kilkeel, Co
Down. Tel: 028 90741166.
*Open May–Sep 10–6;
Oct–Apr 10–4.*

[10] Rostrevor
Kilbroney Park
Kilkeel Road, Rostrevor,
Co Down. Tel: 028
41738134.
Open daily.

Back to Nature
Murlough National
Nature Reserve Visitor
Centre
Dundrum, Co Down.
Tel: 028 43751467.
*Open access daily, visitor
facilities May–Sep.*

INDEX

Index & Acknowledgements

The Automobile Association

wishes to thank the following libraries and photographers for their assistance in the preparation of this book.

BORD FAILTE 18; MICHAEL DIGGIN 59, 151; NORTHERN IRELAND TOURIST BOARD 123, 137, 147, 148, 149.

The remaining transparencies are held in the Association's own library (AA WORLD TRAVEL LIBRARY) and were taken by:

L BLAKE 40, 82, 99, 102, 104, 109, 112, 114/5, 118; J BLANDFORD 6, 28, 30, 31, 32/3, 35, 36, 37, 52, 56, 56/7, 58, 106; C COE 79; S L DAY 7, 12, 45, 50, 63, 65, 70, 71, 96/7, 98, 120/1, 121, 146; M DIGGIN 8, 17, 27, 114, 117; D FORSS 49, 110, 130; C HILL 100, 101, 102/3, 105, 107, 111, 113, 116, 127, 160; S HILL 5, 9, 10/11, 13, 26, 34, 48, 50, 51, 54, 129; J JENNINGS 135, 141, 144, 171; G MUNDAY 122, 125, 128, 131, 133, 138, 140, 142, 143, 145, 153, 154/5, 156, 157; M SHORT 2, 38/9, 41, 42, 44, 46, 47, 53, 55, 61, 69, 73, 74, 75, 76, 77, 80, 81, 84, 85, 86, 87, 88, 89, 90, 92, 94, 95; A STONEHOUSE 29; P ZOELLER 14, 15, 16, 19, 21, 22/3, 24, 25, 60, 62, 64, 66, 78, 90/1, 93, 97, 166.

Contributors

Verifiers: Penny Phenix and Anna Phenix **Designer:** Jo Tapper **Indexer:** Marie Lorimer

Atlas

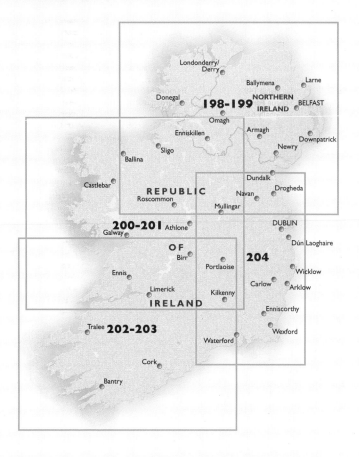

Londonderry/Derry

Ballymena
Larne

Donegal

198-199 NORTHERN IRELAND
BELFAST

Omagh

Enniskillen

Armagh
Downpatrick

Newry

Ballina

Sligo

Castlebar

REPUBLIC
Roscommon
Dundalk
Navan
Drogheda

Mullingar

200-201 Athlone

Galway

DUBLIN
Dún Laoghaire

O F

Birr

Portlaoise

204

Ennis

Limerick

Kilkenny

Carlow
Arklow
Wicklow

IRELAND

Enniscorthy

Tralee **202-203**

Wexford

Waterford

Cork

Bantry

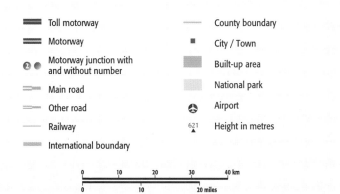

▬▬	Toll motorway	⋯⋯	County boundary
▬▬	Motorway	■	City / Town
➋ ●	Motorway junction with and without number		Built-up area
⇒	Main road		National park
⇢	Other road	✈	Airport
—	Railway	621 ▲	Height in metres
▬	International boundary		

0	10	20	30	40 km
0		10		20 miles

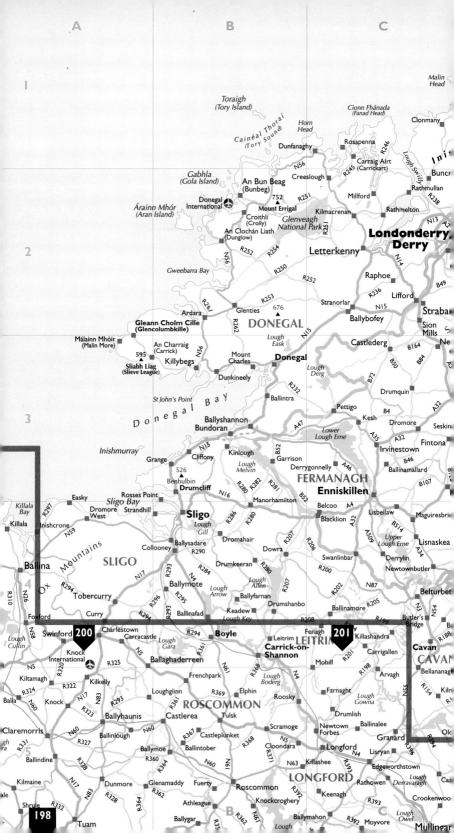

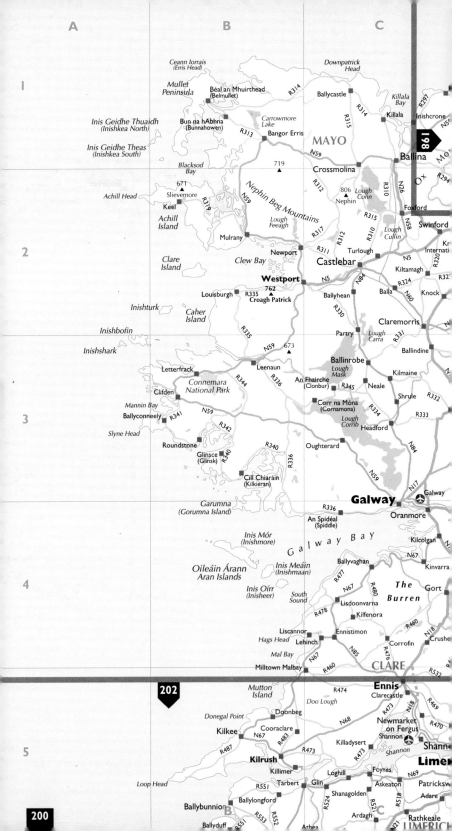

1

Ceann Iorrais
(Erris Head)
Mullet
Peninsula
Béal an Mhuirthead
(Belmullet)
Downpatrick
Head
Ballycastle
R314
Killala
Bay
Killala
Inishcrone
R297

Inis Geidhe Thuaidh
(Inishkea North)
Bun na hAbhna
(Bunnahowen)
Carrowmore
Lake
R313
Bangor Erris
MAYO
R315
R314
Ballina

198

Inis Geidhe Theas
(Inishkea South)
Blacksod
Bay
719
Crossmolina
R312
806
Nephin
Lough
Conn
R310
N26
R294

Achill Head
671
Slievemore
Keel
Achill
Island
R319
N59
Nephin Beg Mountains
Lough
Feeagh
R317
R315
Lough
Cullin
Foxford
N58
Swinford

2

Clare
Island
Mulrany
Clew Bay
Newport
Castlebar
Turlough
N5
Kr
Internati
N320
R32

Westport
762
Croagh Patrick
Ballyhean
N84
Kiltamagh
Balla
R324
Knock
N60

Inishturk
Louisburgh
R335
R335
Ballyhean
R330
Claremorris
Ballindine
R331

Inishbofin
Caher
Island
Partry
Lough
Carra
Ballinrobe

Inishshark
N59
673
Lough
Mask
Kilmaine
Shrule
R332

3

Letterfrack
Connemara
National Park
Clifden
R344
Leenaun
R336
An Fhairche
(Clonbur)
R345
Neale
R334
R333

Mannin Bay
Ballyconneely
R341
N59
R342
Corr na Móna
(Cornamona)
Lough
Corrib
Headford
N84

Slyne Head
Roundstone
Glinsce
(Glinsk)
R340
R340
R336
Oughterard
N59

Cill Chiaráin
(Kilkieran)
Galway
Oranmore

Garumna
(Gorumna Island)
R336
An Spidéal
(Spiddle)
Kilcolgan
N67

Inis Mór
(Inishmore)
G a l w a y   B a y
Ballyvaghan
N67
Kinvarra

4

Oileáin Árann
Aran Islands
Inis Meáin
(Inishmaan)
R477
R480
The
Burren
Gort

Inis Oírr
(Inisheer)
South
Sound
R478
Lisdoonvarna
Kilfenora
R460
R18
Crushe

Liscannor
Lehinch
Ennistimon
Corrofin
R476
R532

Hags Head
Mal Bay
N67
N85
CLARE

Milltown Malbay
R460

202

Mutton
Island
R474
Doo Lough
Ennis
Clarecastle
R473
N18
R469

5

Donegal Point
Doonbeg
N68
Newmarket
on Fergus
Shannon
R470

Kilkee
Cooraclare
N67
R483
Killadysert
Shannon
Shann

Kilrush
R487
R473
Loghill
Foynes
Limer

Loop Head
Killimer
Tarbert
Glin
R524
Shanagolden
Askeaton
R518
Patricksw

R551
Ballylongford
Glin
R521
Ardagh
Adare
Rathkeale

Ballybunnion
Ballyduff
B
R553
R552
Arbea
C
LIMERICK

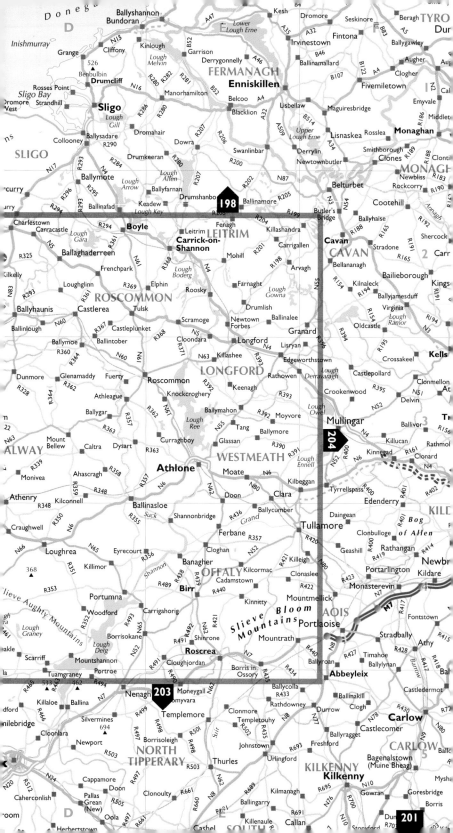

A   B   C

1

2

3

4

5

Inis Mór
(Inishmore)

G lway Ba

Oileáin Árann
Aran Islands

Inis Meáin
(Inishmaan)

Ballyvaghan
R477
N67
Lisdoonva
R478   Kilfe
Ennistimon

Inis Oírr
(Inisheer)

South
Sound

Liscannor
Hags Head   Lehinch
Mal Bay   N67
Milltown Malbay   R460   N85

Mutton
Island   R474

Doo Lough

Donegal Point   Doonbeg   N68

Kilkee   Cooraclare
N67   R483   Killadysert
R487   R473   R473

Kilrush   Killimer   Loghill
Tarbert   Glin   Shanagolden
R551   R524   Ardagl

Loop Head   Ballylongford   Athea   R523
R551   R553   R552

Ballybunnion   R555   Newcastle
Wes

Ballyduff   R551   Abbeyfeale   R5
Kerry Head   Causeway   Listowel   Bro
Ballyheige   R556   N69   409

Ballyheige
Bay   Abbeydorney
Rough   357
Point   Ardfert   R551
Brandon   Tralee   N21   Castleisland   Newmar
Bay   950   Bay   Scartaglin   R578
Cnoc Bréanainn   824   Camp   852   Tralee   R571   Ballydesmond
(Brandon Mountain)   Beenoskee   Baurtregaun   N70   N23
R559   Dingle Peninsula   N86   Castlemaine   Farranfore   Boherboy   R582
Anascaul   R561   Milltown   R561   Kerry   Rathmore   R58
An Blascaod Mór   An Daingean   Inch   N72   County   R582
(Great Blasket   (Dingle)   Killorglin   R563   KERRY
Island)   Killarney
Ceann Sléibhe   Glenbeigh   Laune   Beaufort   Muckross   N72
(Slea Head)   N70   Lough   Killarney
Dingle Bay   Leane   National
Macgillycuddy's Reeks   1039   Park   837
Doulus Head   Carrauntoohil   Mangerton   Poulgorm
Valentia   Mtn   Bridge
Island   Cahersiveen   R568   Kilgarvan   Ballymakeery   N22
R565   Uíbh Ráthach   Kenmare   R569   Béal Átha an
R566   (Iveragh)   Ghaorthaidh   R584
Sneem   N70   (Ballingeary)   Inchigeel
Sceilg Mhichíl   Waterville   Parknasilla   N71   Lee   K
(Great Skellig)   Ceann Bhólais   R571   705
(Bolus Head)   Cathair Dónall   Lauragh   Knockboy   R585   R5
An Scairbh   (Caherdaniel)   Kenmare River   Ardgroom   R574   Glengarriff   R584   Bandon   R5
(Scariff Island)   R575   685   Adrigole   Bantry   Dunmanway
Cod's Head   R572   Bear Island   Bantry
Allihies   Castletown   Bay   Drimoleague   R5
Bearhaven   R586   R594   R593
Dursey   Bear Island   Sheep's Head Peninsula   Durrus   Leap   R
Island   Muntervary/   Sheep's Head   R591   Ballydehob   N71
Sheep's Head   Dunmanus Bay   407   R592   Skibbereen   R595   Castletownsher
Goleen   Toormore Skull   Baltimore   Toe Head
Mizen Head   Crookhaven   Roaringwater Bay
Oilean Cleire
(Clear Island)

ATLAS INDEX

Atlas Index

Atlas Index